IN HIS FOOTSTEPS: The History of Wilhelm Friedrich Eduard Klier - 1834-1907

**Letters and History of the Julius Schlickum,
Julius Ransleben,
and the Johann Striegler Families**

By

LaVerne Heiner

Preface

Mein Lieber, Wilhelm, *Mein Lieber*, Gross Opa, that is how I have come to think of my great-grandfather, Wilhelm Klier. I just could not let his story go untold: emigrating to America at the age of fourteen without parents or siblings. What a brave and courageous young man!

Wilhelm's amazing story of getting caught up in the Civil War, being a "Union" sympathizer, surviving the Nueces Massacre, almost being hung, and going on to get married and have fourteen children ... what a story to pass down to generations of our Klier family. My heart is filled with pride when I think about the sacrifices made by him so that we can have this wonderful life here in Fredericksburg, Texas and beyond ... and let's not forget, we are related to so many because of all the children born to Wilhelm and Ida Striegler Klier which includes my Opa Klier. The love for this family is indescribable and will be forever in my heart.

The accomplishments of the Wilhelm Klier, Julius Schlickum, Julius Ransleben, and the Johann Striegler families are preserved for future generations, what these pioneers did for us, and why their memory should be revered. May the memory of their courage, faith, and perseverance be an inspiration to their descendants and to others who came here in the years that followed.

In Robert Penniger's book, *Fredericksburg, Texas - The First Fifty Years*, it states that a "New generation has arrived, the graves of the old Union supporters have caved in, their purpose has perhaps been atoned and they themselves are probably half-forgotten by their

descendants in their own struggle for their daily bread."
This is a testament by the Wilhelm Klier family that we did
not forget!

I hope this provides you with insight of our ancestral
history. Enjoy your journey in our ancestors' footsteps!

Dedication

(1928-2021)

IN LOVING MEMORY
OF
ALTON WILLIAM KLIER
A Christian Gentleman
This Volume is Reverently Dedicated

My uncle, Alton Klier, was my inspiration to
follow in my great-grandfather's footsteps.

LaVerne Heiner
Fredericksburg, Texas, January 2022

Acknowledgements

I wish to express my gratitude to the following who have so graciously assisted in the preparation of this history:

- Hans Dahlmanns (Hans' great-grandmother was Therese Klier Schlickum).
- Christoph Dahlmanns (*great, great-grandson of Therese Klier Schlickum*).
- Chuck and Carrol Klier Timmerman *(Carrol was a great-granddaughter of Wilhelm Klier)*.
- Alton Klier *(grandson of Wilhelm Klier)*.
- Martelle Luedecke (*great, great-granddaughter of Wilhelm Klier*).
- Kim Otte Gibbs (*great, great-granddaughter of Wilhelm Klier*).
- Alan Saenger *(great-grandson of Wilhelm Klier)*.
- Lesa Brown-Valades (*great, great-granddaughter of Wilhelm Klier*).
- Patrick Klier *(great-grandson of Wilhelm Klier)*.
- Evelyn Weinheimer, Gillespie County Historical Society.
- Val Anderson, Boerne Convention and Visitors Bureau.
- Bryden Moon (Boerne).
- Betty Ransleben, *(wife of Calvin Ransleben, a descendant of Julius Ransleben)*.
- Vicki and Craig Hollmig.
- Hector J. Cardenas, Archivist, San Antonio Fire Museum.
- Roslee Lochte.

- Jonathan Baethge, Bethany Lutheran Church.
- Dr. Peter Worm, Oberbürgermeister, Muenster, Germany.
- Cibolo Nature Center, Boerne.
- Pioneer Memorial Library.
- Gillespie County Courthouse.
- Former Texas Rangers Association.

Finally, I thank the staff at Watercress Press for their assistance.

Introduction

In 2017, the journey for this book began when I received copies of the letters written by our ancestors, from my uncle, Alton Klier. In November 1997, Hans Dahlmanns in Germany, was looking for relatives of the Klier family in Texas. Ralph Klier, my first cousin, who worked at Texas A&M was contacted and he referred Hans Dahlmanns to the Kliers in Fredericksburg!

The book of 48 letters (previously written in German) and pictures from the Dahlmanns, had been passed down to the Klier families in Texas. Due to the generosity of Chuck and Carrol (Klier)Timmerman, the letters were translated from German to English, in June 2012. The translated letters have been inserted into the timeline of the book and, therefore, preserved for present and future generations.

The book of letters and pictures from Germany were dedicated to the memory of Hans Dahlmanns. With the generosity of Hans, the letters and photographs were made available to you and me, your children, your grandchildren, to enjoy. Special mention must be made of Hans' son, Christoph Dahlmanns. In the latter years of Hans, Christoph was instrumental in locating many images, which he shared and also put in touch with "cousins" in Germany who also shared many photographs of their side of the Schlickum-Klier connection.

I wanted to tell the story of Wilhelm Klier (1834-1907), my great-grandfather, and did not realize that the Julius Schlickum and Julius Ransleben families were such a big part of our family history. I tried to write this as a factual account of Wilhelm Klier's life. My journey in his footsteps took me to the following places:

o Camp Davis site, Gillespie County.
o Camp Pedernales site, Gillespie County.
o Cascade Caverns, Kendall County.
o Cibolo Nature Center, Boerne.
o Der Stadt Friedhof, Fredericksburg.
o Firehouse Jail site, San Antonio.
o Former Texas Rangers Association, Fredericksburg.
o Fort Martin Scott, Fredericksburg.
o Fort Mason, Mason.
o Fort McKavett, Menard.
o German Immigrant Trail: Indianola, Victoria, Cuero, Hochheim, Gonzales, Seguin, New Braunfels (Faust Street Bridge), Boerne, Behr Farm (Boerne), Sisterdale, Fredericksburg Luckenbach, and Cain City.
o Gillespie County Courthouse.
o Henderson Farm and Cemetery, Ingram.
o Herff Farm, Kendall County.
o Hollmig Farm, Stonewall.
o Holy Ghost Lutheran Church, Fredericksburg.
o Location of "Schlickum and Holzapfel" store, Boerne.
o Location of Schlickum's home, Boerne.
o Lochte Farm, Meusebach Creek, Gillespie County.
o Main Street, Fredericksburg.
o Marketplatz, Fredericksburg.
o Meusebach Creek Cemetery, Gillespie County.
o Meusebach Creek school ruins, Old Comfort Road, Gillespie County.
o Nimitz Hotel, Fredericksburg.

o Old Jail, Fredericksburg.
o Pioneer Library (Former Second Gillespie County Courthouse), Fredericksburg.
o Pioneer Museum, Fredericksburg.
o Prison Town, Boerne.
o Ransleben Cemetery, Gillespie County.
o Ransleben Farm, Gillespie County.
o Route to Kinney County (Battle of the Nueces): Headwaters of Turtle Creek; Headwaters of the South Fork of the Guadalupe River (Kerr County); Head of the North Prong of Medina River (Bandera County); Headwaters of West Prong of Frio River; Bullhead Mountain; Bullhead Creek; Bullhead Creek meets East Prong of Nueces River (Real County); and West Prong of the Nueces River (Kinney County).
o San Fernando Cathedral, San Antonio.
o Schumacher's Crossing, Kerr County.
o Spring Creek Cemetery (on private property), Gillespie County.
o Stonewall, Gillespie County.
o Texas Ranger Museum and Offices, Fredericksburg.
o Texas Rangers Heritage Center, Fredericksburg.
o Treue der Union, Comfort.
o Trinity Lutheran Church, Stonewall.
o U.S. Army Headquarters (Gunter Hotel), San Antonio.
o Vereins Kirche, Gillespie County.
o You Tube – Tour of Muenster, Germany.

If you are interested in what historic homes and buildings were in existence during Wilhelm Klier's life in Fredericksburg (1850-1907), I recommend the following books that are available at the Pioneer Memorial Library in Fredericksburg:

o Kowert, Elise, *Old Homes And Buildings Of Fredericksburg*, Fredericksburg Publishing Co., Fredericksburg, Texas 1977.

o Kowert, Elise, *Historic Homes In and Around Fredericksburg*, Fredericksburg Publishing Co., Fredericksburg, Texas, 1980.

o Hafertepe, Kenneth, *A Guide to the Historic Buildings of Fredericksburg and Gillespie County*, Texas A & M University Press, College Station, Texas, 2015. Hafertepe's book is also available for purchase from the Pioneer Museum.

One of the most significant discoveries that I found in the letters was the fact that Wilhelm Klier and Julius Schlickum pledged their allegiance to the United States of America. They did not want to be instrumental in tearing up one of the most beautiful forms of government the world had ever seen [our democracy], in order to build a new government founded solely on the principle of expansion of human slavery!

There is an interesting quote from Guido E. Ransleben's book, *A Hundred Years of Comfort in Texas*, that caught my attention: "The day may come when the Southern loyalists will be awarded the honor due them for their patriotism and sacrifice by even their fellow citizens of the South who espoused the wrong cause, but who today sit peacefully under the nation's roof tree and devour the fatted calf." Guido E. Ransleben is a descendant of Julius Ransleben.

We are here because of the bravery of our ancestors. We have been bought with a great price and should value their genes in us. We feel their presence in us. Their features, smiles, and characteristics still line our faces and influence who we are. Let us linger awhile during the time of our family reunions and remember who they were and that they continue to live in us.

As part of the 175th celebration of the founding of Fredericksburg, Texas, I am honored to present a history of our heritage based on the life of Wilhelm Klier.

Table of Contents

Chapter I - A Short Sketch of Wilhelm Friedrich Eduard Klier's Parents and Grandparents

Friedrich Wilhelm Klier *(hereinafter referred to as Father Klier)* was born on December 9, 1799, in Elberfeld, Rheinland, Preussen (Prussia), Germany; he was baptized on December 13, 1799. At age 25, Friedrich Wilhelm Klier (Father Klier) married Anna Marie Josepha Elisabetha Judith Baar,* (hereinafter referred to as Mother Klier) on December 31, 1824, by Priest Rev. Emanuel Doering in Duesseldorf Stadt, Rheinland, Prussia. Anna Marie Josepha was born March 21, 1804; baptized March 23, 1804, in Sankt Anna Katholische, Dusseldorf Stadt, Rheinland, Prussia; and married at the age of 20 years.

Left: Friedrich Wilhelm Klier (Father Kier) as a small boy.

Father Klier's parents were Johann Abraham Klier (1771-1843) and Anna Christina Charlotte Boeck (1776-?), who were married August 15, 1797, Evangelisch, Elberfeld, Rheinland, Prussia. Mother Klier's parents were Laurentius Baar, and her mother was Josepha *nee* Rosbach, wife of Martin Louvens. Friedrich Wilhelm Klier (Father Klier) passed away on May 1, 1879, at age 80 years, in Muenster, North Rhine-Westphalia, Germany; and Josepha Klier (Mother Klier) passed away on April 7, 1881, at age 77 years, in Muenster, Germany.

Above, left: Christina Charlotte Boeck (1776-?) above left, Johanne Abraham Klier (1771-1843)

December 31, 1824
Interpretation
227 Marriage of Friedrich Wilhelm Klier and Anne Marie Josepha Elisabetha Judith Baar.

In the year one thousand eight hundred twenty-four (1824) 31 December in the afternoon at 6PM. Came before me Emanuel Doering, the Mayor of town of Elberfeld.

Groom: Mr. Friedrich Wilhelm Klier, merchant in Elberfeld and Legitimate son registered at the local Parish 13 Dec 1799 son of Merchant Johann Abraham Klier and Mother, Charlotte Boeck.

Bride: Anne Marie Josepha Elisabetha Judith Baar born 21 Mar 1804 in Duesseldorf. Not yet 21 years of age. The mother has agreed as witness before the Royal local peace court to agree to the Marriage of Daughter of Laurentius Baar and Mother, Josepha Rosbach wife of Painter, Martin Louvens.

Officer of the court issued certificate about 11AM 23 of Sep to approve the wedding of three bands verbally. Mother of the Bride gave permission to marry.

Right of the local father: Both partners passed on papers of the lawful parish Priest the signed certificate that is signed by witnesses.

Hans Franz Becker 30 Years Old

Heinrich Shaffer 30 Years old, Saddle maker

Johann...Meyer

After reading all agreed—

Signed by Priest

Rev. Emanuel Doering

Lobens-Louvens-Lovens was not Josephine's last name. Louvens was her stepfather's name, Martin Louvens (1781 - ?).

Chapter II - Background of the Schlickum Family

The following poems were written by Julius Schlickum prior to his emigration to America in 1849:

A poem entitled *Goods Village*, written to his sister, Wilhelmine (Julius was 15 years old) on January 8, 1841.

The Decision to Emigrate written in June 1849.

Der Wanderer written on July 4, 1849.

Goods Village (Translated *somewhat* into English below-January 8, 1841).

Fully I heut was all day long. Wines, probably cries, and hear, Much-many Ms soeur! There it always to the new year In dulci jubilo mode was, To lie not behind thick books, to divert itself probably however with Punsch, There hatt' also I me made, This time the anniversary should come, Me to probably do with Punsch and wine And the whole world - world let be. Thinking now, went already well, So, which one wanted already courage. And one has always merrily money, Thus the whole world stands to purchase. Thus, I thought in my sense And, the days let go. -Knowing: "Time will tell!" Everyone for itself to provide has. But blows! Oh, I yielded poorer! Money did not bring me the New Year. The lütte monthly pocket money Was already in advance half ordered. I can you tell long and broadly Of my terrible embarrassment. I put it to you quite to the heart: Sister, considers means pain! Gladly want I, describing, move, but tears my Wort' suffocate, - I know, o sister, no more cannot! Because I must cry too much. 0 sister, I inserts please you, Put a good word for me. Provide for me nevertheless good much money, Is also the best Lütt of the world. O, is terrible humans the matter, It Fortuna does not sit in the lap! Therefore, loves sister, bitt' for me! For my tears pity you! You, you loves sister mine, In this emergency trust I yours. - I love you, o Minna very much and your more honoured frère remains, Your dear Julius Schlickum, Without money does not come around.

Translation from Julius Schlickum's *Decision to Emigrate* written in June 1849 from Riesenrodt (*in present-day Germany*).

"I am standing in front of the Rubicon, and today I have decided to cross over it. (*Fig, of speech*). This is not, however, a crossing similar to proud Caesar's farewell, although Caesar and I do share similar names. The fate of the world doesn't hang in the balance because of my intentions, nevertheless, it is for me a much more important step than that of the Romans was for him.

I want to go to America! I want to leave my fatherland, my Germany so that I can see the other side of the ocean and establish a new homeland for myself A different homeland? Well, I am forgetting that for a long time I haven't had one. My father's hearth (*place of comfort: fig, of speech*) has been desecrated for years. My mother and my father have been laid in their graves in Beilstein [Beilstein is in the Cochem-Zell district in Rhineland-Palatinate, Germany], and my sisters and brothers are scattered out in the world. There are no binding ties to hold me back because my siblings will accompany me (*to America*), or follow me at a later date. No loving eyes will fill with tears on my departure, nor will white handkerchiefs wave from windows (above) as I leave. Nevertheless, I am sad to leave.

I leave the land of my youthful dreams, leave my German land behind me, and I find myself grieving for its struggle and its humiliation, because I cannot fight these battles. I have seen with my own eyes the way freedom's rays of morning light can break up the dark clouds. There the Germans were men!! These men looked for their forgotten birds of prey and eagles, while scavenger have drunk the blood of your heart. You were able to grind your teeth, and you have tasted the gall while holding the sword high in your hand, but why haven't you used it (for the good)? I don't want to scold you in your own language, in the language that the gods speak. I simply must depart because I can no longer bear your disgrace. However, in Spite of your disgrace, I am proud to be a German.

Live well, my country. Live well!!"

July 4, 1849
Der Wanderer translated from German to English:
The Wanderer
So worried the dim longing
is sneaking into my heart,
And all my songs
must be sad.

Even if I am walking
Or roaming on the wild sea,
I always stay mournful,
With my heart blank.

Heiner

Why should I stay at home
At the abandoned fireplace!
There the dear happiness
Of my life was destroyed.

And all I love,
which alone is my joy,
That is scattered
in the far and distant world.

And if I go on wandering
And wander all the time,
I will never find
calmness in my dim heart.

But at the end I will come
To a cool grave,
Where the tired wanderer
Is called for a soft rest.

Julius Schlickum (1825-1863)

The following was a petition written by Friedrich Wilhelm Klier (Father Klier) in Muenster, Germany on behalf of Julius Schlickum. The letter is dated October 3, 1846, and the addressee is unknown – clearly a copy.

<u>*Letter #1*</u>

Petition by Wilhelm (Papa) Klier on behalf of Julius Schlickum (son-in-law).

Well-born Sir,

You had made an official announcement on the serious and rather hopeless illness of the worthy Inspector Schlickum on the 30th of the previous month. I consider it my holy duty to confidentially call to your attention the precarious situation of this family of 6 destitute children, and to the fact that it could be prevented, and am asking for your support and powerful intercession. If the Inspector would be so unfortunate and pass away, the oldest son Julius who is a volunteer serving at the local 13. Infantry Regiment could be released based on the addendum in § 69 and also on § 95 of the ordinance pertaining to reservists and conscription, if his father's position would be assigned to him, even if only temporary. I'm completely and thoroughly convinced that he would be perfectly qualified. I'm counting on your help, and the help of your son-in-law, and that of Town Mayor Heide, based on the solicitousness and friendship all of you had extended to the old Schlickum at all times and under any circumstances, when he was still a minor. I'm quite confident that in the future you will act the same towards his bereaved children after he has passed away, out of respect to him. And I'm counting on the fact that Julius will be able to perform the duties of this appointment very well, based on his excellent and scholarly education, and his particularly good knowledge of economics. He will certainly apply all fervor and diligence to the satisfaction of his superiors, especially in these circumstances, and based on the fine duty arising from them: to be the support and bread-earner of this helpless family likely about to be abandoned to privation and misery without him.

Please take care of this family who is on the verge of such a threat, with all of your intent and power, in the manner suggested above, and please be so very kind as to inform of your favorable decision with a short note. Assuring you of my highest respect Well-born Sir, I'm remaining your most humble.

Klier
Muenster

The following letter was written by Friedrich Wilhelm Klier (Father Klier) in Muenster, Germany, to Julius

Schlickum, in Muenster, Germany, following the death of Julius' father, Johann Jakob Schlickum. The letter was dated October 6, 1846. (Julius Schlickum was born on October 27, 1825, in Muenster, Germany.)

Letter #2

Letter by the Government Inspector Friedrich Wilhelm Klier to (Jakob) Julius Schlickum, following the death of his father (Johann) Jakob Schlickum (on 6 October 1846 in Marsberg/ Westphalia). (Johann) Jakob Schlickum, born on 26 December 1787 in Elberfeld [North Rhine-Westphalia, Germany], had been educated at an Institute in Strassburg, and thereafter resided in Avignon [France], where he worked as a merchant in a trading-firm. He joined the War as Quartermaster of the l. Hussar Regiment in Münster in 1814 and remained in that position until 1828 [1]; from 1829 to 1835 he worked as a civil servant at the Land-Registry Office in Coblenz [Rhineland-Palatinate, Germany], and thereafter as Inspector at the State's Insane Asylum in Stadtberg [Brandenburg, Germany] close to Marsberg. In 1823 he was married to Katharina Pokorny from Wesseling [North Rhine Westphalia] in the Cologne, Germany] area, who died in 1839 before she turned thirty-nine years of age. Two very beautiful charcoal drawings of both of them still exist. Johann Jakob Schlickum died at the age of 59 and left behind his children Wilhelmine (Minna), 22 years of age; Jakob Julius, 21 years; Catharine, 19 years; Ferdinand, 17 years; Albert, 13 years; and Otto, 11 years old. We can assume that the economic situation these brothers and sisters were facing was quite dismal. Chances are that Uncle Karl Pfleiderer, brother-in-law of Johann Jakob Schlickum, took care of the orphans. Jakob's son Julius, the recipient of this letter, was married on 1 October 1849 [September 27, 1849] to Therese, daughter of Friedrich Wilhelm Klier.

6 October 1846

Dear Schlickum,

May God grant that you might overcome the first, difficult blow of fate in a manly fashion — I don't know of anything to write that might be comforting; chances are that you didn't find any of that in my first letter either. *(Remark in margin:) Did you receive it right away? I had enclosed it when writing to the Director.*

I had been completely confounded by the news and would have loved to answer the holy Vicar Schneppendahl to his condolence letter, but was not able to do so, and even now am not up to it. Please be so kind and tell him for now that I first have to await orders pertaining to a substitute there. I cannot come myself and don't have permission to do so; probably Walther will be sent over there very soon, in order to transfer to Heide management of the financial administration, inventory, and produce, for the time being. At the same time, the Director will likely be asked to submit proposals for temporary and future occupancy of the Inspector's position. In my capacity as Chief Treasurer I'm otherwise not involved in the matter and can only exert my influence through my colleague Hasenkamp, who is in charge of the department at this time. However, as I had mentioned in my previous letter, all hopes of having you appointed as successor appear to be thwarted! If only we could arrange for you jointly take over, or for you to become co-administrator, that would at least give you the reason needed to submit for release from the Military, and you and your brothers and sisters would be able to remain at the Institution and be able to look for another residence before the position is reassigned otherwise. Just about everything depends on the Director's proposal, and therefore please make sure to develop a good relationship with him! And especially so in view of Walther's upcoming report. In regard to the latter, I request that you search my private letters sent to your late Father, as I had corresponded with him openly and in confidence about many a matter and person, and chances are also about the Director and Walther, which could possibly be misconstrued by them to your disadvantage. If possible, please separate the entire private mail, and keep it in your personal possession for now.

Once you can find some time and privacy as needed, please don't tarry, and as soon as possible share your opinion with me, as well as events of vital interest from there as soon as possible and tell me openly and frankly how you are faring, and what your wishes and hopes are, and so on, and also exemplify on your relationship to your relatives. Please let me know where, and how, I can best act on your behalf, in counsel and deed. Above all, recollect yourself and your thoughts, take counsel with Vollmer on everything, and possibly also with Schneppendahl, and don't neglect to do everything you can the more effort you invest, the more you work and are effective, the faster and easier you will get over the justified pain of the difficult and bitter loss.

Sincerely Your *Klier*

Muenster, October 6th

Heide, Ulrich Dürr, and Judiciary Schumacher have already applied for the job, and several people here as well, and Inspector Schmitz is also planning to apply. Haken from Medebach [North Rhine, Westphalia, Germany] as well — it won't be long, and we'll have 100 of those same applications.

¹The editor/transcriber is not completely clear, but apparently Jakob Schlickum fought in the War of 1814 (against Napoléon) and thereafter remained in his position of quartermaster until 1828.

A letter was written by Therese Klier to her future sister-in-law, Minna Schlickum, about two months before her groom Julius Schlickum emigrated to America. Father Klier suggested that Therese not make the trip until her future husband, Julius Schlickum, had established a foothold in the new country. Julius Schlickum was in the process of preparing for the trip by the following: leaving his position as a teacher of economics at an agricultural institution in Westphalia, making arrangements for his siblings to stay with their Aunt and Uncle Pfleiderer; and making travel arrangements to America.

Letter #3

(There is no date, but it can be dated to the beginning of August 1849, about two months before her groom Julius Schlickum emigrated).

August 1849

My most beloved Minna,

Chances are that you have waited for a letter from us already for a long time — I can only imagine and am wondering if you might have been angry at us at one time or another about our baffling silence. Should I begin with long winded explanations why we were prevented from writing until now? But no, in that case I would be filling the page without fulfilling the purpose of today's letter. Julius wrote to me already four times since your departure; but only in his last letter which I received yesterday he wrote about something specific, and I shall report its contents and the most important points of the other letters, as accurately as possible. He wrote that he was received by Goskers very kindly, so much so that it was even more difficult for him to make said disclosures. It appears however that the conversation with Mr. Gosker turned out better than expected, with the result that he was permitted to leave as soon as he would be able to find a worthy replacement for his position. It looks as if he already found one, as he is about to leave Riesenrodt already next Wednesday, on August 8th, with the intention to travel to Mettmann [North Rhine, Westphalia, Germany] and thereafter to meet me on the 11th of the month in Elberfeld. From there we were supposed to travel to Mettmann.

Meanwhile however, things were decided otherwise. Yesterday morning we received the letters from Uncle Pfleiderer,[1] who also wrote to me, and in such a cordial manner that you wouldn't believe it — he wrote a long letter to Father. If he can manage, he would like to visit us this week to talk about the details with Father and Julius. According to his letter he had planned for quite a while already to visit his foster children in Ibbenbüren [North Rhine-Westphalia, Germany], and at that occasion he'd like — to use his expression — to kill two birds with one stone. He doesn't appear opposed to the plan to emigrate, however is not clearly taking a position and is saving everything up until he can talk in person. I'm planning to write to Julius today, to let him know that he should come here right away instead of traveling to Mettmann; he should be here latest by Thursday then. In his last letter Julius enclosed two letters he had received from Uncle and Aunt Pfleiderer that were just as cordial.

Once Julius is here again, we'll also travel to Warendorf [North Rhine, Westphalia, Germany] once where we shall meet the Councilor of Commerce Delius, who can tell Julius much about America that is of great interest to him. Delius will be traveling to Bremen [Lower Saxony, Niedersachsen, Germany] on the 15th of this month in order to arrange the passage for us. His cousin travels to America several times per year, and he'll take especially good care of us. And now, dearest Minna, what is your decision? Julius is also asking about it. Are you still inclined as formerly? Alas, Minna, I so much would like for you to come along. However, I won't talk you into it by force, I quite realize how great your sacrifice would be on our behalf. In case you would make that decision, I would appreciate it for all times and would forever be grateful to you. We would certainly do anything in our power to make your life comfortable, and your future a cheerful one, and every slightest wish would be fulfilled, if possible, I'll stand security for that. However, matters of the heart are more important, and I cannot ask you to sacrifice your happiness on behalf of mine. But the Lord, whom we are all imploring in unison these days, will lovingly take care of all of us, and I shall confidently rely on him.

Father wrote to Julius that it would be better if he first sailed over there alone. Still, he doesn't seem to be comfortable with that; although he would, as he is writing, make this sacrifice if I wished so, however added two buts, and dashes and exclamation marks. Now he would like to hear my opinion, which has been so far to follow him, if you are going to accompany us. In that case we would have to be in Bremen already in six weeks. Goodbye for today, Minna, I'll write more these days. You won't believe how difficult it is around here to find time to write. My dear little Mother is still mourning every day, you wouldn't believe how much this makes me suffer, and I'm forcefully suppressing everything and displaying a cheerful mood. Please include her in your pious prayer as well.

I still have to write to Julius today although it is already late; I always kept putting him off until Sunday. And now may God watch over you, I'm embracing you in spirit faithfully, and a thousand times.

Please write soon to your sister *Therese* who loves you faithfully,

---

¹ Karl Pfleiderer, 1800-1875, factory owner in Mettmann, married to Luise Schlickum. 1797 – 1865, the sister of (Johann) Jakob Schlickum and thus an aunt of Julius. Chances are that Pfleiderers had taken in the children after (Johann) Jakob Schlickum died. They are often mentioned in Minna 's and Therese's letters.

Where did Julius Schlickum get the money to go to America? He was a teacher at Riesenrodt. With the death of both his father and mother, his younger siblings were destitute. Because of Father Klier's wealth, it is assumed that he financed or loaned the money for the trip to America for Julius Schlickum and Wilhelm Klier. The cost to emigrate to America included money for transportation from Bremen, Germany; across the Atlantic to the port of Galveston (food, water, and supplies included in this cost); transportation to Indianola; cross-country transportation including baggage to Fredericksburg, Texas; incidental expenditures; and a dwelling in Fredericksburg.

Julius Schlickum and Caroline Therese Klier were married on September 27, 1849, in *Sankt Ludgeri Katholische* Church, Muenster, Westfalen, Germany. Julius and Therese Klier Schlickum had a very short honeymoon before Julius Schlickum and Wilhelm Klier left for America.

left: Sankt Ludgeri Katholische, Muenster, Germany

Chapter III - Fourteen Going on Fifteen

Wilhelm Klier was 14 years old! What 14-year-old leaves his family, his home and everything he has ever known for a new country at this age? Who does that? Why? With a heavy heart but overwhelming anticipation and excitement, Wilhelm Klier bade farewell to his family at the Klier *Haus* in the *Aegidii Leischaft* District, Muenster, Germany at the end of September 1849. The Klier family had so many visitors that many friends called it "Hotel Klier!" Father and Mother Klier said their goodbyes (*auf wiedersehen*) to their son, Wilhelm, who would be considered an adult at age fifteen. Wilhelm's brothers and sisters had mixed emotions, being happy and sad for their brother's new adventure! They could not believe Wilhelm was leaving. Would they ever see him again? It was time to leave for America!

Wilhelm Friedrich Eduard Klier was born at Muenster, Nordrhein-Westphalia (North Rhine-Westfalen), Germany, on December 9, 1834, and named for his father (Friedrich Wilhelm Klier) who was born on the same date in 1799. His mother's birth name was Anna Marie Josepha Elisabetha Judith Baar. She was born March 21, 1804.

Wilhelm Klier was the son of wealthy parents. His father was a distinguished, well-educated man, an accountant (Chief Treasurer) on the Military Staff in Germany. Muenster was home to the staff of the General Command of the Seventh Army Corps, making Muenster one of the most important army bases in Prussia. The VII Army Corps/VII AK (German *VII Armee-Korps*) was a corps level command of the Prussian and then the Imperial German Armies from the 19th Century to World War I. The General Staff alone sat in the most diverse places in Muenster. Many military authorities were housed in the former episcopal castle, *Schloss*, or in the buildings on *Neuplatz.*

Schloss, Muenster, Germany (Former Episcopal Castle)
and Schlossplatz (Neuplatz)

Schloss Muenster, officially *Fürstbischöfliches Schloss Muenster*, is the *schloss* built as the residence of the prince-bishop of Muenster, now the modern-day North Rhine-Westphalia, Germany. It was built between 1767 and 1787 in baroque style as a mansion for the next to last prince-bishop, *Maximilian Friedrich von Königsegg - Rothenfels.* The architect was Johann Conrad Schlaun. The castle was constructed with the typical Baumberger sandstone of Muenster. Since 1954 it has been the seat and landmark of the Westphalian Wilhelms University.

Today, the Westphalian Wilhelms University uses these *Gebäude* (buildings). The University of Muenster is a public research university. The *Schlossplatz* is a square in Muenster, located west of downtown, in front of the castle, called *Neuplatz* from 1759. From 1927 to 2012 it was called *Hindenburgplatz*.

During the time Wilhelm Klier immigrated to America in 1849, the Klier family lived in the *Aegidii Leischaft* District, No. 238. Today, you will find the place where the house stood, *Konigstrasse* 10, opposite house number 53.

Wilhelm Klier received a good education before coming to America. Wilhelm Klier left Germany when he was about to be inducted into the compulsory three years military training which was required of every able-bodied young man. In addition to the compulsory three years military training in Germany at age 15, the reason for Wilhelm's emigration was not economic although there are some hints that the emigration as a romantic adventure was a great attraction for him. Wilhelm was making the trip to Texas with his brother-in-law, Julius Schlickum, then 24 years old.

The Councilor of Commerce Delius had traveled to Bremen on August 15, 1849, in order to arrange passage to America for Wilhelm Klier and Julius Schlickum. Documents required by the German Immigrants were: 1) baptismal certificate; 2) official evidence concerning business profession or trade and place of residence; 3) a certified copy of good conduct from their home church congregation; and 4) official information regarding financial status.

The reason for Julius Schlickum's emigration was more about the death of both of his mother and father and having no reason to stay in his homeland (see Julius Schlickum's *Decision to Emigrate* from June 1849. It fully describes his reasons for emigration). They were hardly economic, because he had a job as a teacher of economics at an agricultural institution in Westphalia. He suffered from the suppression of the 1848 "revolution" in Germany, although there are some hints that the emigration as a romantic adventure was a great attraction for him as well. Julius desired a better life.

After a very short honeymoon, Julius Schlickum said goodbye to his bride, Therese Klier Schlickum, whom he had married three days earlier (September 27, 1849). Wilhelm and Julius were required to be in Bremen a day before departure to America. How long would it be until Julius saw his bride again? How long before his bride would join him in America?

Muenster, Germany

Wilhelm Friedrich Eduard Klier & siblings:

- Josephine Wilhelmine Klier Ransleben (1826-1888) immigrated to Fredericksburg, Texas.
- Caroline Therese Klier Schlickum (1828-1905) lived in Fredericksburg and Boerne, Texas; returned to Germany during the Civil War in 1864 after the death of her husband, Julius Schlickum.
- Hugo Klier (1832-unknown) stayed in Germany.
- Wilhelm Friedrich Eduard Klier (1834-1907) immigrated to Fredericksburg, Texas.
- Carl Georg Franz Klier (1839-1861) immigrated to Fredericksburg, Texas, and died in an accident; buried at the Ransleben Family Cemetery.
- Maria Friederica Klier Neuhaus (1841-1867) remained in Germany and died at age 26.
- Gustav Rudolph Klier (1843-1908) immigrated to St. Louis, Missouri.
- Antonie (*Toni*) about (1845-1893) remained in Germany, a nun of the Monastery of the Poor Clares.

Chapter IV - Emigration Begins: Germany to America (1849)

Julius Schlickum and Wilhelm Klier took a train from Muenster, to Bremen, Germany, a distance of 106 miles. Bremen was a German emigrant port of departure. They were required to be in Bremen before October 1, 1849. The Bremen port is some 37 miles south of the mouth of the Weser River on the North Sea. The vessels would take emigrants to American ports, unload the immigrants, load up with cargo for the return voyage to Europe.

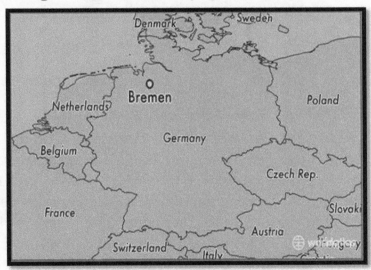

Bremen, Germany

As Wilhelm and Julius boarded the ship, they could see the disarray but were overwhelmed with excitement! This was the first time they had set foot on such a massive ship. Passengers were loaded along with baggage, water barrels, and provisions. Early emigrants were allowed to take some of the following items: seeds and cuttings; money; plows; an unassembled wagon; bed clothing; weapons; utensils; ropes; carpenter and gardening tools; harness; clothes; and weapons.

Left: Typical 3-mast schooner emigrant ship

The *Barque Franziska*, under the command of Captain Hagerdom, was preparing for the Atlantic crossing from Europe to America. On October 1, 1849, the *Barque Franziska*, a three-masted wooden vessel, departed Bremen carrying 138 passengers. The cargo ship was retrofitted for transporting emigrants, had few basic amenities, poor food, limited toilet use, and no privacy.

Julius Schlickum and Wilhelm Klier were finally on their way to America! On board, they met other people who were going to settle in Texas. On the passenger list was Hermann Holzapfel who became a trusted friend of Julius Schlickum and Wilhelm Klier. This friendship would develop into a life-saving event for Wilhelm Klier during the Civil War.

Entry by Aunt Minna into the book where she kept her copies *(perhaps a diary)*. On 1 October 1849, on his wedding day, Julius Schlickum traveled to Texas together with his brother-in-law Wilhelm Klier. After having many a bitter experience, and exploring the country and circumstances there, he wrote down the results in a long manuscript and sent it to his father-in-law Klier, who had it lithographed. *(This lithograph has never been located.)*

The food during the voyage consisted of meat, potatoes, sauerkraut, barley, soup, beans, port, zwieback, coffee, tea, and water. Emigrant passengers were housed in the steerage section. Sleeping berths contained a mattress, blanket, and pillow. Typhus was rampant on emigrant ships. The long days at sea consisted of a choppy ocean, harsh winds, freezing weather, gloomy living quarters, insects, and unclean living quarters. The journey was dismal with seasickness and disease. As the long voyage progressed, the German emigrants were on a crowed sailing ship for almost ten weeks. Many passengers died on these voyages and were buried at sea.

The *Barque Franziska* had departed Bremen and traveled to the mouth of the Weser River on the North Sea. One of the common routes from ports in Germany was to the North Sea on the England coast; southerly through the English Channel, to the Bay of Biscay, past the coast of France; past Portugal and the entrance to the Mediterranean Sea; past the northwest corner of Africa and then west on the Atlantic Ocean; on to the West

Indies; through the Straits of Florida; into the Gulf of Mexico; and finally arriving at Galveston, Texas.

Letter #4

The following written by Therese Klier Schlickum in Muenster, Germany, to her sister-in-law Minna Schlickum in Germany, before she emigrated to America. Her groom, Julius Schlickum, and brother, Wilhelm Klier, were enroute to America on the sailboat, Barque Franziska. It took 67 days to make the perilous voyage. Julius Schlickum wrote Therese Klier Schlickum after he had been on board for six hours stating that he suffered a little from sea sickness but his brother-in-law, Wilhelm Klier, did not. The letter mentioned the upcoming 25th anniversary of Father and Mother Klier who were married on December 31, 1824.

Muenster, 25 November 1849

My most precious sister,

How comforting to one's heart are external influences that manage to transport one's spirit close to a precious object; the distance seems to dwindle away, and I feel as if we were chatting together. Such feelings were aroused by your dear and precious letter, wherein you, my dear and precious Minna, spoke straight to my heart. I felt your presence in every line, as if sitting right next to you — your beautiful heart filled with warm love and compassion intelligible to me. I read and reread your letter again and again, and quite lost myself in it-- and I?-- have to cover my face with both hands, red from shame, in order to hide it from myself. I have to admit that it is unforgivable of myself to have let not weeks, but months pass by without sending you any sign of life, especially since Julius had asked me in his last letter to send his regards to you, and to ask you to forgive him in case he might have hurt you in his last letter. All of these assertions of my deepest and most boundless affection to you must appear like empty talk to you — but no! You have already reached out with your right hand in love, and I'm grasping it with longing and am drawing it to my violently beating heart, which is relating to you more than my words can tell. After having heard my excuses for my prolonged silence you'll have to concede to yourself that I'm not quite as worthy of condemnation as it might appear on first sight.

Since your departure I kept working for Father incessantly, from early in the morning until evening. Thus, I felt exhausted in soul and body, and my former zest for writing letters was replaced by greatest aversion, and not by any stretch of the imagination or best intentions was I able to compose a letter. On weekdays I put it off until Sunday, but on Sundays I was never alone; either we had visitors, eternally boring visitors at that; or I was afflicted by the worst headaches, and whenever I was spared from it all week, I could be sure to expect it on Sunday,-- God be praised, late last night I finished up with Father's work this afternoon I began by writing a letter to Aunt Pfleiderer, since Father wrote to her and I wanted to include my letters. This evening I would like to turn my attention solely to you and won't rest any longer until I have shed my tears at your faithful heart, and until I have shared with you whatever bothers and rejoices my mind. After all, you are the only one who understands me, and whom I can tell openly how I feel. Oh Minna, my sister! If I was able to express as I truly desired, I wouldn't hide any weakness of any of my faults from you. My sister! — while writing this I am rejoicing in my heart as cannot be described; I would like to cry for joy and on my bare knees give thanks to my God who has bestowed on us so incredibly much. He has given you to me as a sister, and therewith fulfilled a wish I had held for many years. Dear Minna, was it a premonition, or how should I call it, considering our lives had always been interwoven in my dreams and plans, and that I always felt you to be at my side in spirit? You, dear Minna, are probably thinking 'what flights of fancy, dear little sister, my love is infinitely greater than that. [1]

And now, dear Minna, I'll happily disclose my heart to you, and I know that you will be pleasantly surprised. Don't worry, you won't find any sorrow or deep suffering in there, instead it looks much fairer therein; the storms are calmed, and it is comparable to a nice spring day now. I can surely share this with you, and you knew anyway that I've had to face terrible storms and have struggled; and I can take comfort from the fact that I have emerged from them victoriously. God's grace was clearly with me. I feel relieved without end, and the good Lord has infinitely comforted my heart since those days when I was joined with Julius forever. I love Julius warmly and sincerely, and with much longing and inner joy am looking towards a future promising me such happiness at my Julius' side. I am filled with joy to have found such a strong and firm support in Julius, — most cheerful scenes of the future surround me while awake and in my dreams. Now I shall continue comforted and jovially on my new path, and by God's grace hopefully shall have the strength to make

Julius happy, and also to be happy myself. And thus, I'm only looking forward, to that beautiful goal in ahead of me, and I keep painting it in ever new colors and splendor. In case I should once be tempted to reach deeper into the past than ever before you will quickly stand by my side, like an angel who protects me, keeping me from crossing that barrier and lovingly pointing me to the goal ahead of me, and how much I am thanking you for it!! I owe you infinite thanks!! I would love to demonstrate that to you by deed and will gladly offer you ....[2] replacement for the years of privation and suffering; I so much would like to see you happy, as you truly deserve. And you haven't received even one letter in that long time, you certainly would rather be in need of one right now, to refresh your depressed mind a little; I'm pretty sure the silence won't keep up for long, through such punishment he is punishing himself as well.

I was with the travelers during the entire trip, tarrying at their side faithfully through storms and all weather, however my mind was more active than yours. While you still imagined them to be in that dangerous archipelago, I permitted them already to land, sending my greetings to them on American soil. I feel much calmer now compared to all the time before, and although I wasn't awakened by bad thoughts or dreams, or premonitions, my heart was still heavily weighed down and I did not know how interpret it. Perhaps I would have felt better if I could have cried, but I seem to be practically devoid of tears, that precious gift of heaven.

I'm not reading or hearing anything about distant lands. I feel infinitely calmer since you have written, and have turned everything, and all worries, over to God.

I doubt that I'll be traveling to Mettmann. They don't want to let me leave here; I would have loved to accompany you. Can't you manage to come to us one of these days, I would so much love to see ... [3] Minna, I'd much prefer if you were here instead of working in such a subordinate situation, it would be such an advantage for me; oh, why can't it be that way? I would have much else to tell you, everything is surging up in my soul, to the extent that it can't line it up in orderly fashion. Besides, I'm surrounded by jovial company again, amusing themselves with pleasantries and playing cards. As you know, Minna, in wintertime one can't help but to be in one room-- in your letter you're asking about Mother's wedding day, which is New Year's Eve; last year we all celebrated together. Now tell me, how are things really with Anna and her fiancé? There are all kinds of talk around here, and I can't make any sense of it. Please, kind Minna, don't take amiss that I'm ending this letter quickly without having answered several of your questions at all. I'm going to make up for it soon. I'm asking you intently to please prove your love and write again very soon. Now, my dear little sister, goodbye, think of me often and especially so in your pious prayer, the Lord will reward you for it. You shall once receive a crown, the size of a tub, for it. Be jovial and cheerful, the Lord will certainly cause everything turns out well. I'm embracing you in spirit and am remaining yours with heartfelt love.

Your faithful sister *Therese*

Why did you address the letter to Miss TH.CL, in haste or as a joke? Father teased me quite a bit and let me wait an hour before handing me the letter, he was going to return it. Quickly: Father, Mother, Josephine, Mrs. Kaldner,[4] Toni, are sending their regards.

I'll send Julius' farewell poem in my next letter.

Goodbye,

Josephine hasn't heard anything from Spiegels yet, not if they have received the items, nor have they sent the money back. What do you think, how will Josephine react to this? *(added in the margin)* Julius wrote his last letter after they were already on board for six hours. The pilot brought it along on his way back. It appears that he already suffered a little from sea sickness. Wilhelm didn't.

---

[1]*The writer forgot the second quotation mark, so the meaning of this sentence is somewhat unclear.*

[2]*Transcriber's blank*

[3]*Transcriber's blank*

[4]*The transcriber was unsure about the surname Kaldner (in brackets and question mark). "Toni" is a younger sister.*

Wilhelm Klier and Julius Schlickum's destination, Galveston, Texas, was nearby. It was December 6, 1849, when Galveston was sighted. The *Barque Franziska* arrived three days before Wilhelm's 15th birthday.

Galveston was considered the port of entry into the United States and all passengers to Texas were registered there. Since the harbor was not deep enough for the *Barque Franziska*, fleet barges would be used to unload passengers and cargo. Passengers were overwhelmed to finally reach Texas soil. After processing with the agent, the emigrants were shipped down the coast in a steamboat or a smaller vessel for the 100-mile trip from Galveston to Indianola, Texas. The port, Indianola, was constructed on Matagorda Bay. *(Indianola was also known as Indian Point as well as "Karlshaven.")* Indianola was a city that was born, flourished, and died on the Texas Coast between 1844 and 1886. They arrived at Indianola in freezing cold and rain.

Indianola

Chapter V - The Trail from Indianola to Fredericksburg

The Fisher-Miller Grant stretched between the Llano and Colorado Rivers westward almost to the Pecos. The grant of 3,800,000 acres was purchased in 1844 by the German Emigration Society from the Texas Republic. John O. Meusebach founded Fredericksburg in 1846 as waystation to the grant. America offered an opportunity to own enormous stretches of unsettled land, to be free people, and the opportunity to better themselves.

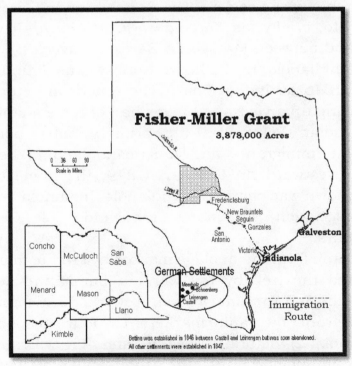

Map of Fisher-Miller Land Grant

Stepping on American soil, the immigrants felt the land promised adventure, great fortunes, and abundance. On December 6, 1849, Wilhelm Klier, Julius Schlickum, and 136 passengers of the *Barque Franziska* had taken a steamboat or smaller vessel for the 100-mile trip from Galveston to Indianola, Texas. Steamships came from Galveston to Indianola near the mouth of Powderhorn Lake. In 1844 a stretch of beach near the point had been selected by Prince Karl Solms Braunfels, commissioner general of the *Adelsverein*, as the landing place for German immigrants bound for western Texas under the sponsorship of the society. The German landing area was referred to, briefly, as *Karlshaven (Carlshaven)*. It was a jut of land between Matagorda Bay and Lavaca Bay. The port of Indianola in Calhoun County was founded in August 1846 as Indian Point. The American settlement had sprung up a year after Texas had become a state. By 1848, Indian Point was the primary entry port for European immigrants and Americans landing here to migrate westward. In February 1849, the name of the growing town was changed to Indianola. Indianola became the destination of many thousands of German Immigrants.

The trail from Indianola is marked by granite markers. It marked the trek by the German immigrants led by Prince Karl and the *Adelsverein*. It marked the four sites along the route by granite markers. The four sites include: 1) Indianola, 2) Victoria, 3) Seguin, and 4) New Braunfels. This trail memorializes the thousands of German immigrants that braved the elements to reach this destination. The markers begin at the foot of the LaSalle statue at Indianola and ends in a flower bed on the Castell Avenue side of the New Braunfels Civic Center.

The Texas Hill Country German Pioneers' Dedication Slab is located on the grounds of the Robert de La Salle monument in the coastal ghost town of Indianola, Texas. It honors the German Pioneers who landed here on their way to the Texas Hill Country. The two inscriptions are separated by a map of the Guadalupe River (which mouths at San Antonio Bay, just a few miles southwest of Indianola) from the coast all the way to the city of New Braunfels and beyond. The slab's inscription is both in English and German, and reads:

"Dedicated to the German Pioneers who traveled along the Guadalupe River in 1845 to settle the Texas Hill Country." 1995 - 150th Anniversary New Braunfels Sesquicentennial "Gewidmet den deutschen Pionieren die 1845 dem Guadalupe folgend das Texanische bergland besiedelten." 1995 - 150 Jubilaeum

Number 1 Granite Marker (Indianola)

A wooden sign can be located that reads, "Welcome to Historic Indianola." When the waters are clear, you can see the foundation of the old courthouse about 50 feet offshore.

Site of the Town of Indianola 1844-1886

"First called by German immigrants Karlshaven, an important port of Texas. Cargoes of ships were hauled to and from points in Texas and Mexico by carts until 1860 when the San Antonio and Mexico Gulf Railroad and the Indianola Railroad were completed to Victoria. The town was partly destroyed with great loss of life by a hurricane,

September 17, 1875. It was rebuilt but completely destroyed by another hurricane, August 20, 1886."
Erected by State of Texas
1936

Covered Wagon With Oxen

After a short stay on the beach, Wilhelm Klier, Julius Schlickum, and the other immigrants were transported approximately 300 hundred miles by ox carts and wagons to Fredericksburg, Texas. The usual average rate of travel with such wagons was about two miles (3.2 km) per hour, and the average distance covered each day was about 15 to 20 miles (24 to 32 km).

The German Immigrants' trail along the Guadalupe River from Indianola to New Braunfels continued through the following communities: Indianola, Chocolate Creek, Victoria, Spring Creek, Hochheim, Peach Creek, Gonzales, Seguin, and to New Braunfels, Texas. The Guadalupe

River is located in the following counties: Victoria, DeWitt, Gonzales, Guadalupe, Comal, Kendall, and Kerr Counties. The Guadalupe River runs from Kerr County, Texas to San Antonio Bay on the Gulf of Mexico.

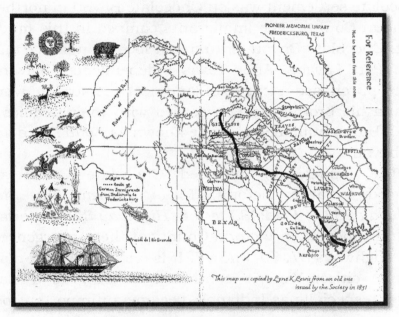

Trail From Indianola to Gillespie County

The tedious 300-hundred-mile journey to Fredericksburg had begun. The immigrants were guarded by riders and marksmen who led them through the wilderness; it was approximately a four-week trip to Fredericksburg. Wilhelm loved adventure, and truly, destiny had many thrilling and some direful experiences in store for him. While on the trail from Indianola to Fredericksburg, Wilhelm Klier celebrated his 15th birthday on Texas soil on December 9, 1849.

The German immigrants departed Indianola and traveled the 12 miles from Indianola to Chocolate Creek (*present day State Highway 316*). They made camp at a site on Chocolate Creek dubbed *Agua Dulce*. The Chocolate settlement was on Chocolate Bayou in northern Calhoun County. The immigrants camped in this muddy spot. Chocolate Bayou is a stream located just 2.7 miles from Port Lavaca. After Texas independence, Sylvanus Hatch purchased a league of land near the stream, where he and his brother Joseph settled with their families in 1846. Hatch built a large home known as *Agua Dulce* near the bayou.

The immigrants departed Chocolate Creek and traveled towards Victoria, Texas (*present day State Highway 238 to FM 2433 to U.S. Highway 87*). Victoria is centrally located in Victoria County at the convergence of U.S. Highways 87, 59, and 77. It is one of the state's old, historic cities. Victoria continued to grow as a trade center, especially as Indianola became an important port of entry for both goods and the thousands of immigrants who settled in the area. The city of Victoria was founded in 1824. There is a German Pioneer Marker located at DeLeon Plaza, 101 North Main Street, Victoria, Texas 77901, dedicated to the German pioneers who traveled along the Guadalupe River in 1845 to settle the Texas Hill County.

Number 2 Granite Marker (Victoria)

"Dedicated to the German Pioneers who traveled along the Guadalupe River in 1845 to settle the Texas Hill Country." 1995 - 150th Anniversary New Braunfels Sesquicentennial "Gewidmet den deutschen Pionieren die

1845 dem Guadalupe folgend das Texanische bergland besiedelten. " 1995 - 150 Jubilaeum

The wagon train made its way northwest from Victoria to Spring Creek (*present day U.S. Highway 87*). Spring Creek is a stream in Victoria County and was named from its source at a clear spring. Spring Creek rises three miles southwest of Fordtran in northern Victoria County. The intermittent stream runs southeast for 17 miles to its mouth on the Guadalupe River.

The German immigrants departed Spring Creek and headed towards the Cuero area (*present day U.S. Highway 87*). Cuero is at the convergence of U.S. Highways 183, 77A, and 87, in central DeWitt County. The first post office in DeWitt County was established in May 1846 in Daniel Boone Friar 's store, four miles north of the present site; it was also called Cuero (*later Old Cuero*). Cuero was not founded until 1872.

The wagon train departed Cuero area and the German immigrants reached McCoy's Creek (*present day U.S. Highway 183*). McCoy's Creek rises 12 miles north of Cuero in northeastern DeWitt County and runs southwest for eight miles to its mouth on the Guadalupe River, six miles north of Cuero. The stream was named for John McCoy, who received a headright on the creek in 1827. McCoy's Creek is located near Concrete, Texas on U.S. Highway 183. James Norman Smith laid out the town in 1846; it was thus the county's earliest townsite, and its nucleus was the old Upper Cuero Creek settlement, which dates from 1827. The trail departed McCoy's Creek and traveled to Hochheim (*present day. U.S. Highways 183 and 77*), at the intersection of U.S. Highway 183 and Texas

State Highway 111 in northeastern DeWitt County. Hochheim was established as a settlement for German immigrants along the Guadalupe River.

The immigrants departed Hochheim and traveled to Peach Creek. Peach Creek *(present day in the vicinity of Texas State Highway 111)* is a stream in Gonzales County. Peach Creek flows southward for 48 miles into the Guadalupe River.

After departing Peach Creek, the immigrants made the trek to Gonzales *(present day Texas State Highway 111 to U.S. Highway 183)*. Gonzales is one of the earliest Anglo-American settlements in Texas. It was established by Empresario Green DeWitt as the capital of his colony in August 1825. DeWitt named the community for *Rafael Gonzáles*, governor of *Coahuila y Tejas*. Gonzales it is at the confluence of the Guadalupe and San Marcos rivers, on U.S. Highways 90, 97, and 183 in the north central part of the county. Rolling, green hills came into view. The Guadalupe River rushed its banks, and this must have been a glorious sight to the weary pioneers.

The German Immigrant Trail continued from Gonzales to Seguin *(present day U.S. Highway 90/U.S. Highway 90A)*. Seguin was founded in 1838. Seguin's cultural identity was shaped by the dominance of German American pioneers. These settlers traveled along the German Immigrant Trail in the 1840s and 1850s from Indianola, on the coast, to Seguin and the Hill Country in New Braunfels. Seguin was on the trail taken by German immigrants from Indianola to the Hill Country.

A historical marker dedicated to the early German pioneers can be found in Seguin's downtown Central Park on the Square (201 S. Austin Street, Seguin, Texas 78155). The small granite marker honoring the German settlement is at the western entrance.

Number 3 Granite Marker (Seguin)

"Dedicated to the German pioneers who traveled along the Guadalupe River in 1845 to settle in the Texas Hill County"
1995 – 150th Anniversary

The immigrants departed Seguin and traveled to New Braunfels *(present day Texas State Highway 46)*. New Braunfels, the county seat of Comal County, is at the confluence of the Guadalupe and Comal rivers. The settlers forded the Guadalupe River *(near the present-day Faust Street Bridge, 554 E Faust St, New Braunfels, Texas 78130)* in New Braunfels. Settlers often waited for prolonged periods of time at this crossing until the waters were low enough to ford. The viewpoint from this bridge (not in existence in 1849) gives us an incredulous view of what our ancestors endured in order to travel to the Hill Country.

New Braunfels was established in 1845 by Prince Karl of Solms-Braunfels, Commissioner General of the *Mainzer Adelsverein*, also known as the Noblemen's Society. Prince Karl named the settlement in honor of his home of Solms-Braunfels, Germany. The *Adelsverein* organized hundreds of people in Germany to settle in Texas. He found the perfect place for them on a site called *"Las Fontanas"* at the confluence of the Guadalupe and Comal Rivers. They named the town New Braunfels in honor of the Prince.

This trail memorializes the thousands of German immigrants that braved the elements to reach this destination. It includes the gray granite marker at 375 S.

Castell Avenue, New Braunfels, Texas 78130. It is located in a flower bed to the right of the front entrance to the New Braunfels Civic/Convention Center.

Number 4 Granite Marker (New Braunfels)

"Dedicated to German Pioneers Who Traveled Along the Guadalupe River in 1845 to Settle the Texas Hill Country" 1995-150th *Anniversary New Braunfels Sesquicentennial*

"Cewidmet Den Deatschen Pionieren Die 1845 Dem Guadalupe Folcend Das Texanische Bergland Besiedelten" *1995-150 Juliaeum*

After crossing the Guadalupe at the fords under the Faust Street Bridge, the German immigrants set up camp on the high side of the Comal Creek *(present day Zink and Landa Street)*. In general, the Dry Comal Creek empties into the Comal River close by Landa Park. The stream was the site of one of the first communities in Comal County, the Comal Creek settlement.

The next leg of the trail went from New Braunfels to Boerne *(present day Texas State Highway 46)*. Boerne was first settled by German immigrants in 1849. Boerne, the county seat of Kendall County is located on Cibolo Creek, Interstate Highway 10, and U.S. Highway 87.

A cutoff at Boerne *(present day Sisterdale Road, RM1376)* from the newly popular Fredericksburg Road preserved access to Sisterdale and beyond to Fredericksburg via the Pinta Trail. The last leg of the journey went north of Boerne to Sisterdale, then cut through the back woods to the north side of today's Boerne. The trail continued to be used above Sisterdale for a period of time, crossed the Guadalupe River near today's Sisterdale.

The German Immigrant Trail continued past the Ottmar (Ottomar) von Behr Farm, established in 1847. The Behr Farm is located on the left 11 miles from Boerne on RM1376 in Kendall County. In Letter #6, dated August 1860, Julius Schlickum described the accident that happened near the Behr Farm at the Guadalupe River crossing. Gustav Thiessens' wife, Ottilie Theissen *(and another lady)*, died by drowning while trying to cross the Guadalupe River by carriage close to the Behr Farm.

There is a historical marker is situated near the Behr Farm. The marker states the following:

Ottmar von Behr

Sisterdale

Kendall County, Texas

"Ottmar von Behr had an influence on German immigration before bringing his family to Texas in 1848. Having toured America in 1846, he published an emigrant's guide, suggesting the life of a Texas farmer. Although Ottmar was the son of nobility in Germany, he left to farm and raise sheep in Texas. German immigrants were moving into Texas with professional credentials and degrees to seek new freedoms. Ottmar and his neighbors brought with them a distinguished collection of books and a passion for intellectual freedom, attributes that to the creation of a Latin colony. The Sisterdale was not a platted community, but a series of large farms populated by German immigrants who left behind prestigious recognition in Germany to take up farming. Ottmar was the second regional pioneer to settle in Guadalupe Valley by the Old Pinta Trail. Thus, his entry in 1848 gave him second settler status in future Blanco County (1858) and Kendall County (1862). Ottmar was also

responsible for the naming of Sisterdale. He suggested changing the Sisty's Creeks to Sister Creeks and put Sisterdale on the map when he petitioned for a post office in 1851 and was appointed first postmaster. He was elected Justice of the Peace in 1851. Ottmar was known for his social skills, hosting visitors, guests, and travelers. Ottmar had returned to Germany in 1855 when the Sisterdale petition was signed to create a new county so his wife, Louise Behr, signed for him. Ottmar never returned to Texas; he died on his return trip back to America. Ottmar only lived in Sisterdale of seven years, but he left a lasting legacy."

The immigrants traveled to Sisterdale *(present day RM1376)*, located in the valley of Sister Creek. Sister Creek rises in two branches in northern Kendall County. Sisterdale was established in 1847. The wagon train departed Sisterdale and traveled towards Luckenbach. The trail followed West Sister Creek *(present day intersection RM1376 and RM473)* to the vicinity of its headwaters. The trail diverted to the northwest along Jung Creek. Jung Creek is a stream in Kendall County, Texas that runs parallel to RM 1376 on the left-hand side as you leave Sisterdale and can be found on the Whitworth Ranch (private property) near Sisterdale. Jung Creek starts past Platten Creek.

Because the trail above West Sister Creek was another difficult stretch of the trail, it was soon abandoned in favor of a road up a gentler slope to the east, passing through Luckenbach *(present day RM1376)*. The trail traversed a ridge and dropped down to ford South Grape Creek *(present day RM1376)*, up the hill, and through a pass, continuing northwest to Luckenbach. According to the Texas State Historical Society, the town was founded by German farmers, including the Engel and Luckenbach families, in the late 1840s, known by the name of South Grape Creek. A new road from Sisterdale through Luckenbach to Fredericksburg emerged. In 1849, Minna Engel opened a trading post on South Grape Creek, "Pioneers' Crossing," that would become the town of Luckenbach.

The immigrants departed Luckenbach (*present day FM1376*) and continued to the Cain City area (*present day Luckenbach-Cain City Road*). Cain City is a ghost town founded in 1915. On the ridge of the Cain City Road, lay before them the breathtaking view of the Pedernales Valley. Seven miles to the northwest, hidden among trees, was the future home of Fredericksburg.

The trail ventured northwest (*present day U.S. Highway 290*), and it crossed the Pedernales at the first inverted horseshoe bend, site of Mormon Colony Zodiac, a Mormon settlement established in 1847 by 150 Mormons under the leadership of Lyman Wight (1796-1858). The colony was abandoned in 1851 after floods destroyed their mill. The Texas Historical Marker was erected in 1936. It is located on U.S. Highway 290 at Schmidtzinsky Road, east 1.4 miles (on private property).

Site of Zodiac

"*A Mormon settlement established in 1847 by 150 Mormons under the leadership of Lyman Wight (1796-1858). Abandoned in 1851 after floods destroyed their mill.*"

A Texas Historical marker on the right side of U.S. Highway 290 West towards Fredericksburg marks the location of the Pinta Trail. The inscription is as follows:

The Pinta Trail

"Origin of the Pinta Trail is attributed to nomadic Plains Indian tribes. Early Spanish and Mexican expeditions followed the general route of the trail, which extended from San Antonio de Bexar to the San Saba River near present Menard. A survey by German immigrants in 1845 provided a wagon road over part of the trail, and, after the discovery of gold in California in 1849, the trail was utilized by U.S. Military companies seeking new routes to the western states. Use of the trail declined with the advent of railroads in the late 1800s and early 1900s."
Texas Sesquicentennial 1836-1986

The trail continued to Fredericksburg *(present day U.S. Highway 290, past Schmidtzinsky Road)*, crossed the Pedernales River and Barons Creek. Fredericksburg was built between two creeks, Barons Creek and Town Creek. Town Creek flows into Barons Creek and Barons Creek flows into the Pedernales River.

The trail passed Fort Martin Scott on the right *(present day U.S. Highway 290)*. The Texas Historical marker inscription at this site reads as follows:

Site of Fort Martin Scott

"Established by the U.S. Army December 5, 1848, as a protection to travelers and settlers against Indian attack. Named in honor of Major Martin Scott, Brevet Lieutenant Colonel, 5th U.S. Infantry, killed at Molino Del Rey September 8, 1847. Its garrison participated in many Indian

skirmishes. Occupied intermittingly after 1852. Held by the Confederacy, 1861-1865 Permanently in December 1866."
    Erected by State of Texas
    1936

The train of immigrants arrived at the site for the new settlement of Texas. Wilhelm Klier and Julius Schlickum arrived in Fredericksburg in January 1850. It had been a long and weary four-week, 300-mile journey. Christmas was celebrated on Texas soil and now the new year would be celebrated in Fredericksburg, Texas!

The Republic of Texas German Immigrant Trail 1844-1846 marker was erected at 325 West Main Street, Fredericksburg, Texas. The marker is located at the entrance to the Pioneer Museum. The following quote from the marker tells the story:

Republic of Texas German Immigrant Trail
"Between 1844 and 1846, thousands of German immigrants under the auspices of the Society for the Protection of German Immigrants in Texas, better known as Adelsverein, landed at Galveston and Indianola. Their ultimate destination was the 3,878,000-acre Fisher-Miller Land Grant located between the Llano and Colorado Rivers.

The experiences of these immigrants on the way to their land grants is testament to the strength of their character. The first German immigrants lived in tents and dugouts on the beach at Indianola awaiting transportation that never came. With frigid weather, heavy rain, no adequate shelter, diseases, and lack of food and clean water, hundreds died. They realized their only hope to find food and shelter was to start toward the land they had been promised. Those who were able set out on foot, leaving behind household goods and even sick relatives. Still more died along the trail and often were not buried. It was written that out of approximately 6,000 German immigrants who had landed in the Republic of Texas, almost half died a miserable death, and no more than 1500 ever reached their destination.

On May 8, 1846, the first group of immigrants arrived in Fredericksburg Many were still ill and died shortly after arriving. Some forged on to the five planned settlements which included Castell in Llano County. Others settled in what became Bexar, Blanco. Mason and surrounding counties. Many remained in Fredericksburg and Gillespie County.

Numerous German communities in Texas had their beginnings from those brave and determined immigrants who traveled the Republic of Texas German Immigrant Trails of 1844-1846. These communities continue to grow and flourish today."

The Daughters of the Republic of Texas Chapters: Alamo Heroes, Blanco County Pioneers, Dr. Wilhelm Keidel and Llano Pioneers

Chapter VI - Gillespie County (1850-1852)

In 1850, cholera took many lives in the Hill Country. Fredericksburg had a total population of 1,253 of which 913 residents were of German descent in the 1850 Census. The community was totally German speaking. Fort Martin Scott provided protection from the Indians, and it was also a market for the local farmers. The Mormons had opened a settlement called Zodiac on 2,200 acres four miles east of Fredericksburg. The Mormon sawmill became an import alternative to the hand sawing of timber. Millard Fillmore was elected as the 13th President of the United States in 1850. In 1850, Peter H. Bell was serving as the Governor of Texas.

German immigrants were adjusting to life in their new country. The residents had a community farm and Sundays were spent worshiping at the *Vereins Kirche* which was a non-denominational church. It was also the first school. Indians had been hostile until John Meusebach had successfully negotiated a non-government peace treaty with the "Penateka Comanche Indians" on May 9, 1847. That treaty has never been broken.

Meusebach Treaty with Penateka Comanche Indians - Fredericksburg Marketplatz

The settlers were just trying to survive. The community needed furniture makers, wheelwrights, farmers, and shoemakers. Existing log homes were improved, or new ones were being built from native limestone. Gillespie County was beginning to see the hustle and bustle of daily living. The German community consisted of hard workers, frugal, and hard-headed Germans. They had come through some tough times and now they were ready to do more than just survive.

Wilhelm Klier and Julius Schlickum arrived in Fredericksburg in January 1850, after a four-week trip. They observed the main street (San Saba Street), wide enough for horse drawn carriages and stagecoaches to make a U-turn. Right in the middle of the street was the *Vereins Kirche (present day 100 W. Main Street, Fredericksburg, Texas)*. The *Vereins Kirche* (which served as a church and a school) was the center of town.

The original church built by settlers in 1847 had two doors; one facing southeast (downtown) and the other faced northwest (uptown), making it possible to walk straight through the church on the way up or down the street. The southeast door was for the men and the women entered on the northwest door. The men were seated on the right side of the aisle and the women at the left side of the aisle. This "segregated" seating carried over for many years in the other churches built later.

Above: Vereins Kirche

Further down the *Haupstrasse* was a general store. The Kammlah House *(present day 309 West Main Street)* was built by Heinrich Kammlah in the first year or two after he settled in Fredericksburg, being one of the city's oldest homes. Henry Kammlah and his wife, Auguste, lived in the front four-rooms; subsequently, the big front room became the two rooms of the store.

Left: The Kammlah House (Pioneer Museum)

The first courthouse for Gillespie County had not been built and all the public records of Gillespie County covering the first two years of its original existence were destroyed by fire when John Hunter's store was burned in 1850. He was the County Clerk and kept all records in his store. John Hunter had evicted a drunk Fort Martin Scott soldier from his store which resulted in a fatal stabbing. The slain soldier's comrades returned to Hunter's store to seek revenge. Hunter, who had been forewarned, fled to a friend's home. The soldiers set fire to the store and burned it, thus completely destroying all county records.

In the ensuing months, Schlickum and Klier made a living by trading and light work. After a few months, Schlickum and Klier began the purchase of land in Gillespie County, Texas. Schlickum purchased 320 acres from Mr. John Twohig for $352 on August 28, 1850. *(Father Klier provided the funds for this purchase and was the lien holder – see contract June 28, 1856)*. Wilhelm was 15 years old and thus, only Julius Schlickum's name appears on the legal document.

xxxxxxxxxxxxx

April 1850

Copy Nr. 14

In the month April 1850 Mr. Louis Wahrmund bought 320-acre land from Mr. John Twohig to be sure that he could select from the section 45 the upper or the lowest and Capt. Engrin, agent to Mr. Twohig would told Mr. L. Wahrmund the piece of 320 acres to measure too. After Mr. Wahrmund selected the upper half, Capt. Engrin divided the section in two halves, so that the lowest or the east part remained with Mr. Twohig.

In the month of July 1850 Mr. Schlickum went to Mr. Twohig to buy land from him also. Mr. Twohig showed him through his agent Capt. Engrin, which was also the land measure here, this 320-acres from the section 45 and Schlickum bought this, and Engrin and Mr. L. Wahrmund gave and showed also the both corners to Mr. Schlickum.

In the month August 1850 Mr. Schlickum got the title about 320 acres from Mr. John Twohig so that was told in the title: the piece from Mr. Louis Wahrmund till to Mr. E. Wagner, and for that Mr. Twohig has guaranteed.

This is the simple fact and no Lourveur (??) or anybody else can dispute my right.

****

John Twohig (1806–1891) was a San Antonio merchant and banker, was born in Cork County, Ireland. After serving as an apprentice on a British merchant vessel and engaging in coastwise trade between New Orleans and Boston, he established a mercantile business in San Antonio, Texas, in 1830. He became a banker and was widely known for his breadline for the unfortunate which he financed personally. In the years prior to the Civil War, he amassed a large personal fortune. His banking business declined because of the effects of the war, but soon recovered. In 1870 Twohig was among the 100 wealthiest men in Texas. He died at his home in San Antonio in October 1891.

Louis Wahrmund, son of Christian Wahrmund, was born in Germany in 1822. He was a farmer, age 28 years; he purchased the upper half of 320 acres from John Twohig.

Vol. B, Pg. 125 August 28, 1850

<u>Jno Twohig</u>   to <u>Julius Schlickum</u>

The State of Texas   }
County of Bexar   }

Know all men by these presents, that I John Twohig of the County of Bexar and State of Texas for and in consideration of Three hundred and fifty two dollars to me in hand paid by Julius Schlickum of the County of Gillespie and State of Texas have granted, bargained, sold and released, and by these presents do grant, bargain, sell and release unto the said Julius Schlickum his heirs and assigns all that tract or parcel of Land lying and being in the County of Gillespie on the South Side of the Perdenales [Pedernales] River being the lower half of survey No forty three containing Six hundred and forty acres the part and parcel here conveyed being three hundred and twenty Acres adjoining on the east a part of the same survey bought by Louis Wharmond [Wahrmund] and on the West a tract purchased by E. Wagner the part and parcel hereby conveyed being an equal undivided half of said survey for 640 acres of Land; together with all and singular, the rights members hereditaments and appurtenances to the same belonging or in any wise incident or appertaining -- To have and to hold all and singular the premises above mentioned unto the said Julius Schlickum his heirs and Assigns forever--And I do hereby bind myself, my heirs executors and administrators, to warrant and forever defend all and singular the said premises unto the said Julius Schlickum his heirs and Assigns, against every person whomsoever, lawfully claiming or to Claim the same or any part thereof.

In testimony whereof, I have hereunto subscribed my name and affixed my Scrawl in place of Seal this twenty-eight day of August One thousand eight hundred and fifty

Signed Sealed & delivered in presence of us:

(sig.) F. L. Paschal
(sig.) Jno Twohig (Seal)
(sig.) Philip F. Bowman

State of Texas   }
County of Bexar   }

Before me J Wilson Cooke a Notary· Public in and for said County, duly commissioned and qualified, this day came Philip F Bowman who having been by me duly sworn deposed and said that John Twohig did in his presence sign, seal and deliver the within instrument of writing and declared the same to be his act and deed, for the purposes and considerations therein set forth and that F L Paschal signed with deponent as Witness.

To certify which I hereunto sign my name and affix the impress of my official Seal at San Antonio this 31st day of August A D 1850.

(L. S.)
(sig.) J Wilson Cooke Notary Public B C

Filed for record on Thursday 5th, Septr A D 1850 at 6 o' Clock P M and recorded Saturday 7th Septr A D 1850.

JMHunter C C G C

per Wm Mogford Depty
****

TRANSCRIBER'S NOTE: In the original volume the clerk's certificate to the foregoing instrument does not show vol. or page of record.

Since the first deed records were destroyed by fire sometime between the first of January and the 15th of July 1850, Gillespie County began to make substitute deeds beginning July 15, 1850. On September 10, 1850, Richard Cloudt was elected as sheriff of Gillespie County.

In September 1850, after purchasing the farm six miles outside of Fredericksburg, Wilhelm Klier and Julius Schlickum started to build a log cabin as a home for their family *(present day in the area of 2653 River Road, Fredericksburg, Texas)*. Cultivating fields in order to plant crops and procuring livestock was underway. The demanding work of making a living off a farm had begun. Wilhelm Klier celebrated his 16th on December 9, 1850.

On July 7, 1851, Friedrich Oestrich was elected sheriff of Gillespie County. Thereafter, George Freeman became the sheriff of Gillespie County on November 28, 1851.

In 1851, a diary entry was made by Aunt Minna into the book where she kept her copies (perhaps a diary). In 1851, his wife [Therese Klier Schlickum] traveled in the company of a family she was friends with to Fredericksburg, where a farm had been purchased in the meantime. She was accompanied by her sister, Josephine Klier, and by her brother, Carl Klier.

In 1851, Therese Klier Schlickum, age 23 years, accompanied by her sister, Josephine Klier, age 25 years (prior to their arrival in America, this would be the last time that Josephine Klier would see Mother and Father

Klier in their lifetime), and brother, Carl Klier, age 13 years, traveled to America, arriving in Indianola on December 1, 1851. Mrs. Ernst Felsing and Mrs. Oswald immigrated to Texas from Germany with Therese Klier Schlickum; they arrived at Indianola, Texas on the same date. After a stopover for a few days to gather necessities, they hurried to Fredericksburg by stagecoach, having expensive and bad accommodations along the way.

After an exhausting trip, they arrived in Fredericksburg on Christmas Eve, December 24, 1851. Julius Schlickum and Wilhelm Klier had been ill and, therefore, the log home had not been completely furnished. The travelers were put up at the Wagner's farm (Edward) for the holidays and thereafter moved to their own farm. It had been two years since Julius and Therese's wedding. Now in December 1851, Therese saw her groom, Julius Schlickum, for the first time since he had emigrated to America on October 1, 1849. When they moved to the farm, the household consisted of Julius Schlickum, Therese Klier Schlickum, Wilhelm Klier, Josephine Klier, and Carl Klier. Wilhelm Klier celebrated his 17th birthday on December 9, 1851.

In 1852, Charles Henry Nimitz erected a sun-dried brick hotel in the shape of a ship and was later enlarged to resemble a steamship. The Nimitz Hotel sat on the lot at 340 East Main Street, Townlot 186. George Freeman became the sheriff of Gillespie County in 1852.

Nimitz Hotel

The following was a letter that Ferdinand Schlickum, in Muenster, Germany, wrote to Josepha Klier (mother-in-law of Julius Schlickum) about Therese Klier Schlickum, Josephine Klier, and Carl Klier's trip to America in 1851; their arrival in Indianola, Texas; their travel by stagecoach; and their arrival in Fredericksburg, Texas on Christmas Eve.

Letter #5

(Letter by Ferdinand Schlickum [1] / Recipient Mother Klier)

Muenster, 14 April 1852

Since you, dear Mother [2], have to read so many letters [3], I'll take the liberty to only briefly share with you the most important items from our dear Texans' letters. [4] Our 4 travelers [5] arrived, as you may have gathered from their first report[6], in Indianola on December 1st (1851), where they were already notified of Julius' and Wilhelm's illness. After a stopover of several days in order to shop for necessities, they hurried to Fredericksburg by stagecoach as quickly as possible, accompanied by a cousin of Mr. Wagner.

They arrived there on Christmas Eve, after an exhausting trip. Among other things, especially bad and expensive overnight accommodations (*often a bed made of straw with those very annoying 'Germanic insects'*), rainy and -very wintry weather, wolves accompanying the coach which the stage-coachman tried to chase away by sounding the horn, and other such experiences, were the cause of many a discomfort. Julius had instructed a friend to greet them upon their arrival in Fredericksburg, and to pick them up there with his carriage. You'll surely spare me the recount of the scene when they met up, as described by Therese, as I'm missing the manuscript right now, and I'm skipping over it to describe their living arrangements.

Due to Julius' and Wilhelm's illness, the log home had not been completely furnished yet to offer accommodations for them. So, they were put up at Wagener's [Wagner's] farm for the Holidays, and thereafter moved to their own farm. They furnished and decorated it in no time at all, to the point of attracting the admiration of the other farmers. They met Wilhelm only late at night as he wasn't permitted to leave the house yet, and found him to have changed so much, that he appeared to Therese and Josephine like a stranger. Julius had changed quite bit as well, both of them were (yellow?) [7] and had become strong[8] , and after nearly one year of having been ill, they were quite worn-out and disfigured.

In their last letters they thought however that both of them had already recovered quite well due to the good and unaccustomed care, and so much so, that Julius would be able to work again after six weeks, and Wilhelm already after two weeks. Until then Julius had tried to make a living by trading and such light work, but hadn't become discouraged at all despite these circumstances, and remained jovial and was quite looking forward to the future. Despite the many privations, Therese feels extremely happy there and said that although there aren't as many amusements there as over here, she is experiencing family life as the greatest substitute, and that it is more comfortable there than in Germany.

Josephine on the other hand appears to feel the privations more intensely, and therefore appears to like it less there. She is however very amused by the cattle and is taking special care of them. Carl on the other hand is rather enjoying it there, and his job is to round up the cattle. Their fare is simple, as is customary everywhere over there: coffee, bacon and eggs or pancakes, and cornbread in the morning; rice at noon and mostly meat, fruit, or such, followed by coffee; and in the evening often as in the morning, but mostly cold food. Thus, they are living in modest, but happy circumstances, and let's hope that they'll have abundant harvests and God's blessing, so they will soon get to where they can cover the losses they have experienced, and able to attain an all-around secure livelihood in the future. [9]

Fer. Schlickum

---

[l] *Ferdinand Schlickum (born 1829) was Julius' younger brother. He immigrated to the US in 1858 and settled in Austin. He was also a customs inspector in New Orleans for*

a long time. After an adventurous life, he died in 1876 in Austin, Texas.

2 "dear Mother" is Josephine (senior) Klier, and thus Julius' mother-in-law.

4 Translator's Note: It appears that the transcriber may have misread several words in this sentence, but hopefully my translation was able to render the original meaning (although I'm unsure of that).

5 Therese Schlickum, her sister Josephine (junior) Klier and Therese's brother Carl, who was only 13 years old.

6 This report is lost.

7 Transcriber's brackets and question-mark — the sentence appears to have been misread or mis-transcribed somewhat, as it appears to not make much sense at all (yellow, strong, and worn-out), I suspect ü should say "weakened", of "enfeebled" instead of "strong."

9 Following bad years and losses of all kinds the farm was sold in 1855. Julius and Therese Schlickum erected a store in San Antonio, which they sold however again at the end of 1860. Thereafter they opened a store in Boerne that was quite successful, until they had to give it up in 1862 due to the flight to Mexico.

*Left: Karl Ferdinand
Schlickum
10/12/1829 -
11/12/1876
Austin, Texas*

In July 1852, the Commissioners voted to build a county jail. The stone 18x14 jail stood near the school building on Marketplatz. On December 27, 1852, John M. Hunter was elected sheriff of Gillespie County.

Chapter VII - Background of the Julius Ludwig Siegmund Ransleben Family

Julius Ludwig Siegmund Ransleben was born on August 17, 1814, in Berlin, Germany. Julius was the eldest of eight children. He joined the Texas immigration government in the mid-forties. Julius, age 29, married his first wife, Marie Spannagel, on November 15, 1843, at the *St. Nikolai-Kirche*, Berlin, Germany. Marie Spannagel was born on July 30, 1827; she was 16 years old at the time of her marriage.

Julius Ransleben and his bride, nee Maria Spannagel, departed Bremen, Germany on August 1, 1846, on the ship *Mathilde*, commanded by Captain Basse. After a lengthy voyage, the ship and passengers arrived in Galveston on October 3, 1846. The Ranslebens traveled in covered wagons pulled by oxen from Indianola to the *Vereins* colony on the Comal. After a short stay in Hortontown and New Braunfels, they joined John Meusebach's colony at Fredericksburg.

Julius Ransleben was issued Townlot 185, Gillespie Country Court Record, Volume D, in 1847; this lot adjoined the present Nimitz Hotel. Ransleben established the first privately-owned general store on this lot. Soon thereafter, another mercantile business opened that furnished supplies to Fort Martin Scott. Faced with this competition, Ransleben sold his store and retreated to his occupation of farming. Ransleben's wife, Marie, became enamored by the glamour of the soldiers' uniforms at Fort Martin Scott and she departed for parts unknown with a member of these troops. Julius and Marie were divorced. On December 15, 1847, Julius Ransleben's signature appears on the petition asking the State Legislature to grant the organization of Gillespie County.

After meeting the charming Josephine Klier, age 26 years, Julius Ransleben, age 38 years, married her on October 28, 1852, Wedding License No. 63. The Texas branch of the Ransleben family tree had its beginning with this marriage. Josephine Wilhelmine Klier, became the second wife of Julius Ransleben; they were married 10 months after she arrived in Fredericksburg. Josephine was born and baptized on August 1, 1826, in Dusseldorf, Rheinprovinz, Preussen. The Rhine Province *(German: Rheinprovinz)* was also known as Rhenish Prussia (Rheinpreussen).

After their marriage, Julius, and Josephine Klier Ransleben lived in a covered wagon in Comfort. Their first-born son, Carl, was born in this covered wagon on June 13, 1853. Julius was working in the Comfort area helping to prepare the land for cultivation. Julius Ransleben had acquired the corner lot in Fredericksburg, which together with his original lot and building, he sold to Charles Nimitz in 1855. Julius Schlickum sold the 320-acre farm on the Pedernales River to Josephine Klier Ransleben and Wilhelm Klier for $500 on June 28, 1856. Friedrich Wilhelm Klier (Father Klier) in Germany was the lien holder of this note.

After a family visit to Germany in 1859-1860, Wilhelm Klier, Therese Klier Schlickum (children, Katchen, Julius), and Carl Klier returned to Texas. Wilhelm and Carl Klier made their home with Julius and Josephine Klier

Ransleben at the Klier-Ransleben farm. Carl Klier, age 21 years, died by accident on the farm within a year after he came to Texas from Germany. He is buried at the Ransleben Family Cemetery on the Pedernales River.

On the 1860 Gillespie County Census, Julius Ransleben was listed as a farmer and the household members included Julius Ransleben, age 43; Josephine, age 32; Carl, age seven; Max, age five; Oscar, age four; Julius, age three; Fritz, age six months; and Wilhelm Klier, age 25 years.

Ransleben was a member of Nimitz's Gillespie Rifles. Although a Union sympathizer, Julius Ransleben was forced into hauling food and other material from coastal ports to the Texas hinterland for Confederate forces during the Civil War (1861-1865). These trips separated him from home for long intervals at times. In the meantime, Mrs. Ransleben was providing refuge for one of her family, her brother Wilhelm Klier who had escaped the Nueces Battle at the beginning of hostilities. During the Civil War in 1863, Fritz Ransleben, son of Julius and Josephine Klier Ransleben, died in Gillespie County at the age of three years.

After the Civil War, the Julius Ransleben's family continued to grow. The 1870 Gillespie County Census lists Julius as a farmer and the household consisted of the following: Julius, age 56; Josephine, age 44; Carl, age 17; Max, age 15; Oscar, age 13; Julius, age 11; Josephine, age eight; Hilmar, age six; Guido, age five; and Herman, zero months.

On November 2, 1872, Wilhelm Klier sells one-half of his land to Julius Ransleben for $300, Vol. L, Page 420;

his sister, Josephine Klier Ransleben, already owned the other half of this 320-acre farm.

Carl Ransleben and his brother, Oscar Ransleben, were blacksmiths and wheelwrights who had their business in the building at 417 E. Main Street. Oscar Ransleben purchased a modest limestone-rock house at 104 South Elk Street, Townlot 217, on September 3, 1885, for the price of $750.00. In 1887, Carl Ransleben built the rock house next to the shop on East Main Street and the family moved in here. Carl and Oscar Ransleben were the sons of Julius and Josephine Klier Ransleben.

Julius and Josephine Klier Ransleben had their share of heartaches. They had nine children and three passed away *(Fritz died in his third year in 1863, Guido died in his 23rd year in 1892, and Herman died in 17th year in 1887).*

Left: Julius and Josephine Klier Ransleben

Josephine Klier Ransleben was born of wealthy parents in Germany, but she endured hardships in a true pioneer spirit. She was ever busy with all of her duties, needlework, sewing, and cooking. She was a graduate of the *Koenigliche, and Kaiserliche Kueche* in Berlin and her cooking skills were widely known. Josephine Ransleben passed away on June 29, 1888, at the age of 62 years. Julius Ransleben died on October 9, 1897, at the age 83 years. The hardest years for Julius were those years without his beloved, Josephine, by his side for some 20 years. They are together again, buried in the family plot on the original Ransleben farm on the banks of the beautiful Pedernales River.

Chapter VIII - Pre-Civil War Era (1853-1860)

Julius Schlickum's brother, Ferdinand, (1829-1876), emigrated to America in 1853. Ferdinand Schlickum was Julius' younger brother. He was a customs inspector in New Orleans for a long time. Franklin Pierce became the President of the United States of America in 1853. James Henderson completed Peter Bell's term when Bell resigned as Governor of Texas on November 23, 1853. Elisha M. Pease was elected as Governor of Texas on December 21, 1853. Louis Weiss was elected sheriff of Gillespie County in 1854. He was elected again as sheriff in 1856.

Wilhelm Klier had spent his teenage and early twenties living and working on the Schlickum property on the banks of the Pedernales. New life began within the family! Julius and Therese Klier Schlickum had a daughter, Katchen (Catharine) Schlickum, who was born on the Schlickum-Klier farm, Gillespie County, in 1854. Schlickum was a participant in the 1854 San Antonio German Convention in San Antonio that attempted to unite the various German settlements into a political union. Schlickum urged the convention to be careful and not go too far in opposing the Texans. Julius and Therese Klier Schlickum resided at the farm on the banks of the Pedernales Road until 1855. Following several bad years and losses of all kinds, Julius and Therese had to sell the farm and moved to San Antonio to open a mercantile store.

In September 1855, Gillespie County's first courthouse was completed on the northwest corner of the courthouse square. The courthouse was a two-story limestone building with a galley in front, two rooms downstairs, and a courtroom upstairs at the cost of $2,200. This stood where the old post office was located and was razed in 1940.

First Gillespie County Courthouse

Wilhelm Klier celebrated his 21st on December 9, 1855. The following legal document was a contract to begin the transfer of the Schlickum property to Wilhelm Klier and Josephine Klier Ransleben in 1856.

April 22, 1856
Vol. H. Pages 332 & 333
The State of Texas }
County of Gillespie }
Before me H. Ochs, Clerk of the County Court of said County personally appeared Friedrich Wrede to me well known, who on his oath deposited and said, that he had been County Clerk of this County at the date of execution of the within instrument of writing and that, while incumbent of that capacity, appeared before him Julius

Schlickum and Therese Schlickum his wife, known to him who separately did acknowledge to him to have executed the within instrument of writing as their act and deed to the purposes and consideration therein stated, and that such acknowledgment were given to him by said Therese Schlickum in the manner prescribed by law in regard to married women.

In Testimony whereof I hereunto set my hand & official seal this 27th day of March A.D. 1856.

(L.S.)

H. Ochs. Clk CCGC

Filed for record April the 21st at 3 o'clock P.M. and recorded April the 22nd 1856 at 3 o'clock P.M. in Book H pages 332 & 333.

H. Ochs, Clk.

****

Following several bad years and losses of all kinds, Julius Schlickum had sold the 320-acre farm to Josephine Klier Ransleben and Wilhelm Klier for $500 on June 28, 1856. Julius and Therese Schlickum had opened a mercantile store in San Antonio. The contract mentioned a debt (or mortgage) of $150 payable to Friedrich Wilhelm Klier (Father Klier), in Muenster, Germany, which the buyers accepted payment of, (but the seller will pay). Julius Schlickum paid off the $150 debt out of the $500 he received from the sale of the 320-acres as stated in the contract. "Julius Ransleben and both Seller hereby thus clarify that Julius Schlickum, through the above sale, has fully satisfied his obligation to Friedrich Wilhelm Klier in Muenster." Julius Ransleben's name was in that last sentence only because he was a witness of both Julius and Therese Schlickum's signatures on the document. Since the 320-acres were purchased by both Josephine Klier Ransleben and Wilhelm Klier (together), the assumption was that the intention was for each of them get one half of the 320 acres.

June 28, 1856 (translated from German)
Vol. H. Pages 332 & 333
Julius Schlickum & c to Jos. Ransleben & c.

Between the signatories Julius Schlickum as seller on the one hand and Josephine Ransleben née Klier and Wilhelm Klier on the other hand, the following purchase contract has been concluded.

1. Julius Schlickum hereby gives the two buyers his farm 320 acres of land on the south side of the Pedernales, together with all the buildings and improvements on it, as an owner and commits himself to the consequence of all and every claim to the said reason.

2. Buyers, on the other hand, have to pay the seller the sum of 500 dollars say five hundred dollars and while 400 dollars in cash and a hundred dollars in three months, without fail, until the first of October of this year.

3. Buyers hereby also accept the payment of the mortgage liable on the farm up to the amount of 150 dollars say a hundred and fifty dollars, whereas seller undertake to pay the now liable debt up to the said amount of 150 dollars.

4. Since Julius Schlickum has repeatedly named the two buyers, behalf settlement with Friedrich Wilhelm Klier, government Chief Accountant, in Muenster, Konige Preussen, at said sum top last, so the undersigned have not fixed a general price of the farm and leave the arrest of the same to their father or father-in-law said Friedrich Wilhelm Klier in Muenster, as the purchasers are committed to the possible additional amount.

Julius Ransleben and both Seller hereby thus clarify that Julius Schlickum, through the above sale, has fully satisfied his obligations to Friedrich Wilhelm Klier in Muenster and as a legal man.

Done San Antonio the 28th of June 1856.

(sig.) Julius Schlickum, Seller

(sig.) Therese Schlickum born Klier

Witness

     Julius Ransleben

****

Julius and Therese Klier Schlickum had a mercantile store in San Antonio in 1857. James Buchanan became the President of the United States in 1857. Hardin R. Runnels was elected Governor of Texas on December 21, 1857. Francis Kettner was elected sheriff of Gillespie County in 1858. Wilhelm Klier, now 23 years old, was issued the State Certificate of Citizenship in May 1858. A Certificate of Citizenship is an identity document proving U.S. citizenship. It is generally issued to derivative citizens and to persons who acquired U.S. citizenship. Ferdinand Schlickum, brother of Julius Schlickum, was married to Emma Wueste on June 1, 1858, in Bexar County, Texas.

On April 11, 1859, the second Gillespie County jail was built. On July 27, 1859, Louis Weiss was elected sheriff of Gillespie County. Meanwhile, in Bexar County, Texas, Julius Friedrich Wilhelm Schlickum, son of Julius and Therese Klier Schlickum, was born November 22, 1859. In December 1859, Wilhelm Klier, his brother Carl, and his sister, Therese Klier Schlickum (now the mother of two children, little Kathe, and Julius) returned to Germany to visit family. Wilhelm Klier turned 25 years old on December 9, 1859, while at his homeplace in Muenster, Germany. Sam Houston was elected as Governor of Texas on December 21, 1859.

In 1859, Hermann Holzapfel, at age 39 years, purchased a tract of land located on the east side of San Pedro Creek in San Antonio, Bexar County, Texas, from Ignacio Perez (Doc #99991695860). That document was witnessed by J. Schlickum and P. R. Schmidt on December 28, 1859.

Holzapfel was born on August 19, 1820, in Baderhorn, Germany and was married to Anna Martha Schmidt. Their marriage date or number of children is not known. Carl Hermann Holzapfel and his brother Gustav Holzapfel emigrated to Texas on the same ship as Julius Schlickum and Wilhelm Klier. Hermann Holzapfel became a trusted and close friend of Julius Schlickum and Wilhelm Klier. The 1860 Census of Bexar County, Texas lists Hermann Holzapfel, a merchant, age 39 years, living in the same household with Julius Schlickum, age 33 years. Other household members were Therese Klier Schlickum, age 26; Catharine Schlickum, age six; Julius Schlickum, age nine months; and Aby Maxfield, age 11.

73

In the 1860 Gillespie County Census, Wilhelm Klier, age 25, was living in the household of Julius Ransleben, a farmer, age 43; Josephine Klier Ransleben, age 32; Carl Ransleben, age seven; Max Ransleben, age five; Oscar Ransleben, age four; Julius Ransleben, age three; and Fritz Ransleben, age six months. Wilhelm's occupation was listed as a wagoner. In farming, a wagoner looked after the horses under his control and drove them in accordance with whatever work was to be undertaken, e.g., ploughing, reaping, harrowing, carting, etc. Otherwise, he drove a horse-drawn heavy four-wheeled wagon, conveying produce or manufactured goods to a market, or railway station.

While on the return trip to Germany, Julius Friedrich Wilhelm Schlickum, son of Julius and Therese Klier Schlickum, was baptized on April 11, 1860, at *Sankt Martini Katholische*, Muenster, Westfalen, Germany. His birth date was November 22, 1859, in Bexar County, Texas.

Left: Sankt Martini Katholische, Muenster, Germany

Ed Maier was elected sheriff on February 6, 1860. Thereafter, Phillip Braubach was elected Sheriff and John Dietz was elected Deputy Sheriff of Gillespie County, Texas in August 1860. In 1860, the population of Gillespie County was 2,736.

On their return to Texas in September 1860, five members of the Klier family, brothers Wilhelm and Carl Klier, one sister, Therese Klier Schlickum, niece and nephew, Catharine, and Julius Schlickum, returned to America on the ship *Gaston*. Two other sisters, Maria and Toni, and brothers, Hugo, and Gustav *(Gustav immigrated in 1866)*, remained in Germany. This would be the last time that Wilhelm and Carl would see Father and Mother Klier in their lifetime. Wilhelm and his brother, Carl, made their home with his sister, Josephine, who became the second wife of Julius Ransleben, Sr.

Wilhelm Klier began working for Johan Frederick G. Striegler, his future father-in-law in 1860. *(Johan Striegler was a Mail Contractor for the U.S. Government for several years beginning in 1860)*. Wilhelm and his partner used a mail wagon pulled by a team of mules to carry the U.S. Mail from Fort Martin Scott near Fredericksburg to Fort Mason, and Fort McKavett during the time of the ever-threatening Indians. *(Camp San Saba was not established until 1864; Fort Concho was not established until 1867.)* They had many thrilling adventures.

The City of Fredericksburg now owns the site of Fort Martin Scott, has a recorded Texas Historical Marker, and is open to the public. Fort Martin Scott is located at 1606 East Main Street (US 290 east) Fredericksburg, TX 78624. The historic site contains one original garrison building, which has been restored, one late 1800s old farm shed and three reproduction garrison buildings.

Historical marker, Fort Martin Scott, Fredericksburg, Texas

A restored reproduction officers' quarters is located at the Fort Mason Museum. Fort Mason is located at 204 West Spruce Street, Mason, TX 76856.

Left: Fort Mason, Mason Texas

Site of Fort Mason

"Established July 6, 1851, by the U.S. Army as a protection to the frontier. Named in honor of Lieutenant George T. Mason, killed in action near Brownsville April 25, 1846. Albert Sidney Johnston, George H. Thomas, Earl Van Dorn, and Robert E. Lee were stationed here at intervals from 1856 to 1861. Evacuated by Federal Troops March 29, 1861. Reoccupied after the Civil War until 1869."

Erected by the State of Texas 1936

Fort McKavett, Menard, Texas

Fort McKavett is considered one of the best-preserved intact examples of the Texas Indian Wars (1850-1875) military posts. Restored structures include the officers' quarters, barracks, hospital, schoolhouse, dead house, sink, and post headquarters. In addition, there are ruins of several buildings, most notably the commanding officer's quarters, which burned in 1941, and the barracks along the north side of the parade ground, which once was the longest building west of the Mississippi River.

Fort McKavett is located at 7066 FM 864, Fort McKavett, TX 76841.

The following was a letter by Julius Schlickum, living in San Antonio, Texas, Ward 3, to his wife Therese, while she was visiting Germany with their children, Julius, and Catharine (Katchen). Julius brings Therese news about their friends in the surrounding areas.

Letter #6

By Julius Schlickum to his wife Therese, while she was visiting Germany with their children Julius and Kathchen[1]

(*The date presumably is August 1860*)

My precious and kindest Therese,

I received your letter dated mid-July only a few days ago. You reported therein of your arrival in Muenster, and that you are all doing well. Thank you for writing this letter, you have lifted my spirits out of great concern and worry and have made me extraordinarily happy with your cheerful description of your way of life, the kindness of your parents, and the diversity of amusements, and so on.[2] And how much more will I be delighted when I'll be able to hear your oral accounts of your pilgrimage. Soon you will be returning! Each day I'm counting the days with greater longing, until I can hold you in my arms again my dearest darling and have my sweet children back again. — It's a good thing that the time of my solitude will finally be over as I'm feeling it more every day and am longing for all of you from all of my heart; I cannot even say how much. This time I can related an entire bunch of news from here. Recently there was a wedding at Lanks[3], where I was invited. Of rather, it was a belated celebration, as the young couple had made a trip to Comfort right after the wedding, and the celebration took place upon their return from there. We were all quite merry, everyone was there with their family except for myself. [4] Everyone mentioned you in greatest love and care, which made me feel quite good. Mrs. Briles[5] had a little girl about 5 weeks ago and is doing better than ever. Mrs. Herzberg, and Mrs. Meier, and Alice Nohl, were in Comfort for 3 weeks; the latter has turned Mr. A. Schmidt down officially. Last week Mrs. vom Stein also left to go to Comfort. Mrs. Theissen is going to Sisterdale this week. Everyone is fleeing this South African heat, which has never been seen here before. The thermometer is showing 100-105 degrees Fahrenheit, rarely less than 95 degrees in the shade at noon.[6] Mr. Fischer is currently in San Antonio, allowing me the opportunity to thank him for his kindness towards you on your trip to Galveston. He is sending kindest regards to you. The ladies' coffee parties were less frequented lately, the new thing is ... [7]. Dances and concerts remain unattended as well, no one has money, and everyone is economizing by necessity. Mr. A. Schmidt sold his store with all its inventory to Dr. Nohl, and he is bankrupt. Due to this sale his creditors in New York are about to lose around 5000 Dollar. What an outrageous trick! I had formerly told you that he had agreed on a partnership with a gentleman in New York. This man, by the name of Tehonian [8], arrived two weeks ago. When he reviewed the accounts, he discovered that the matter was not quite in order. He and Schmidt asked me to act as arbitrator between themselves....... [9] after a short examination I discovered that Schmidt still had 45,00 Dollars' worth of payments due, and a shortfall of a minimum of 2000 Dollar ... [10]. Schmidt himself had no clue of his actual situation. Naturally, nothing came of the partnership, and as a result Nohl, who had granted surety for about 1000 Dollar, made the bogus purchase, showing both men in an odious light, and as swindlers. This morning one of Mr. Nette's [11] boys cut his finger off with a ... [12] cutter. Several days have gone by, and this letter hasn't left yet. I was kept from writing to you in the last days repeatedly. Since then there we've received terrible news. First Mr. ... [13] ... was murdered in Arizona by his workers. Mr. ... [14] is from Westphalia, his mother supposedly is still alive, and he has relatives in Dortmund [North Rhine-Westphalia, Germany] or Amsberg; he leaves behind a sizable estate. I had mentioned above that Mrs. Theissen was going to Sisterdale, and last week she traveled to and took Miss ... [15] along. Mr. Theissen had no time to accompany her. A Mexican took her there. When they ... [16] at Behrs farm, the drawbar of the carriage broke, and it rolled over, and Mrs. Theissen and her ... [17] drowned. The Mexican was only able to save Miss ... [18]. The bodies haven't been found yet. It is too horrible, and poor Mr. Theissen is in despair. He traveled to Sisterdale still in that same night after he received news of the accident, despite terrible weather and wolves. Mrs. Stein is now in Comfort as well. Mr. Defoe is entering a business partnership with ... [19].

Hopefully, you'll receive this letter before you're preparing to leave these last news have so disturbed me that I'm very worried. I haven't made any decisions yet in regard to the plans here[20], but I expect that I'll stick with Boerne. In any case, I'll remain here another four weeks and won't make any decisions until then, perhaps I'll find a better opportunity.

[1] *Kathchen — little Kathe.*

[2] *Translator's Note: transcriber was unsure about some of the words, however I expect to have correctly understood and related the gist of the sentence.*

[3] *Transcriber was unsure of the surname.*

[4] *Translation is a good guess, as the sentence appears to be transcribed incorrectly.*

[5] *Transcriber was unsure of the surname.*

[6] *Some words are obviously transcribed incorrectly, but hopefully my translation reflects the meaning in the original more closely.*

[7] *Transcriber could not decipher.*

[8] *Transcriber was unsure of this surname.*

[9] *Transcriber could not decipher.*

[10] *See 25.*

[11] *Transcriber was unsure of this surname.*

[12] *See25*

[13] *See 25.*

[14] *See 29.*

[15] *See 25.*

[16] *See 25.*

[17] *See 25.*

[18] *See 25.*

[19] *See 25.*

[20] *Transcriber was unsure of this word.*

Abraham Lincoln was elected President on November 6, 1860; his term was from 1861-1865. Wilhelm Klier had turned 26 years old on December 9, 1860. Julius and Therese Klier Schlickum had sold their store in San Antonio at the end of 1860. Thereafter, they opened a store in Boerne (*on a monthly rent basis*) at the corner of Main Street and Blanco, Lots 104, 105, 106, and 107, in Kendall County. The store was quite successful.

J. F. Stendebach had sold Lots 104, 105, 106, and 107 in Kendall County to Erastus Reed and Seaman Field, Volume 1, Pages 173-174 on December 15, 1860. A copy of that Indenture (deed of trust) stated that Stendebach purchased the lots from Gustav Theissen.

It stated the following: "with all the improvements thereon and all the improvements that the part of the first part may put thereon as per his contract with J. Schlickum. Also, the monthly rent for said place from said Schlickum, as per his contract with said party of the first part."

State of Texas   }
County of Blanco   }

This Indenture made and entered into between J.F. Stendebach of the first part, and Erastus Reed, of the second part = Trustee and Seaman Field of the third part. All three parties living in the aforesaid State of Texas and County of Blanco. Witnesseth -That the said part of the first part, for and in consideration of the sum of Fifteen hundred dollars, to him in hand paid (and the receipt of which is hereby acknowledged) by the said party of the second part – and for the further consideration hereinafter mentioned, have granted, bargained and sold, and does by these presents grant, bargain, and sell unto the said party of the second part, a certain lot or lots of land – as follows – being the same purchased of Gustav Theissen by said party of the first part, and known as lots Numbers 104,

105, 106, and 107 on the map of the town of Boerne in said County and State, with all the improvements, thereon and all that the said party of the first part may part thereon – as per his contract with J. Schlickum – Also, the monthly rent for said place from said Schlickum, as per his contract with said party of the first part, at any time where said party of the first part may desire to sell the foregoing, enumerated property. To have and to hold so the said party of the second part, to his heirs, executors, administrators and assigns forever. And the said party the first part does hereby command to warrant and defend same forever the title to the above bargained premises and property of the said part of the second part, his heirs, executors, and administrators and assigns forever.

But this Deed is executed the trust and conditions following, that is to say, Whereas the said party of the first part is in debt to the said party of the third part in the sum of fifteen hundred dollars by his name for that amount. Dated Boerne, Blanco County, Texas, December fifteenth eighteen hundred and sixty, and payable twelve months after Date to the order of said Seaman Fields for value received with twelve percent Cert. Int. from Date until paid. Now it is the intention of this instrument to secure the said party of the third part in the payment of said Debt. And if the said party of the first part shall fail to pay off and discharge the same on or before the maturity of the aforesaid Note – Than and in that case, it shall be the duty of the said party of the second part, when required so to do, by the party of the third part. And the said party of the second part is hereby authorized in that contingency. After giving notice of the time and place of sale by posting up written notices thereof. One at house of A. Staffel and one on each house of the aforementioned premises in the town of Boerne. To offer for sale to sell at public auction on the premises to the highest bid for each in hand the said herein described property improvements and increase. And to convey the same to the purchaser or purchasers thereof to his or their heirs forever, by deed and according to law and in that event to apply the proceeds of sale to the discharge of said debt and to the payment of the execution of this trust. And should then be a surplus remaining after the payment of this, to pay the same to the said party of the first part. But should the said party of the first part pay off and discharge the said debt before any sale can take place under this Deed, then this Deed shall be void to all intents and purposes.

In testimony whereof, I the said party of the first part have hereunto set my and on this the fifteenth day of December Eighteen hundred and sixty.

J. F. Stendebach
Signed and delivered.
In presence of
Fisher N. K. Kichling
Staffel.
****

Chapter IX - Background of the Johan Frederick Gottlieb Striegler Family

The patriarch of the Striegler family in Gillespie County was Johan Frederick Gottlieb Striegler, born in Denmark, December 5, 1813. His father, Carl F. W. Striegler, was a Norwegian whose name was originally spelled Strigler; his mother, Agatha nee Sindegaard, was Danish. Johan was the oldest of five children, the others being Rudolph, William, Amalie, and Theodore. Johan Striegler received a good education in his native Denmark, and he was gifted in music and a composer of music. Johan Striegler was confirmed in 1828 at the age of 15 years.

When Johan Striegler was 21 years of age, he was issued a character recommendation by the Danish Government in 1834. This document states that he was a man of good character, honest, industrious, and reliable. On January 15, 1837, at the age of 23 years, Johan Striegler married Jensine Amalie Adamine Fredericke Lange, born on March 14, 1814, a daughter of Architect Klaus Christian Lange and wife, Christophine Petrine Lange. Jensine Lange was baptized in 1814 and confirmed in 1830. They were members of the Lutheran Church.

A Danish Document issued under seal of the Government certified Johan Frederick Striegler's appointment to the Office of Assistant Mayor of Svendborg for a term of six years. While in Denmark, the Johan Striegler family moved four times, finally residing in Svendborg. Johan Striegler and his family owned and

operated several business establishments; one business was a weaving and dyeing establishment where linens were hand-woven from flax. They were dyed, and then the material was sold by the yard in their dry goods store. In 1851, Johan invented a loom which was then used in his business to produce woolen goods. Then, they began the weaving of woolen cloth, in addition to the process of linens.

For several years, Johan owned two farms, one of which was on an island of Jutland. Striegler sold one of the farms in order to expand his factory and store in

Svendborg. Despite his family's many activities, he was desirous of providing for them on a better and more extensive scale.

In 1854 and early in 1855, the Strieglers' thoughts were turned towards Texas by the reports from Rasmus Frandsen [Frantzen]. A former schoolmate of Johan Striegler, Rasmus Frandsen [Frantzen], had gone to America—to Gillespie County, Texas. Frandsen [Frantzen] wrote in glowing terms of the possibilities in Texas and urged them to come to America. It was a great sacrifice for them, but with the spirit of self-abnegation characteristic of their lives, they decided it would be best for their children. Then, they made arrangements with Waldemar Lange, his wife's brother, who took charge of the store and factory in Svendborg, and his brother, Theodore, who took charge of the farm. (Waldemar Lange later left Denmark for Brazil, South America, and was never heard from again).

On August 3, 1855, the Johan Frederick Gottlieb Striegler family left Hamburg, Germany on the ship *Gutenberg* with Captain N.C. Peterson for America. Fifteen belonged to the Striegler group: father, mother, nine children (two had died in Denmark), two servants, and two young men who were former employees in the Striegler factory. The Striegler family included the following: Johan, age 41; Jensine, age 41; Antoinette, age 18; Olfert, age 16; Arthur, age 15; Ove, age 13; Atilla, age 12; Ida, age 10; Frederick, age seven; Amalie, age four; and Inetz, age three months. The two young men were William Otte, Antoinette's fiancé; Carl Frandsen [Frantzen], a nephew of Rasmus Frandsen [Frantzen]; and two servants. Both Otte and Frandsen were employed in the Striegler factory before leaving Denmark. (Carl Frandsen [Frantzen] worked at the Nimitz Hotel about six months, then— disappointed in Texas—he returned to Denmark.) One of the servants, Caroline Steffenson, later married Henry Kirchner on February 8, 1857, and moved to San Antonio. When the Strieglers left Denmark, William Otte concealed himself on the boat until they were well out at sea. Antoinette was the only one of the family who knew that he was on the ship. The young couple had agreed that the Atlantic Ocean would not separate them!

To their dismay, the passengers on the *Gutenberg* soon learned that the ship had a leak so, they were obliged to take turns in pumping water out of the boat to keep it from sinking. It took seven weeks to make the perilous voyage. The Johan Striegler family arrived in Indianola, Texas on October 2, 1855. The covered wagons, drawn by oxen, were guarded by riders and marksmen, who led them through the wilderness to their destination, near Fredericksburg.

On their arrival in Gillespie County in October 1855, the Strieglers lived in a house on the Rasmus Frandsen [Frantzen] place for several months. Johan Striegler purchased land on the Pedernales River in the Rocky Hill community. Here he built a substantial home on a bank of the Pedernales. Those were the exciting days of occurring episodes relative to the Indians. However, they were determined and willing to fight for their new home. Now began the demanding work of subduing this new land to make it yield a livelihood for the family. Antoinette Striegler was married in the spring of 1856 to William Otte in the *Vereins Kirche.* Fernanda Striegler was born May 14, 1857, in Gillespie County, to Johan and Jensine Lange Striegler. Alice Striegler was born in 1859, in Fredericksburg, Texas.

In 1860 John Frederick and his three oldest sons obtained their Citizenship and Naturalization papers from the United States Government. Thereafter, John Frederick Striegler was a Mail Contractor for the Government for several years. The 1860 Gillespie County Census included the following in the Striegler household: Johan, farmer, age 47; Jensine, age 46; Olfert, age 21; Arthur, age 19; Ove, age 17; Atilla, age 16; Ida, age 15; Frederick, age 12; Amalie, age eight; Inetz, age six; Fernanda, age three; and Alice age three months.

The 1860 Gillespie County Census listed the following members of the Rasmus Frandzen [Frantzen] household: Rasmus, a farmer, age 43; Johanna, age 32; Andreas, age 13; Emma, age 12; Henry, age 11; Carl, age nine; Edward, age eight; William, age seven; Martha, age five; Robert, age one; and Johanna Hasse, age 58 years.

Alice Striegler, daughter of Johan and Jensine Lange Striegler, died of diphtheria in1861, in Gillespie County, Texas, at the age of two and one-half years.

Crisis faced the Strieglers in1861; there was the Civil War, and the call came for soldiers for the Confederate States. Johan's three oldest sons answered the call. The three oldest sons, Olfert, 22, Arthur, 21, and Ove, 19, served in the Confederate Army during the war. They all survived the war. Arthur, who was a linguist, proficient in French, Danish, English, German, and Spanish, was employed as an interpreter for the Government in the

State of Louisiana during a part of the time of the War between the States. Johan, who was past the military age at the time, joined the Home Guard with his two youngest sons, Attila, 17, and young Frederick, who was only 14 years old. They all survived the war.

At an election held on August 1, 1864, Johan Striegler was elected County Commissioner of Gillespie County by 267 votes, which was most of all votes cast for said office. He served until the military government took over at the end of the war. In the 59th year of his life, Johan Striegler died November 13, 1872. He had lived an active, fruitful life; he had met the challenge. Jensine Lange Striegler died 15 years later, on October 25, 1887, in her 74th year.

Mr. and Mrs. Striegler had 13 children; 11 were born in Denmark and two were born in Gillespie County, Texas. Of these, one infant daughter died in 1838 in Denmark. Another daughter, Olga Emilie Striegler, born August 7, 1847, in Svendborg died November 16, 1847, in Svendborg, Denmark, at the age of three months. One daughter, Alice, the youngest child, died of diphtheria in Fredericksburg, Texas at the tender age of two and one-half years.

The 10 children, five sons and five daughters, who grew to manhood and womanhood were: Antoinette Striegler Otte, (Mrs. William Otte), Gillespie County, Texas; Olfert Striegler, (m. Lucy Ann Robinson Roberts), Menard County, Texas; Arthur Striegler, (m. Marie Lorentzen), Gillespie County, Texas; Ove William Striegler, (m. Anna Pueschel), Gillespie County, Texas; Attila Nicolai Striegler, (m. Margaret Gates), Kendall County, Texas; Ida Striegler Klier, (Mrs. Wilhelm Klier), Stonewall, Texas;

Frederick Christian Striegler, (m. Mary Louise Mogford), Gillespie County, Texas; Amailie Striegler Nelson, (Mrs. Charles W. Nelson), Kendall County, Texas; Inetz Striegler Pickett, (Mrs. Cassius Pickett), Sand Springs, Oklahoma; and Fernanda Striegler Falder, (Mrs. Amos Falder), Sedalia, Missouri.

They have all passed away. Their biographies, and short sketches of all the descendants of John Frederick G. Striegler may be read in *Striegler History Book*. Their record shows that they were good, law-abiding, progressive citizens. The name has been kept untarnished through the years. All the descendants have reasons to be proud of their ancestry. May the young generation, and those not yet born, emulate their example.

Chapter X - The Civil War Years (1861-1865)

In January 1861, Julius Schlickum ,and Hermann Holzapfel opened a store in Boerne named "Schlickum and Holzapfel," *(present day 211 W. Main Street, Boerne, Texas)*. They had previously signed the contract for monthly rent on December 15, 1860.

Gillespie County opposed secession by an overwhelming 400 to 17. But Texas seceded from the Union on February 1, 1861, and joined the Confederacy. The total statewide vote on the Texas Ordinance of Secession in February 1861 was 61,337. A total of 46,188 voted for secession and 15,149 against. Jefferson Davis was elected Provisional President of the newly formed Confederate States of America on February 10, 1861.

The Hill Country Germans really wanted nothing to do with the Civil War. They thought if they kept their heads down, worked their farms, protected settlers from the Indians, remained loyal to the United States, that they would be left alone. They did not want to be instrumental in tearing up one of the most beautiful forms of government the world had ever seen, in order to build a new government founded solely on the principle of expansion of human slavery.

Wilhelm Klier served Gillespie County by becoming a member of the Minute Company, Gillespie County, Texas State Troops. Private Klier enlisted February 25, 1861, at Fredericksburg, Texas. The Commanding Officer was Captain Phillip Braubach, Minute Company, Gillespie County, Texas State Troop; called into service of state by Act of February 7, 1861.* The frontier troops, Gillespie

County Minute Company, were paid by Texas and provided protection from Indians, renegades, and bandits.

The Texas Ordinance of Secession was the document that officially separated Texas from the United States in February 1861 and joined the Confederate States on March 2, 1861.

```
Name & Rank:    Klier, W., Pvt.,
Comm. Off:      Braubach, Phillip, Capt.,
Organ:          Minute Co., Gillespie Cty., TST.

Enlist:         F 25-61 at Fredricksburg, Texas

Disch:          Serv. 35 days - Recd. $52.50
Descrip:        Age 26

Remarks:        R&F 40; Val.Horse $65;Chief Justice
                Gillespie Cty. En.Off.; Called into
                service of state by act of F 7-61;
                1 muster roll and four payrolls;
```

On March 2, 1861, Texas officially seceded from the Union and Texas joined the Confederate States of American. Abraham Lincoln was inaugurated as the 16th President of the United States on March 4, 1861. Sam Houston was Governor when Texas seceded from the United States but refused to declare any loyalty to the new Confederacy. Lieutenant Governor Edward Clark replaced him. Clark filled the rest of Houston's term on March 16, 1861.

Fort Sumter in South Carolina was fired upon by the Confederacy on April 12, 1861. The Civil War exploded driving a wedge between German immigrants and most other Texans. During this time, records show that Private Wilhelm Klier was on the muster roll of the Minute Company ending May 25, 1861, and paid $10.50.

Shortly after the promulgation of the Ordinance of Secession, a "Union Loyal League" was organized in June 1861. The purpose of the league was not to cause strife between Unionists and Confederates but to take such actions necessary from being compelled to bear arms against the Union and to protect their families against hostile Indians.

Texas Governor Edward Clark issued a proclamation on June 8, 1861, telling everyone that they had 20 days to take the Confederate Oath of Allegiance or leave the state which was the same month the "Union Loyal League" was formed in the Hill Country.

Jefferson Davis (Provisional President of the Confederacy) issued a proclamation on August 14, 1861. This proclamation gave all male citizens 40 days to either take the oath of allegiance or leave the Confederacy. The Unionists would later claim that the Germans were traveling under this proclamation. Private Wilhelm Klier was on the muster roll of Minute Company for Gillespie County, Texas State Troops ending August 25, 1861; and paid $27.00 for 18 days.

The 1861 Texas gubernatorial election was held on November 4, 1861, to elect the Governor of Texas. Incumbent Governor Edward Clark was running for his first full term but was defeated by Francis Lubbock by a margin of 124 votes. The election was the first of two held in Texas during the American Civil War. On November 6, 1861, Jefferson Davis was elected President of the Confederate States of America.

Private Klier was on the muster roll of Minute Company for Gillespie County, Texas State Troops, ending November 25, 1861; and paid $15.00 for 10 days. In 1862, Julius Schlickum was the commander of Company B, 3rd Regiment, 31st Brigade District. Kendall County. Julius Schlickum had refused to join the "Union Loyal League."

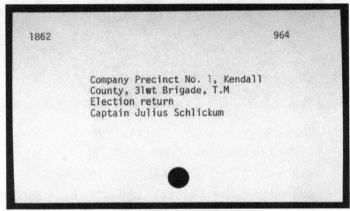

Schlickum Muster

In January 1862, the Texas legislature created Kendall County, carving it out of Kerr, Blanco, and Bexar counties. The voters chose Boerne as the county seat and elected John Sansom, as the county's first sheriff.

Julius Schlickum and Hermann Holzapfel continued to operate their store in Boerne in January 1862. The store was quite successful and was called "Schlickum and Holzapfel." The store was located on the corner of Main

Street and Blanco Road in Boerne. Hugo Schlickum, son of Julius and Therese Klier Schlickum, was born January 14, 1862, in Bexar County Texas. He was cared for by a nanny, Mrs. Anna Holzapfel, wife of Hermann Holzapfel. Julius Splittgerber was elected sheriff of Gillespie County in 1862.

Two-Story St. James Hotel on the left; location of
"Schlickum and Holzapfel" Store

Private Wilhelm Klier served under the Commanding Officer Captain Jacob Kuechler; Ranger Company for Gillespie, Kerr, and Hays Counties; Frontier Regiment, Texas State Troops. Klier enlisted on February 12, 1862, for 12 months unless sooner discharged. Captain Kuechler was the Enlistment Officer. This Company was organized under Act of December 21, 1861.* This Company was dissolved by the Governor and the new Commander (Capt. Davis')** was enrolled.

```
Name & Rank: Klier, Wilh., Pvt.
Comm. Off:   Keuchler, Jacob, Capt.
Organ: Ranger Co.for Gillespie,Kerr & Hays Cntys.
       Fron.Rgt., TST
Enlist:F 12-62 for 12 mos unless sooner dischrg.

Disch:
Descrip:

Remarks:R&F 75;Capt.Keuchler,En Of;H:$100;HE:$30;
        Rifle & Shotgun :$60;Navy Pistol:$40.Co.
        org.under act of D 21-61.Co.dissolved by
        Gov & new Co.(Capt.Davis') enrolled. 1 MR:
        F 12-62.
```

The Frontier Regiment was the name history had given to a regiment of rangers authorized by the Ninth Legislature of Texas on December 21, 1861,* for the protection of the northern and western frontier of Texas.

**Captain Henry T. Davis, Company A, Frontier Regiment, was the commanding officer of the company organized under Act dated December 21, 1861.

The Colt Model 1861 Navy cap & ball .36-caliber revolver *(listed above as Wilhelm Klier's Navy pistol valued at $40)* was a six-shot, single-action percussion weapon produced by Colt's Manufacturing Company from 1861 until 1873. The term "Navy" refers to the caliber of the revolver, not necessarily the branch of service. The .36 caliber revolvers are called "Navy" and the .44 caliber revolvers are called "Army." It incorporated the "creeping" or ratchet loading lever and round barrel of the .44-caliber Army Model of 1860 but had a barrel one-half inch shorter, at 7.5 inches. The total production was 38,000 revolvers. (see p. 99)

On March 8, 1862, Julius Schlickum was sworn in as Justice of the Peace, Kendall County, Texas. When Kendall County was formed in early 1862, Hermann Holzapfel served as the Clerk to the Kendall County Commissioners Court. Hermann Holzapfel was sworn in as Kendall County Clerk, Volume 1, Page 8 as follows:

.......of which well and truly to be made unto said Governor, we bind ourselves, our heirs, executors, and administrators, jointly and severally, firmly, by these present. Signed with our hands and sealed with our seals, the seals being sprawls the eighth day of March 1862. The condition of this obligation is such, that whereas said Hermann Holzapfel has been elected Clerk of the County Court of Kendall County, if the said Herman Holzapfel shall well and truly discharge and perform all the duties of the above-named office, required of him under said Section, according to law. Then this obligation shall be null and void, otherwise to remain in full force.

(L. L.) Herman Holzapfel

(L. L.) T. Werner

(L. L.) Julius Schlickum

****

State of Texas, {County of Kendall} The foregoing annexed hand of Hermann Holzapfel as County Clerk was recognized and approved by me this eighth day of March in the year 1862.

Jos. Graham

P.T.K.C.

I Herman Holzapfel, do solemnly swear, that I will well and truly discharge and perform all the duties of the office of County Clerk of County of Kendall according to the best of my ability, agreeable to the Constitution and laws of the Confederate States and the State of Texas, and I do further solemnly swear, that since the twenty first day of May, last, nor at any time before, I being a citizen of this State, have not fought a duel with deadly weapons within this State, nor out of it, nor have I acted as second in carrying a challenge, or aided, advised or assisted any person thus offending – so help me God.

(Sign.) Hermann Holzapfel

****

State of Texas   }
Kendall County   }

I the undersigned Chief Justice of Kendall County certify that Herman Holzapfel, scribed, and swore to the foregoing oath at the town of Boerne before me this day the 8th of March 1862.

Sign. Jos. Graham

C.J.K.C.

Filed in my office for registration this eighth Day of March A.D. 1862 at five o'clock P.M.

H. Holzapfel

C.C. Kendall County

****

"The Enrollment Act" was a bill signed into law by President Jefferson Davis (President of the Confederacy) on April 16, 1862. It was a military draft that required all white males between the ages of 18 and 35 to register for military service.

On April 21, 1862, the Confederate Congress issued the "Partisan Ranger Act." It was intended as a stimulus for recruitment of irregulars for service into the Confederate Army during the Civil War. Under this act Captain James Duff's Partisan Texas Rangers became part of the Confederate States of America Army.

The First Confederate Conscription Act, passed on April 26, 1862, which made any white male between 18 to 35 years old liable to three years of military service. Service in the Texas State Troops had pre-empted the "Conscription Act" but soon it became apparent to all young men of Texas that service in the Confederate Army was mandatory.

Hermann Holzapfel's first entry as the County Clerk to the Kendall County Commissioners' Court was on May 19, 1862. The first signature by Hermann Holzapfel appears on May 28, 1862, as Clerk to the Kendall County Commissioners' Court.

Volume 1, Page 32

I, Jacob Theis, do solemnly swear, that I will faithfully and responsibly discharge and perform all the duties incumbered on me as Constable for the first Precinct of the County of Kendall, State of Texas, according to the best of my skill and ability agreeable to the Constitution and the law of the State of Texas, and also to the Constitution and the law of the Confederate States of America, as long as the State of Texas shall remain a member of that Confederacy. And I do further solemnly swear that hence the second day of March 1861, I being a citizen of the State, have not fought a duel with deadly weapons within this State nor out of it, nor have I tendered or accepted a challenge to fight a duel with deadly weapons, nor have I acted as second in carrying a challenge or aided, advised, or assisted any person thus offending – so help me God.

(Sign.) Jacob Theis

****

The State of Texas }

County of Kendall }

Sworn to and subscribed before me the signed Clerk of said county this 28th day of May 1862.

(L. L.)   In testimony whereof I herewith lift my hand and affix the Seal of the County Court of the said County at day and year last above written.

Signed H. Holzapfel, Clerk County Court Kendall Co.

****

There is a $500 Debt Power of Attorney (obligation), dated May 28, 1862, recorded in Volume 1, Pages 33, of the Kendall County Deed Records that mentions Jacob Theis along with Julius Schlickum and William Kuhfuss.

Volume 1, Page 33

The State of Texas }

County of Kendall }

Know all men by these present as we, Jacob Theis, as principal, and Julius Schlickum and William Kuhfuss, as parties, are held and firmly bound unto the present Governor of the State of Texas and his successors in office in the sum of five hundred dollars for the payment of which well and truly so be made we bind ourselves, our heirs, executors, and administrators, jointly and severally, firmly by these presents. Given under our hand this 28th day of May. A.D. 1862. The condition of this obligation is such, that where, as said Jacob Theis has been elected constable for the first Precinct of Kendall Cunty, if the said Jacob Theis shall not well and truly perform all the duties required of him by law, then this obligation shall be null and void, otherwise to remain in full force and effect.

William Kuhfuss, Jacob Theis, Julius Schlickum

(L.L.) Approved 5th June 1862

Jos. Graham C.J.K.C.

Filed for record at office in town of Boerne this 28th day of May A.D. 1862 at 8 o'clock A.M.

Hermann Holzapfel, C.C.C.K.C.

****

General Hamilton P. Bee declared martial Law in Bexar County on May 28, 1862. Resistance to the draft in the Hill Country was bitter; these communities had not been in favor of secession. Hence, on May 30, 1862, Brig. Gen. P.O. Hebert proclaimed martial law over the State of Texas, requiring every male over 16 years of age who was an alien to swear allegiance to Texas and to the Confederacy.

General Bee sent confederate units to enforce the martial law in Gillespie County on May 30, 1862. James Duff, Partisan Company, was sent to the Hill Country as one of these units. Duff's company arrived in the Hill Country on May 30, 1862. Duff, after arriving in Fredericksburg, declared martial law in Gillespie County, giving residents six days to come in and take the Oath of Allegiance to the Confederacy.

There was open resistance to the martial law proclamation. Citizens rebelled against taking the

103

Confederate Oath of Allegiance during the spring and summer of 1862. This resulted in what was commonly known as "the reign of terror" in the Hill Country. Men were hung when they refused to take the oath. Food and livestock were confiscated. Fields were burned, crops were burned, homes were burned, and property was destroyed. Families were harassed as Duff searched for dissidents. Duff became known as the "Butcher of Fredericksburg."

As per the deed below, Hermann Holzapfel purchased the four lots for $500 in Boerne on June 5, 1862. The lots are the location of the "Schlickum and Holzapfel" store at the corner of Main Street and Blanco Road.

The State of Texas   }
County of Kendall   }

Know all men by these present, that I Seaman Field, of the County of Kendall, State of Texas, for and in consideration of the sum of Five Hundred Dollars, to me in hand paid by Hermann Holzapfel, of the aforesaid County and State, the receipt whereof is hereby acknowledged, before the signing, sealing and delivering of these present, have granted, bargained, sold, released and conveyed, and by these present do grant, bargain, convey and deliver unto the said Hermann Holzapfel, his heirs and assigns, all those tracts or parcels of land lying, and being in the county of Kendall and town of Boerne, consisting of four lots, according to the Map of said town, to wit:

Lot Number one hundred and four (104), twenty-five varies square;

Lot Number one hundred and five and one hundred and six, (105 & 106) the same size; and Lot Number one hundred and seven (107), twenty-five varies by twenty-five varies.

Paid first mentioned Lot being situated on the corner of the Public Square and the Main Street and the others adjoining this, being the same the property purchased by me of Gustav Theissen under Deed bearing, Date August the second A.D 1861 – together with all and singular the rights, members, here it amends and ap. Pertinence to the same belonging or in anywise incident or appertaining: to have and to hold all and singular the premises above mentioned unto the said Hermann Holzapfel, his heirs, and assigns forever.

And I do further bind myself, my heirs, executors, and administrators, to warrant and forever defend, all and singular the said premises unto the said Herman Holzapfel, his heirs and assigns against every person whomsoever, lawfully claiming, or to claim the same, or any part thereof.

In testimony whereof I have hereunto subscribed my name and affixed my seal, using for ands, for my Seal, in the city of San Antonio this nineteenth day of March A.D. one thousand eight hundred and sixty-two.

Signed and delivered in presence
of C.E. Jefferson
Seaman Field (SF)
****

The State of Texas }
County of Bexar   }

Before me, C.E. Jefferson, a Notary Public of Bexar County, personally appeared Seaman Field, to me well know, who acknowledged that he signed, sealed, and delivered the foregoing; instrument of writing, and he declared the same to be his act and deed for the purposes and consideration therein expressed.

To certify which I hereto set my official Seal (C.E.) and signature this 19th day of May, A.D. 1862.

C.E. Jefferson, Notary Public

Be it remembered, that in this original deed, in the 5th line on the second page thereof, the word "Seal" is underlined instead of the erased word "Self", and also the words "City of San Antonio" instead of the erased words "town of Boerne."

H. Holzapfel

Clerk County Court Kendall Co.

Filed for registration in my office of Boerne this fifth day of June 1862, at four o'clock P.M. Recorded same day at five o'clock.

(Sign.) H. Holzapfel Clerk Commissioner's Court Kendall County.

****

The "Schlickum & Holzapfel" store was located at 211 W. Main Street, Boerne, Texas. Later, the old two-story St. James Hotel was located at 211 W. Main Street, Boerne *(see picture of the two-story building on the left; this was the location of "Schlickum and Holzapfel's" mercantile store in 1862).* The Julius and Therese Klier Schlickum family lived in a home about 500 feet from the store on a hill, surrounded by fields and gardens. See home (indicates location only) on the hill (with windmill) to the right of the

Old St. James Hotel, (*present day 402 Blanco, Boerne*). They owned 30 Morgens of land surrounded by a wall. A Morgen is a unit of measurement of land, varying in size from 1/2 to 2 1/2-acres, depending on each German state or area.

211 N. Main, Boerne (left two-story building) + 402 Blanco Road, Boerne (home & windmill on hill, upper left in the background)

Therese Klier Schlickum became deathly ill in June 1862. As she lay ill, Julius Schlickum was arrested on June 19th, by Captain James Duff, at his home in Boerne by the Confederates. Captain James Duff reported that the prisoner had been in contact with Federal prisoners at Camp Verde, with Hill Country Unionists, and with the North. Since martial law had been declared, Schlickum had not taken the Confederate Oath of Allegiance. Although upset that Therese was so ill, Schlickum was not surprised when the arrest happened. Through the help of rich friends, he offered the captain $25,000 for bail if he would leave him in the house until the doctor arrived and gave him the results of Therese's illness. The request was denied and Schlickum was arrested.

Schlickum was transported to San Antonio by Confederates with other prisoners and permitted to ride his own horse. He was brought to a firehouse that had been turned into a jail where 17 fellow sufferers were staying. *(The present-day location of this firehouse jail is 231 W. Commerce, San Antonio, Texas, San Fernando Cathedral Hall.)* The city's first firehouse included a large storage area in the back that had been turned into a holding cell for the various defendants. The prisoners awaited their day in court, often chained to heavy metal balls. All were German and most were educated and wealthy men. Phillip Braubach, the Sheriff of Gillespie County, was shackled with two balls and chains. Then there was H. J. Richarz *(1822-1910)*, the Chief Judge from Medina County and originally from Dusseldorf, Germany; as well as a friend Radeleff from Fredericksburg; and others. The prisoners were heavily guarded and treated illiberally. Their meals were delivered from a hotel for $20 per month since they did not want to eat soldiers' fare.

Shortly after Schlickum's arrest, Hermann Holzapfel wrote Julius Schlickum in the San Antonio jail. He stated that Therese Klier Schlickum's health was improving but she had to wean the poor little one, Hugo, who was four months old. The prisoners had to wait for months until someone tried to tell them the reason for their imprisonment. It took six weeks until Julius Schlickum and the other prisoners were interrogated although they had complained every day. Schlickum was accused of being disloyal.

On July 2, 1862, a Confederate Military Commission convened in San Antonio to hear testimony and put on trial dozens of insurgency leaders and Unionist sympathizers suspected of being traitors to the rebel cause. The sessions, which lasted through October 10, 1862, were held at the old U.S. Army headquarters on East Houston Street, a two-story structure that would be later

be reopened as the Vance House. *(Today the site of the Gunter Hotel. The historical Marker is located to the right of the entrance to the Hotel.)*

On July 4, 1862, not less than 500 male Unionists met where Bear Creek originates on the watershed between Fredericksburg and Comfort and proceeded to perfect the "Union Loyal League." The Gillespie County Company elected Jacob Kuechler, Captain and Valentine Hohmann, Lieutenant. The "Union Loyal League" had a spy in their midst by the name of Basil Stewart. The League became aware of this spy and an informant to James Duff. They decided to execute this traitor, drawing straws to the person who would do the deed. Ernst Besler drew the straw and shot Stewart to death as a traitor (Stewart was ambushed) on July 5, 1862.

On July 17, 1862, Julius Schlickum, previously arrested by the Confederates, was tried before the Military Commission in San Antonio, Texas. The charge was that "in his general deportment he is calculated to create discontent and dissatisfaction with this Government and its currency."

July 17, 1862 - Confederate States vs. Julius Schlickum

Erastus Reed, [sworn] says:

I have known Mr. Schlickum about one year. Judging from his conversations I don't think he has any sympathy for the Confederate States. I know of no act that he has ever done against the Government, his general conversations has been such as would lead anyone to suppose that he was opposed to the Confederacy. Knows of nothing particular except his manner of expression at the reception of the news.

He never appeared to believe anything coming from the Confederates, but on the contrary would always credit the news from our enemies. His associates generally were those who were looked upon with suspicion. He always appeared to know a great deal of those who were looked upon with suspicion. He once told me that he did not believe that Radeleff and Doebbler were any more disloyal than he was. He said he asked Radeleff and Doebbler if they belonged to that organization, to which they answered in the negative. The Accused said he knew of such an organization, but that it was for self-defense. He said he knew there were over one hundred men out in the woods, said he did not belong to the organization. About the time Duff's Co was there the Prisoner asked me whether he would be arrested, said rather than be arrested he would have to go into the woods. He finally said that he done nothing and would not go.

He also told me that there was an organization in San Antonio. He said that he believed they were mostly boys, and they could be easily put down. He believed he knew men who belonged to it. He assured me that he did not belong to such an organization. I have never known him to construe any news favorable to the Confederacy.

By the Defendant:

I never saw the accused associate with anyone looked upon with suspicion, except persons who came to the Defendant's store. Do you recollect after a singing festivity in Boerne, I told you as follows - Doebbler and Radeleff were passing through Boerne from San Antonio? I told Mr. Reed that rumors were floating about our vicinity that secret organizations were up in the mountains. Answer. So, you told me and told me that he believed that Judge Scott and men like him had started such organizations by threatening the lives of those who did not believe as they did about Political matters and that it was for self-defense.

I remember the accused told me he had had a conversation with Radeleff and Doebbler about such an organization, and that he, "the accused," had told Radeleff and Doebbler that he did not believe they were such fools, as to be guilty of joining such an organization, which would only bring destruction on the people and bloodshed on the frontier. I know he told me that there was such an organization in San Antonio. I think Holzapfel was present when this conversation took place. The whole neighborhood frequented his store. Judge Scott is an Ultra Southern man.

Signed

Erastus Reed

Geo. Wilkins Kendall a witness, was then called before the Commission and being duly sworn deposed as follows:

I live in four or five miles of the accused. I never heard the accused say anything by which I could judge whether he was in favor of one Government or the other. I know nothing of the accused opinions on the Slavery question. I never heard anyone say that the accused was a friend to the South. I never asked anyone whether the accused was friendly to the South.

Signed

George Wilkins Kendall

Erastus Reed was then recalled before the Commission and being duly sworn, deposed as follows:

I have heard the accused say that he was born in Europe and was in favor of free labor and opposed to the institution of slavery. He told me this in his own store. I don't remember who was present. I cannot tell what brought on the conversation, it was some time ago.

I took it that this referred to Slavery in Texas. I think anyone entertaining such views is an Abolitionist and would be in favor of abolishing Slavery.

Signed

Erastus Reed

Joseph Graham was then called before the Commission and being sworn deposed as follows:

I live three miles from Boerne. I make my visits to town as short as possible. I sometimes called at the store of the accused, he always appeared to be in possession of news, more favorable to the North than to the South. I have never heard him express his opinion on the justice or injustice of the war. When Capt. Duff's Co was up the country the accused told me that he heard he was to be arrested, asked my advice as to what he should do.

He said that if it depended on Capt. Duff he would go and report himself but that he might have Orders to arrest him. He said he might have sung some Yankee songs, but that he was drunk, and did not think it treason. I told the accused that he was accused of being an Abolitionist. He said, "I was brought up in Europe and my views and yours differ."

He did not say that he was opposed to the institution here but remarked as above. I have never been intimate with the accused. I have not heard accused spoken of, as regards Abolitionism, more than the generality of Germans. I know that the accused was opposed to Secession, and I have seen nothing since to induce me to think he had changed his views. Accused knew that I was one of four or five out of a hundred who voted for Secession, and when I was a Candidate for Chief Justice, he did more for me than I did for myself.

Signed
Joseph Graham
****

July 18, 1862 - Confederate States vs. Julius Schlickum

The Case of J. Schlickum coming up the accused was brought before the Commission.

Seaman Field, 1st sergeant. in Duff's Co T.P.D. being duly sworn and deposed as follows:

I know of nothing particular against the accused but have always supposed him to be against us. He was not in the habit of presenting our successes in a fair light. I mean by that, that he never had any good news on our side, but generally had something bad to tell. I have regarded him as being dangerous, from the fact, that those to whom he would communicate his news were governed by what he would say. I know of no open acts, further than as stated, except depreciating Confederate Currency. I know of his being opposed to taking Confederate currency and advised others not to do so. This was previous to the proclamation establishing Martial law. I have lived in four miles of the accused for two years, except the last three months. I know the general reputation of accused in his section, as regards his loyalty to this Government, and it is bad. Accused is a man of considerable influence in his section, he is a merchant, he is a man of more than ordinary intelligence, or more than the majority of the people he lives with. He informs himself of transpiring events.

By the Accused.

I heard about the month of February last, that accused refused to take Confederate Money. I have heard you advise people not to take Confederate Money. Accused advised me not to take it. He told me if I had any, I had better get shut of it, as it would be worth nothing in a short time. That the U. S. Army was getting the best of us, and we would be whipped in soon and the money would be worthless. I have seen accused associated with no suspicious character, except countrymen of the accused who I regarded as being influenced by accused's advice. Slasson was constantly about the accused's Store, and I regarded him as a very suspicious and dangerous character.

Signed

Seaman Field

****

Julius Schlickum took on his own defense and told the Military Commission that their witnesses had only voiced their opinions of himself but had not proven any facts; that he requested the right to his own opinion, that a Military Court was no Revolutionary Tribunal, and therefore could not judge matters of faith.

July 19, 1862 - Confederate States vs. Julius Schlickum

The Prisoner J. Schlickum was brought before the Commission and presented the following defense:

To the Honorable Military Commission San Antonio Gentlemen,

In conformity with your desire, I submit to you in the following my defense against the accusations brought against me. My charges were couched in such general terms that I concluded to call three gentle- men as witnesses, or rather references, who were known as good and loyal Citizens, though I was not so well acquainted with them, that they could give other than general evidence. These gentlemen all state, that I have often communicated news, unfavorable to the South, but Col. Graham admits, that, at the time, there was no other news to communicate. I do not deny, that, in some instances, I have doubted the reports of News Papers, which, I believe everybody did, more or less.

Mr. Reed says that he had often seen me in Company with people, who were looked upon with suspicion, but he was forced to admit, never outside my Store. I am a Merchant and have no business with my customers politics, how Mr. Reed can make this out to be a crime, as it appears to be his intention, is more than malicious.

A similar malice is contained in the repetition of a conversation, which I had some time ago with this gentleman, about a secret society, which was said to have organized in the mountains. He said at first that I had said, I know of such association, but on being cross questioned, was forced to admit, that I had only talked about floating rumors.

Mr. Reed says further that I had talked about a similar society in San Antonio, but could not produce the witness who he said, had been present. I most emphatically deny ever having said such things and consider my No! to be entitled to just as much credence as Mr. Reed's Yes!

The testimony of the three gentlemen is clear, I do not consider it necessary, to say much about it; but that Col. Graham, the only one of my accusers, who voted for Secession has treated me more favorable in his evidence, than the other two gentlemen, who formerly held the same political opinion with me. Do they try, by accusing me, to make their antecedents forgotten?

I have always obeyed the laws of the land, have taken the Oath, prescribed by law, and committed no illegal act, and I am willing to do my duty as a Citizen of these Conf' States. May the Court take into consideration, that I am a man of small means, have a large family, and that my wife is continually ailing and that from your decision, the welfare, nay, the existence of a whole family is now depending. Hoping soon to receive a judgment, which will enable me to return to my family.

I remain.

Gentlemen

Your Obedient Servant

Julius Schlickum

****

On July 19, 1862, Schlickum and two others escaped from the San Antonio jail, hid in the deep woods some 20 miles outside of the city until the hunt for them ended, and made their way to Matamoros. *[Julius Schlickum's letter dated February 20, 1863, stated that he had planned to escape on July 18th or July 19th. According to the Military Commission, Schlickum, Braubach, and Doebbler escaped in August 1862.]*

See excerpt below from Letter #8 that Julius Schlickum wrote to his father-in-law, Friedrich Wilhelm Klier, in Germany on February 20, 1863, with a detailed account of their escape from the San Antonio jail.

"I had prepared for a 'climate change' already before the sentence was passed down to me. At that moment I sent a message to my friends, telling them the time had arrived, and I decided on the night of July 18th to 19th. Braubach and Doebbler received the same sentence and wanted to accompany me. I received weapons and one bottle of nightcaps (whiskey for the guards), and the news that horses would be ready and waiting outside of town at 1 a.m. Our friends had been very busy. On the 18th in the afternoon, imagine my fright, Therese arrived, I could hardly believe my eyes.

She knew of my plans, and her worry, concern, and love, had prompted her to come see me one more time. I was quite worried and told her that she had gotten herself into grave danger and that I now would have to give up my plans so as not to compromise her safety. She adjured me not to pay any regard to her, and under no circumstance wanted me to give up my plan. She remained only a short time. — I haven't seen her since. Our prison had 4 windows (No. 3, 4, 5, 6). There were guards posted outside of 3, 4, and 6. Door 2 is leading to the room where fire-equipment was kept, and door 1 to an open plaza, opposite to the

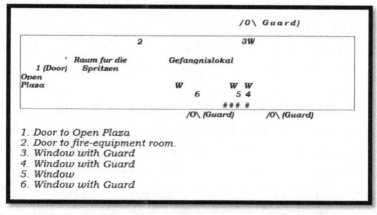

1. Door to Open Plaza
2. Door to fire-equipment room.
3. Window with Guard
4. Window with Guard
5. Window
6. Window with Guard

main guard house. Door 2 was locked and bolted, but we had discovered a way to unlock it already a long time ago.

Night had fallen, and we had retired early, but no one could sleep.

By 1 a.m. there was a changing of the guards. The moon lit up everything as brightly outside as if in daylight. One of the guards sat at the window, looking inside. We had no choice. We deliberated if we should offer him a drink mixed with strong whiskey. We always had liquor at our place since the soldiers never refused a drink. Then his comrade called out: "Let me have ... your ... ." He turned around, and — through the shadows, we slid out the door that was standing half open, while it was squeaking. — Door 1 in the fire house was opened quickly.

A few people passed by. In the shadows of the courthouse across the street there were two figures, with hats in hand. They were our friends. With loaded revolvers we slipped outside. The guard didn't see us and kept walking up and down. Their backs turned, we dared to jump. If the man would have seen us, he would never again open his eyes. Our friends were posted close, next to other houses, in dark doorways, in case there might have been an emergency and we might have needed their gun fire to cover us. We kept walking quietly. Finally. Outside of town we heard a whistle from thick underbrush. — We gave the counter sign, and six men on horseback, leading three saddled horses, rode up.

A short greeting, a deep breath, and an even deeper sip from our bottle of cognac which was making the rounds, and we dashed off through the prairie, avoiding all roads and bridges, until the horses had covered 22 miles in 2 hours. At daybreak we camped in a narrow and remote valley, in thick brush. "Over there in a dry riverbed in the middle of the woods is a cave, hide there! You will find food, goodbye!" and our friends chased on to hide the horses, which otherwise could easily have given us away.

We were free! — in this forest, probably the size of 100 Morgen, 2 miles from water, we spent about 6 weeks, until the pursuer's zeal had died down. We soon were told that all troops were patrolling along the frontier night and day in order to catch us, and that the Rio Grande, the river at the border between Texas and Mexico, was heavily guarded. They had orders to shoot or hang us, wherever they would come across us. The homes of our numerous friends were searched repeatedly.

Naturally, nobody believed that we would be staying so close to town, and so they kept searching us far away, as we had correctly figured beforehand. We were extremely vigilant in standing guard, never lit a fire, and got our water 6 miles from the spring at the farm of our friend Wilhelm Hester, who came every day in person to bring us groceries, bread, and salted meat. (Hester had helped rescue us, and he had done the same for others. Subsequently he was sentenced to death, but that was mainly based on the suspicion to having freed us. Pray for him!)."

Schlickum and the others obtained water six miles from the spring at the farm of their friend William Hester, who came every day in person to bring groceries, bread, and salted meat. Hester lived on a farm near Leon Springs which is about six miles from the cave. The 1860 Bexar County Census listed William Hester, as a stock raiser, age 24, living in Leon Springs, Bexar County, Texas. The household members included Catherine Ann Hester, age 35, Elizabeth Hester, age seven, and Julia Hester, age five.

The cave is in all probability was Cascade Caverns* in Boerne which is 22 miles from downtown San Antonio as the crow flies. The Confederates were searching for them in the opposite direction from San Antonio to Mexico. The letter stated that they stayed close to town, likely Boerne. The cave was well known by Kendall County residents.

On July 20, 1862, Major Fritz Tegener, while at work in his grist and sawmills, received information that the Counties of Gillespie, Kendall, Kerr, Edwards, and Kimble were declared to be in open rebellion against the Confederate States of America.

Cascade Caverns once known as Hester's Cave, is a historically, geologically, and biologically important limestone solutional cave three miles south of Boerne, Texas, United States, on 226 Cascade Caverns Road, in Kendall County. It has been commercially operated as a show cave and open for public tours since 1932. Informal tours were run as far back as 1875, when Dr. Benjamin Hester (no relation to William Hester was found though possible) owned the cave property. The cave was known by the native Lipan Apache people who lived in the area prior to 1800.

Captain James M. Duff had been ordered by the Confederacy to take such prompt and vigorous measures as, in his judgment were necessary to put down the rebellion in said counties. On July 22, 1862, Phillip Braubach (1829-1888), former Sheriff of Gillespie County, was brought before the Military Commission. Braubach was born in Wiesbaden, Germany, on July 28, 1829. He was educated there before immigrating to Texas on the *Neptune* in 1850. Braubach was elected Sheriff of Gillespie County, Texas in August 1860, and in 1861 joined Jacob Kuechler's frontier company. In 1862 he became captain of a Unionist militia company and was arrested in June by Duff's men.

On July 24, 1862, J. Rudolph Radeleff (1829-1880) from Fredericksburg, appeared before the Military Commission. J. Rudolph Radeleff was a Gillespie County Unionist and likely an original member of the "Union Loyal League." He was born about 1829 in either Holstein or Denmark. On July 25, 1862, Julius Schlickum was found guilty and sentenced to imprisonment for the duration of the Civil War, for lack of loyalty and antipathy towards the Southern States (disaffection of the Confederate Government); he was locked up in the San Antonio firehouse jail. Others were banished, and yet others sentenced to high fines. See excerpt below from Letter #8 that Julius Schlickum wrote to his father-in-law, Friedrich Wilhelm Klier, in Germany on February 20, 1863.

"Nevertheless, I was sentenced to imprisonment for the duration of the War, for lack of loyalty and antipathy towards the Southern States (disaffection of the Confederate Government). Two of my friends fared the same. Others were banished, and yet others sentenced to high fines. Texas was ruled by a sword-rattling militarist of the most loathsome kind. They suspended Civil Law completely. The slightest allegation by any boy was all it took to throw honorable men into jail, where they had to wait for months until someone made an effort to tell them the reason for their imprisonment. (To he hauled off into jail for the duration of the War was in affect about the same as going to be hanged from one of the first trees along the way; that was the fate of many)."

July 25, 1862 - Confederate States vs. Julius Schlickum

The defendant Julius Schlickum is charged with being a disloyal person to the Confederate States of America. That in his general deportment he is calculated to create discontent, and dissatisfaction with this Government and its currency.

Signed

John Ireland

Judge Advocate and Recorder

The statements of parties being thus in possession of the Commission, the Commission was cleared for deliberation and having maturely considered the evidence adduced, fined the accused Julius Schlickum, Guilty of Charge and Specification. And the Commission do thereby sentence the said Julius Schlickum to be "Imprisoned until peace is ratified between the United States and the Confederate States."

****

On July 25, 1862, Friedrich Wilhelm Doebbler (1824-1913) appeared before the Military Commission. He was the Grapetown innkeeper and Unionist from Fredericksburg. Captain James Duff had arrested him in early June 1862. On the same day, Eduard Degener (1809-1890) from Sisterdale came to the home of John W. Sansom on Curry's Creek and told him about the organization of the "Union Loyal League." Degener had immigrated to the United States in 1850 and settled in

Sisterdale, Texas, where he farmed. J. Rudolph Radeleff from Gillespie County offered his defense before the Military Commission on July 26, 1862. Phillip Braubach of Fredericksburg offered his defense to the Military Commission on July 27, 1862. Friedrich Wilhelm Doebbler from Fredericksburg was found guilty on July 28, 1862, and sentenced to imprisonment for and during the term of the present War.

Eduard Degener invited John Sansom to their meeting place on August 1, 1862, at Turtle Creek (now known as Bushwhack Creek). Fritz Tegener would be leading the group to Mexico; Sansom had previous knowledge and experience as a guide to the Edwards Plateau and the crossings on the Rio Grande. Sansom agreed to attend the assembly area meeting on August 1, 1862, below Kerrville on Turtle Creek.

The Hill Country Germans found themselves in the middle of the Civil War. Had they not left the nasty politics in Germany? Now they lived in Texas which had seceded from the Union. Their Oath of Allegiance had been to the United States of America. The German Unionists decided to head to Mexico where they would be able to travel to a Gulf of Mexico port, board a ship bound for New Orleans, and join the Union army. The German Texans thought they had had been offered a 30-day amnesty by the Governor of Texas and that they had an opportunity to depart Texas unmolested, rather than take the loyalty oath. But there was no such amnesty in effect. On August 1, 1862, the members of the "Union Loyal League" gathered at the headwaters of Turtle Creek. In response to the call from Fritz Tegener, 60 men cast their lot with

Tegener which included Wilhelm Klier and Jacob Kuechler. Fritz Tegener's sawmill was on a stream named Tegener Creek which was just beyond the meeting point at Turtle Creek. Tegener was familiar with the first part of their journey. The Unionists spent the night at Turtle Creek on August 1, 1862.

The headwaters of Turtle Creek are located near Farm to Market Road 1273 in the vicinity of the intersection of Hog Trot Trail and Aime Real Ranch Road in Kerr County. Even today, the headwaters of Turtle Creek are remote, lying-in rugged hills, southwest of Kerrville. *(The source or headwaters of a river or stream is the furthest place in that river or stream from its estuary or confluence with another river, as measured along the course of the river.)*

The Tegener's sawmill was located below Schumacher's Crossing at the confluence of the Guadalupe River and Tegener Creek. Tegener Creek, which flows into the Guadalupe River, sits between Ox Hollow and the of the Guadalupe just four miles from Ingram, Kerr County, near Hunt, Texas. Ox Hollow is a valley located in Kerr County. A historical marker is located at Schumacher's Crossing, Texas State Highway 39, near Hunt, Kerr County, Texas, which states the following:

"Christian Schumacher emigrated with his family from Germany to Texas in 1845, the year he was born. He came to Kerr County in 1880, later marrying Sarah Brazeal Sublett and moved to land along the Guadalupe River, near the site of an antebellum sawmill operation built by Gustav and Fredrich Tegener. In the 1920's son John Randolph Schumacher built a series of dams across the river

providing security from raging floodwaters for a steam crossing and new road to Hunt. Today, the dams remain, and an improved highway bridge crosses the stream. Schumacher's Crossing is still enjoyed for its scenery and access to the river."

The location of Duff's and Donelson's Companies and detachments of Taylor's 8th Battalion Texas Cavalry were at Camp Pedernales in Gillespie County. On August 1, 1862, these Companies spent the night at Camp Pedernales (Confederates' Camp). Camp Pedernales was located at Morris Ranch on the Pedernales River, which is off Texas State Highway 16 South in Gillespie County on the Morris Ranch Road. There is no historical marker.

On August 2, 1862, the Unionist continued to meet at the Union Assembly Area at Turtle Creek in preparation for trip to Mexico. The Unionists spent the night at Turtle Creek on August 2, 1862. The location of Duff's and Donelson's Companies and detachments of Taylor's 8th Battalion Texas Cavalry continued to meet at Camp Pedernales (Confederate Camp) in Gillespie County. The Confederates spent the night of August 2, 1862, at Camp Pedernales. On August 3, 1862, the Unionists continued to meet at the Union Assembly Area on Turtle Creek in preparation for the trip to Mexico, and where they received supplies from supporters. Charles Burgmann informed Captain James Duff of the route that the Germans were taking to Mexico when he had supplies taken from him by the Germans. A few days earlier, militia members had met Burgmann in an open field who had stumbled across a store of provisions. The militia took possession of the food out of hunger or as a joke. Burgmann became angry and out of revenge, put the pursuers on the trail of the Hill Country Germans. When Duff received information from Charles Burgmann regarding the intended route, Duff ordered Lt. Colin McRae (1835-1864) to hunt down the Unionists.

The Unionists departed Turtle Creek on August 3, 1862. The Hill Country Militia headed southwest. The Unionists arrived at the Main Unionists Camp near the headwaters of the South Fork of the Guadalupe River. This is where the Unionists spent the night of August 3, 1862. The headwaters of the South Fork of the Guadalupe River rises three miles southwest past the Intersection of Texas State Highway 39 and Ranch to Market Road 187 in Kerr County. The group was under the impression that they had 30 days to leave the state. They traveled leisurely on this 140-mile trip. The Unionists had good horses with sufficient pack animals and were well armed.

On August 3, 1862, Confederate Lt. Colin D. McRae left Camp Pedernales with a detachment of 94 men, as ordered by Captain Donelson, to hunt down the Unionists. Lt. McRae's Confederate detachment spent the night of August 3, 1862, at Camp Davis, which was the location of Davis' Company F, The Frontier Regiment in Gillespie County. McRae was with Donelson's Company K, 2nd Regiment Texas Mounted Rifles. Camp Davis was located in Gillespie County, Texas, four miles from the junction of White Oak Creek and the Pedernales River. Camp Davis was established in March 1862 by James M. Norris as a ranger station for the Frontier Regiment. There is no historical marker there. Captain John Donelson arrested four men about August 3, 1862, near the Guadalupe

River: Sebird Henderson, Hiram Nelson, Gustav Tegener, and C. Frank Scott, who were later hung near Spring Creek on August 22nd, 1862.

On August 4, 1862, the Unionists departed the Main Unionist Camp near the headwaters of the South Fork of the Guadalupe River in Kerr County. The Unionists arrived at the Head of the North Prong of the Medina River where the Unionists spent the night of August 4, 1862. The Head of the North Prong of the Medina River rises four miles northwest of the Lost Maples State Natural Area in northwestern Bandera County near Ranch to Market Road 187. *(Head is where the river starts, and the mouth is where it lets out into a body of water like a lake or ocean.)*

The Confederates departed Camp Davis midday and headed southwest on August 4,1862. The Confederates arrived at Henderson Farm, most likely Sebird Henderson's farm, where the Confederates spent the night of August 4, 1862. Sebird Henderson, Hiram Nelson, Gus Tegener, and Frank Scott had been taken into custody by a regiment of the Confederate soldiers for refusing to take the Confederate Oath of Allegiance. The Henderson Farm was located a few miles west of Ingram on Texas State Highway 27 and Henderson Branch Road, Ingram, Kerr County, Texas. There is a historical marker.

HENDERSON CEMETERY (Two Miles North)

"Howard Henderson (1842-1908) came to Texas in 1857. He was a survivor of the Civil War Battle of the Nueces in 1862 in which he and other Unionists were ambushed by a Confederate Force near the Nueces River. He later served as a Texas Ranger. Henderson married

Narcissa Turknett in 1866 and they settled near this site. In 1870, upon the deaths of their infant twin sons Thomas and Philip, they began a family burial ground which became known as Henderson Cemetery. Other family members and neighbors were also buried in the graveyard."

The Unionists departed the Head of the North Prong of the Medina River on August 5, 1862. The Unionists arrived at the Headwaters of the West Prong of the Frio River where the Unionists spent the night of August 5, 1862. The West Prong of the Frio River flows 19 miles roughly parallel to Farm Road 336 to join the East Prong of the Frio River at U.S. Highway 83 in Leakey. The Headwaters of the West Prong of the Frio River is approximately eight miles south of Texas State Highway 41 and Farm Road 336 in Real County, Texas. Sometimes referred to as "The Swiss Alps of Texas," area elevations range from 1,500 to 2,400 feet with deep canyons cut by the Frio River.

The Unionists had proceeded at a leisurely pace because they felt safe and were unaware that they were being followed. The Unionists believed they had sufficient time to leave Texas, and therefore did not guard their trail by keeping a scout in the rear. They moved through the hills very slowly and were not in a hurry as they hunted deer, searched for honey, and had barbecues. They also moved at a slower pace because the horses were unshod and carried heavy supplies. The Unionists had to travel close to rivers and creeks for water because the Hill Country was experiencing a drought. The Confederates departed the Henderson Farm on August 5, 1862. They headed to the Guadalupe River. When the Confederate pursuit force reached the river, at that point they turned west. The Confederates arrived at Tegener Creek where the Confederates spent the night of August 5, 1862.

On August 6, 1862, the Unionists departed the West Prong of the Frio River. The Unionists arrived at the Head of Bullhead Creek where they spent the night of August 6, 1862. The head of Bullhead Creek is a spring-fed stream that rises in the upper elevations of the divide separating the Nueces and Frio canyons in central Real County in the vicinity of Ranch to Market Road 335.

On August 6, 1862, the Confederates departed Tegener Creek. On the morning of August 6, Lt. McRae found the trail of the Germans which he had followed in a southwesterly direction. Charles Burgmann was probably a guide for McRae. The Confederates arrived near the headwaters of the South Fork of the Guadalupe River where the Confederates spent the night of August 6, 1862.

The Unionists departed the Head of Bullhead Creek on August 7, 1862. The Unionists arrived at the location where Bullhead Creek meets East Prong of the Nueces River; this is where the Unionists spent the night of August 7, 1862, and where four Texan Anglos joined them. Howard Henderson, William Hester, Thomas J. Scott, and Warren Scott joined the Unionists which increased the size of the group to 64 Unionists. The East Prong of the Nueces River flows through a canyon of remarkable beauty paralleling Ranch to Market Road 335 in Real County. Bullhead Creek runs west for 20 miles, passing to the southeast of Bullhead Mountain, before joining the Nueces River just below Vance. Bullhead Mountain is located north of Vance, Texas on Ranch to Market Road 335.

The Confederates departed the South Fork of the Guadalupe River on August 7, 1862. The Confederates arrived at the Head of the North Prong of the Medina River on the morning of August 7, 1862. The Confederates continued toward the Headwaters of the West Prong of Frio River which the Confederates reached on the afternoon of August 7, 1862. The Confederates arrived at a point on a high plateau, a "dry camp," where the Confederates spent the night of August 7, 1862. This dry camp was in the northern part of Real County. A "dry camp" is a camp that has no source of water.

On August 8, 1862, at the Military Commission in San Antonio, Phillip Braubach, Sheriff of Gillespie County, was found guilty and sentenced to imprisonment for and during the period of the present war, then to be sent out of the Confederate States and never to return, under the penalty of Death. On that same day, the Unionists departed Bullhead Creek area where it meets the East Prong of the Nueces River. The Unionists arrived at a "dry camp," a point "deep in mountains," in Real County where the Unionists spent the night of August 8, 1862. The horses were mostly unshod, and they had begun to go lame on the treacherous mountain trails.

The Confederates departed a "dry camp," a point on a high plateau on August 8, 1862, and arrived at the Head of Bullhead Creek at 10 a.m. on August 8, 1862. They continued to where Bullhead Creek meets the East Prong of the Nueces River around 2 p.m. on August 8, 1862. The Confederates arrived at a "dry camp," at a point "high in mountains" in Edwards County where the Confederates spent the night of August 8, 1862.

The Unionists departed a "dry camp," a point "deep in mountains" on August 9, 1862. They arrived at the West Prong of the Nueces River about mid-morning on August 9. 1862. Tegener decided they would pitch camp near the west branch of the Nueces River in Kinney County. The camp was about 150 yards west of the stream in an open place under cedar trees so scattering as not to obstruct the breeze. They were close to water on this very hot Saturday afternoon. The Unionists had spotted a suspicious rider on a ridge the day before, but the Unionists decided to make camp. Sixty-four men were in the camp when the group went to sleep on August 9. The West Prong of the Nueces River crosses Ranch Road 334 in Kinney County approximately seven miles west of Texas State Highway 55. The battle site is on private property. There is no historical marker. The Confederates departed a "dry camp," a Point "high in mountain" on August 9, 1862. They arrived at another "dry camp" at a point "deep in mountains" about midday on August 9, 1862. The Confederate Scouts reached the West Prong of the Nueces River mid-afternoon on August 9, 1862.

The battle of the Nueces took place on the West Nueces River on August 10, 1862. In this battle, 64 German Unionists, attempting to reach Mexico and then New Orleans to join the Union Army, were attacked by a Confederate force of 96 men. The following 19 Unionists died outright in the assaults on the camp or were executed at 4:00 P.M.: Leopold Bauer, Frederick "Fritz" Behrends, Ernst Beseler, Albert Bruns, Ludwig "Louis" Boerner, Hilmar Degener, Hugo Degener, Pablo Diaz, George Christian "John" Kallenberg, Heinrich Wilhelm "Henry"

Markwordt, Christian Schaefer, Sr., Ludwig "Louis" Schierholz, Emil "Amil" Schreiner, Heinrich August "Henry" Steves, Wilhelm Telgmann, Adolph Vater, Friedrich "Fritz" Vater, Heinrich "Henry" Wiershausen and Michael Weyrich.

From an excerpt from Letter #8, which Julius Schlickum wrote to his father-in-law, Friedrich Wilhelm Klier, in Germany on February 20, 1863. While in Mexico, Jacob Kuechler relayed to Julius Schlickum in detail what happened at the Battle of the Nueces.

"During my imprisonment, my friend Jakob Kuechler had retreated into the mountains with 20 men and decided to go to Mexico as the expected invasion of Northern troops failed to materialize. Sixty-eight of his companions, among them Wilhelm Klier, were ready to follow him. The others returned, took the Oath of Allegiance, and let themselves be drafted into the army. Kuechler is a fearless man who knows his way around the forests, and despite Cooper's Leatherstocking Tales a good hunter, while also educated in science. But he is phlegm personified. 'Just don't push me!' He is a true jungle-drifter. He moved through the mountains with his people very slowly and was not in a hurry. They hunted deer, searched for honey, had barbecues and meals, and in the evening sang songs. Towards the end of July, while moving through the forests, they came upon the Western edge of Nueces springs, only a one-day journey or about 40 miles to the Rio Grande. They stopped at the spring, cooked dinner, and tied their horses in the grass. Two men stood guard, and the group camped under a few cedar trees at the edge of some brush.

Across from the camp was a huge, steep rock wall. The night was soft, southern, and warm, and there were bright stars in the deep, blue sky. Around three o'clock in the morning the guard called out: 'Wake up, we are betrayed! To your weapons!' At that same moment there was crackling and flashing all around, and bullets whistling from all sides into the camp. Such was accompanied by screaming and shouting, as if 1000 Indians had been possessed by the devil. 'Don't stick your neck out! Keep your weapons ready! Don't shoot! Keep cool!' Kuechler shouted. The attacking troops had planned to chase the men outside the camp, and then to take them prisoner. Since no one moved this plan was thwarted. So, the enemies, 175 men, quietly occupied the cedar forest, the spring, and the road.

After the firing stopped, eight Americans sneaked out of the camp of the Union people. Others followed, and at daybreak Kuechler had 35 men left. This small number decided to fight by the sword[2] and die. They positioned themselves as well as possible and used the sparse trees as cover. Each had a six-shooter and a rifle. All of them Germans, and many of them had a wife and children at home, German youth of West Texas in their prime of life.

All were fearless hunters, sure shots who had been raised at the frontier, at home in pathless flatlands and wild forests, most of them intelligent, good-hearted boys, whom we had known when they grew up. At the break of daylight, the commando of the advancing troops sounded 'Forward, attack, the hell with them, kill them all!' — On the other hand, Kuechler shouted: 'Don't shoot your powder in vain! Whoever shoots, make sure to get your man!' They sent a hail of bullets into the camp of the Union followers, and then stormed towards it while howling like Indians.

In silence they allowed them to approach up to 50 feet, and then shot into the rows of attackers with deadly precision, whose' Sharps rifles that could be loaded with rounds from behind. The Germans on the other hand shot with taped bullets Brave Wilhelm had taken his position next to Kuechler, and as the latter assured me, he stood like a man, was undaunted, and held out to the very end. He was a credit to you, dear Father. He was one of the few who were not wounded. After the last attack had been repelled there were only seven fighters left, and in addition eight wounded who could still walk. Nineteen brave boys lay dead, or grievously wounded on the battlefield. Two sons of my old friend Degener from Sisterdale lay dead on the ground. They had been the joy and pride of their parents (their mother went mad because of this). They were famous bear hunters, and well liked everywhere.

Karl Besler lay there, their close friend, who had been as brave as they were. He had been shot at night while standing guard. And there lay Paul the Mexican, who had been bought from the Indians as a child and had been raised as a German. There lay my friend Wilhelm Telgmann from Braunschweig [Lower Saxony, Germany] who had been pierced by three bullets, still fighting with his sword while he was dying. — On the other hand, 44 rangers [the Confederates] had been shot, 18 of them mortally wounded, who have since died. The Germans had shot with such deadly precision that there were only few rangers [the Confederates] who were lightly wounded. —

But now their firepower was too weak, and they foresaw that they would not be able to withstand another attack. They decided to retreat, and in order to cover them, Telgmann and a few others who lay on the ground mortally wounded, opened fire powerfully with their still loaded revolvers. Thus protected, the survivors climbed the rocks on the opposite side at a passable place covered by wood and scattered in the thicket.

Kuechler safely escaped with his people. Among greatest deprivation he was able to reach settlements again, together with those who had recovered after having been sick. Naturally, they had lost everything, horses, clothes, provisions. After the Confederates had plundered the camp, they murdered all of the living in cold blood. A great number of those who had left before the fight were taken prisoner by them and hanged without due process."

After the Nueces Battle, either individually or in small groups, the surviving Unionists made their escape, either to Mexico or back to the Hill Country. Some were caught and hung, others captured and brought to trial and still others eventually impressed into the Confederate frontier force after signing the Oath of Allegiance. A number of those who made it to Mexico sailed to New Orleans to join the U.S. First Texas Cavalry.

On August 10, 1862, Wilhelm Klier survived the Nueces Battle in Kinney County, Texas. Wilhelm Klier was one of the last ones to leave the camp at the Nueces River. Bullets whirled from all directions when he fled across an open plain, but miraculously, he escaped injury. He was separated from the others and made his way alone through the wilderness for hundreds of miles, without food *(prickly pear fruit, apples, and bear grass made up his main diet)* or clothes other than shirt and pants. He took a new route from which he came and managed to evade anyone in pursuit. Wilhelm returned to Fredericksburg with his Colt .44 on his hip and strapped to his leg. It took Wilhelm approximately ten days to make his way back to the Klier-Ransleben farm.

The following excerpt is from Letter #8, which Julius Schlickum wrote to his father-in-law, Friedrich Wilhelm Klier, in Germany on February 20, 1863. While in Mexico, Jacob Kuechler relayed to Julius Schlickum what happened to Wilhelm Klier after the battle at the Nueces.

"From then on, my special account of Wilhelm, your dear oldest son, ends. I heard however that he was separated from the others and made his way alone through the wilderness for hundreds of miles, without food or clothes other than shirt and pants. Half-starved and sick he arrived one night at his brother-in-law Ransleben's place, who thoughtlessly, shocked, like a fool, walked to town the next morning to ask for advice. He went from one place to another and didn't know what to do for fear. As a result, the news that Wilhelm had returned had already spread by afternoon."

August Luckenbach, Adolph Ruebsahm [Ruebsamen], and Louis Ruebsahm [Ruebsamen], survivors of the Nueces Battle, were executed on August 20, 1862, in West or Northwest San Antonio, Texas. Confederate Captain John Donelson *(who had previously arrested four men on August 3, 1862, near the Guadalupe River)*, hung Sebird Henderson, Hiram Nelson, Gustav Tegener, and C. Frank Scott, near Spring Creek on August 22, 1862. They were buried on the banks of Spring Creek and to this day are interred in the small cemetery *(private property)* at Spring Creek. Heinrich "Henry" Stieler and Theodor Bruckisch, all survivors of the Nueces Battle, were executed at Goat Creek in Kerr County on August 22, 1862. Goat Creek runs south for about nine miles to its mouth on the Guadalupe River, west of Kerrville in central Kerr County

Wilhelm Klier was one of the survivors who finally reached his home around August 22, 1862. He arrived half-starved and sick one night and was given refuge by his sister, Josephine Klier Ransleben at the Klier-Ransleben Farm. Wilhelm's brother-in-law, Julius Ransleben thoughtlessly, walked to town the next morning on August 23, 1862, to ask for advice. As a result, the news that Wilhelm had returned had already spread by afternoon. That same evening Wilhelm, who was sick in bed, was picked up by the Confederate Military and imprisoned. He was transported the next morning, August 24, 1862, to Prison Town near Boerne along with two friends, Conrad Bock and Fritz Tays. The 1860 Gillespie County Census lists Conrad Bock, age 24, as a farm laborer and the household included Pauline Bock, age 16. Julius Ransleben accompanied Wilhelm and gave him a ride in his carriage.

Klier was forced to watch the hanging of Conrad Bock and Fritz Tays, on August 24, 1862, by the Confederate soldiers. A detachment from Duff's company had captured these two Unionists and subsequentially hung them at Prison Town. Prison Town was located near the confluence of Cibolo and Menger Creek, just north of Boerne, Kendall

Texas Prisoner of War Camps

P.O.W. Camp Name	Prison Type	Operation Years	Max Prisoner Capacity	Max Prisoner Held	Escapes	Deaths
Boerne (Prison Town)	6	1862	—	350	0	0
Camp Ford	6	1863-1865	—	4,900	4+	232+
Camp Groce (Hempstead)	3	1863	—	500+	—	20
Camp Van Dorn (Salado Camp)	7	1861	—	—	—	—
Camp Verde	7	1861-1862	—	350	0	0
Galveston	3	1863	—	100	0	0
Houston	3	1863	—	100	0	0
Huntsville (Texas State Penitentiary)	1	1863	—	232	0	—
San Antonio	3	1861	—	360+	—	0
San Pedro Springs	7	1862	—	350+	0	—

Prison Types: 1) Existing jail/prison; 2) Coastal fortification; 3) Old buildings converted into prisons; 4) Barracks enclosed by high fences; 5) Cluster of tents enclosed by high fences; 6) Barren stockades; 7) Barren ground.

County *(present day Cibolo Nature Center, 140 City Park Road, Boerne, Texas, 78006).* Due to an impression, marked by thorough honesty and sincerity, which Wilhelm Klier made on his friend, Hermann Holzapfel, he came to the prison camp just at the opportune time and interceded for Wilhelm; thus, saving his life. Also, Julius Ransleben stood guard next to the sleeping and ill Wilhelm; Ransleben convinced the Confederates not to hang Klier.

Ferdinand Peter Herff (1883-1965) recounts that during the Civil War, "A company of Rangers (Confederates) commandeered the most fertile part of the ranch land that he, Dr. Ferdinand Ludwig Herff (1820-1912) had acquired in Boerne, using it as a prison camp for captured troops." Pastures were damaged and horses, sheep, and cattle confiscated. A Confederate prisoner of war camp—referred to as "Prison Town" is known to have operated near Boerne in 1862. While it is generally agreed that the camp was on Ferdinand Herff's property, possibly near the confluence of the Cibolo and Menger creeks, the actual location has not been determined.

In his undated account, Ferdinand Peter Herff mentioned "stone ruins of the campsite, still visible after so many years." The Herff Farm is located at 33 Herff Road, Boerne, Texas. There is a Historic Marker for Dr. Ferdinand Ludwig Herff located on Malakopf Mountain, 1.5 miles northeast of Boerne Via FM 474 and Kennon Ranch Road.

Dr. Ferdinand Ludwig Von Herff
(Nov. 29, 1820-May 18, 1912)

"The son of a prominent Germany family and a veteran of the Prussian Army, physician Ferdinand Ludwig von

Herff first came to Texas in 1847. By the 1860s he had set up practice in San Antonio, where he was an active civic leader. His medical innovations made him a prominent physician in the Southwest.

Dr. Herff and his wife Mathilde (1823-1910) owned a ranch at this site and, through their interest in the area, led in the development of Boerne. Local residents honored their many contributions with a monument here on Malakopf Mountain, a site favored by the Herffs." (1982)

Confluence of Menger and Cibolo Creek Cibolo Nature Center, Boerne, Texas (Location where Wilhelm Klier was almost hung).

On August 25, 1862, two survivors of the Nueces Battle, Wilhelm F. Boerner and Herman Flick, were executed in the Hill Country likely by Captain Davis' men.

By August 29, 1862, the Military Commission had worked its way around to Mrs. Therese Klier Schlickum, who had been arrested in Boerne more than two months earlier. During the time Mrs. Schlickum had languished in her apartment in San Antonio, a lot had happened in the Hill Country. From Letter #8 which Julius Schlickum wrote to his father-in-law, Friedrich Wilhelm Klier, in

Germany on February 20, 1863, "When our flight was discovered in the morning [either July 19, 1862, or August 1862], my wife was asked to appear in front of a panel at the Military Commission, just as I had feared. She was accused of having helped me to flee, and they tried to intimidate her with threats, so she would tell them where I could be found. She remained firm and fearless. She was forbidden to leave town by a penalty of 5,000 Dollar. Therese rented an apartment and had the children brought to her. She had the message related to me that I should not worry, and that she was in good spirits.

After repeated questioning they realized that she wouldn't say anything and was permitted to move back to Boerne due to the mediation of acquaintances that were kindly disposed to her, while the General [General P.O. Hebert] who was angry with her was absent for several days. Her bail was dismissed. — I heard from different people that Therese had conducted herself very discreetly, bravely, and with dignity throughout this affair. She was admired by friends and respected by enemies."

The following was addressed by the Judge Advocate to Mrs. Schlickum:

Office of the Military Commission
San Antonio, August 29, 1862

To all whom it may concern, Mrs. Schlickum is hereby released and has permission to leave for her home at her convenience.

Signed
William Edwards, Captain
Judge Advocate and Recorder
****

After six weeks (in all probability September 1862) of escaping the San Antonio jail and hiding in a cave six miles from William Hester's farm, Julius Schlickum, Phillip Braubach, and Friedrich Wilhelm Doebbler made plans to leave Texas. Two acquaintances, who had taken part in the fight at the Nueces, had meanwhile been brought into their camp by friends, and then a third joined them. One evening, after horses, provisions, and weapons had been procured for everyone, they left for Mexico on horseback.

In this excerpt from Letter #8 that Julius Schlickum wrote to his father-in-law, Friedrich Wilhelm Klier, in Germany on February 20, 1863. Julius related how he had escaped from jail, hid out in a cave for six weeks, and made preparations to leave Texas in September 1862.

"In September we made preparations to leave Texas. Two acquaintances, who had taken part in the fight at the Nueces, had meanwhile been brought into our camp by friends, and then a third joined us. One evening, after horses, provisions, and weapons had been procured for everyone we left on horseback. This story of our escape, the account on how we were betrayed, how we avoided settlements and sentries; and how we had to be on the alert at all times not to leave any traces, much like Indians; and the means we used to trick the keen eyes of roaming hunters, — it would fill pages if I described in detail. — Finally, we arrived at the border. — We came upon the Rio Grande when it was high and impassable. We were at the river three times, in places at a distance of a day's journey. Once we found ourselves in the middle of a Ranger's camp [Confederates' Camp] in the light of day, but nevertheless got away unnoticed.

Finally, we had nothing left to eat, our powder was drenched and unusable, and we had to return back to a settlement again. Indeed, on this trip we spent once three entire days without enjoying one bite of food. Those were difficult days, though not as unbearable as one day in agonizing heat without as much as one sip to quench the dreadful, and torturous thirst. After we had managed to buy provisions without getting recognized, and were rested again and our horses had recovered, and I had bought powder, we set out again and finally crossed the still torrential river at night, close to the stockades of the Confederate Fort Duncan [near the town of Eagle Pass, Texas], on a small boat sent there to us by friends from Mexico. We greeted Mexican soil at 1 AM.

For the first time in quite a while we were able to breath freely, without any danger of showing our faces in public! But our adventures had not yet come to an end. We had left our horses on the other side in Texas, and as soon as we had arrived in Piedras Negras (the latter is a Mexican border town), they hired a Mexican who swam across that same night to get them. He found the horses at the place we had described and brought them to the river at daybreak. About to swim them across, he was stopped by Americans, taken prisoner, and led to the Provost Marshall in the little town of Eagle Pass, naked as he was. But he already found an opportunity in town to get away on one of the horses. He was not hit by the shots fired after him.

Piedras Negras is located across from Eagle Pass and Fort Duncan, separated by the Rio Grande flowing in between them. We soon heard that our horses had been given into the care of the same man who had stopped the Mexican, and since we heard that not more than three men were staying at that farm 9 miles away, we decided to retrieve our horses again. We sent a reliable Mexican across who reported that the horses were tied down not far from the house. Four of us went, unnoticed, to the place at the river across from the farm. We built a small raft from dry tree trunks.

When nighttime fell, we set it into the water, packed our weapons and clothes in covers, tied them to it, and pulled and pushed the raft with the help of a Mexican, while swimming across the rapidly flowing stream, about 750 feet wide. We made it across safely, and after getting dressed and our weapons in order we approached the farm carefully. But — no horses were to be found there. Then the moon was setting, but the night was lit brightly by stars. To begin with we approached the buildings. Braubach and myself crawled closer on hands and feet, carefully making sure that the dogs did not notice us. We soon discovered that horses were tied up between the house and the barn.

We cautiously retreated approximately 50 feet from the house, behind a few low bushes where our companions lay hidden. But the dogs had become restive and were barking. While we were still contemplating what should be done, the door of the suddenly brightly lit house opened, and lots of armed men came outside. I just about believed in magic when people came from all sides. We were nearly surrounded, and therefore had no time to lose. Those guys were so close to us. We aimed our guns, and when it barely cracked, downright pellet-fire started on all sides. We had laid down close to the ground, protected behind the dense, low brush and undergrowth. They did not see us, and the bullets kept flying over us without causing us any harm. We did not owe the attackers an answer, and all of them soon retrieved to the house, cursing and moaning, while carrying a soldier hit by 9 bullets who died that same night. A number of others were wounded. As soon as the firing began the Mexican had disappeared. Then I looked around for my comrades, but to my astonishment found none. I didn't feel like running after them and did not want to leave without any of the horses. Carefully I sneaked around the farm, circling it from a distance, as I heard the sound of horses, and right thereafter saw how a man led two horses.

Before he knew I was there, took hold of him with one hand and with the other held my revolver to his head. 'Don't move, or you're a dead man!' I said to him in English. 'Oh, Don Julio, don't kill me, it's me!' he answered in Spanish. It was our faithful Mexican, who used the confusion of the battle to cut the horses loose and had brought them out. loose and had brought them out. 'Where are the missing horses?' I asked. 'Only three were there, and I brought them outside the fence; the third did not want to be led, so I was happy to get these out.'

I thought for a moment, went back to the fence where I found the third one, wound the rope around its nose, jumped on its back and followed the Mexican through the bushes. No one followed us, the people were afraid. At the

Rio Grande we met up with our guys, who didn't believe their eyes when they saw the horses. These were then driven into the water, the raft was made ready, and soon we arrived at the other bank. Apparently, this must have been trap. The horses were probably brought to the farm so we would try to get them, and that is why 30 military men had been sent there quietly at night. Why they were so easily intimidated remains inexplicable to us.

Only after having arrived at the other side, we discovered to our amazement that we were in possession of completely different horses. Well, that wasn't our mistake, and I sent them away that very night to Monterrey [Mexico], together with three of our people. Braubach and I stayed in Piedras Negras, where Kuechler, W. Hester, and 15 others traversed the river several days later, 15 miles further up."

Schlickum, Braubach, and Doebbler avoided settlements and sentries; and had to be on the alert at all times not to leave any traces, much like Indians. They arrived at the Rio Grande (September 1862) and made their way to the border town of Piedras Negras, located across from Eagle Pass and Fort Duncan, divided by the Rio Grande. Braubach and Schlickum stayed in Piedras Negras.

Wilhelm Klier was kept in tight detention in San Antonio for several months (August/September 1862). A capable lawyer advocated his case, and there was no lack of intercessors since he was always well liked, and thus he was finally pardoned. Then he was put into a soldier's jacket; after giving his Oath of Allegiance to the Confederacy, Wilhelm Klier was conscripted to join

Company B, Luckett's Third Infantry of the Confederate Army by Captain John Herman Kampmann, on October 1, 1862.

John Hermann Kampmann (1819-1885), Confederate officer, was born in Leveringhausen, Markischer Kreis, Nordrhein-Westfalen, Prussia, on December 25, 1819. Before immigrating to Texas, Kampmann was raised as a Catholic and attended the University of Cologne. He left Europe in 1848 and settled in San Antonio. When the Civil War began, he raised a company of Germans for service in the Confederacy. This unit was incorporated into the Third Texas Infantry in the autumn of 1861, with Kampmann elected as captain, and served along the Texas coast at Brownsville and Galveston but never saw action. Men of the Third came largely from Central Texas; specifically Bexar, Gillespie, San Patricio, and Travis counties. As these counties were heavily populated with recent German immigrants and persons of Mexican descent, a large number of the regiment's men were foreign-born.

Wilhelm Klier served from October 1, 1862, through May 26, 1865, when he was mustered out of the Confederacy. The Third Texas Infantry saw little action during the course of the war. They began their duty in San Antonio from 1861 through 1862. In January 1863, the regiment proceeded to Brownsville to protect cotton shipments and guard against raids from Mexico. On May 14, 1863, the regiment left Brownsville for Galveston. In March 1864, Luckett's Third Infantry Regiment occupied much of its time firing at Union gunboats along the Brazos and San Bernard Rivers on the Texas coast. Near the end of the war, the Third was ordered to Hempstead,* Texas, where the regiment was disbanded, and the troops returned to their homes. Gen. Edmund Kirby Smith officially surrendered the regiment at Galveston on May 26, 1865.

Survivors of the Nueces Battle were as follows: Peter Burg, Ernst Cramer, Richard Doebbler, Kasper "Caspar" Fritz, Jacob Gold, Peter Gold, Carl William "Charles" Graf, Howard Henderson, William Hester, August Hoffmann, William "Karl" Itz, Sr. (wounded), Peter Jacoby, Jr., Henry Kammlah II (wounded), Sylvester Kleck, Wilhelm Klier, Jacob Kuechler, Jacob Kusenberger, Mathius Pehl, Heinrich "Henry" Rausch, John Sansom, Henry Joseph Schwethelm, Thomas J. Scott, Warren Scott, Ferdinand Simon (wounded), Frederick "Fritz" Tegener (wounded), William Vater (wounded), Carl "Charles" Vetterlein, Adolphus "Adolf" Zoeller (wounded).

Jacob Kuechler, survivor of the Nueces Battle eventually made his way home. In October 1862, Kuechler organized another attempt to flee to Mexico. A group of approximately 17 men joined him and they took the same route that was taken in August 1862. When they arrived at the Nueces battle site, they gathered the bones of their dead friends and built a stone monument in their honor. Word spread that Kuechler, and his group were once again on their way to Mexico. A Confederate unit was dispatched

During the Civil War, Hempstead served as a Confederate supply and manufacturing center. It was also (used intermittently by Confederate troops during the Civil War and was the site of a Confederate military hospital; three Confederate camps were located in its vicinity.)

from Camp Wood and to intercept them. The Confederates located the Union group on the Rio Grande near Del Rio on October 18, 1862. On reaching the ford in the river, the Unionists drew Confederate fire and attempted to cross the Rio Grande while firing back. They lost their horses and only 11 of 17 reached the free shore. Kuechler and Tegener were wounded but made their escape to Mexico. Among those killed were two friends of Wilhelm Klier, the Weiss brothers, as well as Mr. Felsing. He was the husband of the lady who came from Germany accompanied by Mrs. Oswald and Therese Klier Schlickum.

The following six Unionists died at the Rio Grande on October 18, 1862: Joseph Elstner, Ernst Felsing, Henry Herrmann, Valentine Hohmann, Franz Weiss, and Moritz Weiss. Fritz Lange and Peter Bonnet were wounded at the Rio Grande; Johannes Christian Frederick "Fritz" Lange died from his wounds after 1866. John Peter Bonnet died in Mexico on March 12, 1863, from wounds he received at the Rio Grande. Others escaped across the river unhurt; however, both Kuechler and Tegener were seriously wounded but survived. All found sanctuary in Northern Mexico.

Julius Schlickum and Phillip Braubach were in Piedras Negras on October 18, 1862. A few days after the battle at the Rio Grande, Schlickum, formerly of Fredericksburg, met up with his friend, Jacob Kuechler, in Piedras Negras. Kuechler related to Schlickum the harrowing story of the midnight attack on the Nueces River and their remarkable escape. Julius Schlickum traveled to Monterey, Mexico and met Gustav Schmidt from Houston who was originally from Hagen, Germany. Schmidt offered Schlickum an opportunity to travel to New York on business. Three weeks thereafter (November 1862), Julius Schlickum and Gustav Schmidt traveled to Matamoros, Mexico. In Matamoros, Julius Schlickum boarded an English frigate on December 8, 1862, for the 17-day passage to Havana, Cuba.

The following was a letter that Julius Schlickum wrote to his father-in-law (Father Klier), in Muenster, Germany, on December 21, 1862, from the Gulf of Mexico, on board *British Frigate HMS Hope*, while he was in his stateroom on a trip to New York, having escaped to Mexico; his wife, Therese Klier Schlickum, still lived in Boerne, Texas. Julius and Therese had three children: Hugo, age 11 months; Julius, age three years; and Katchen, age eight years. Their nanny/maid, Mrs. Holzapfel, had left earlier. He stated that Wilhelm Klier was a soldier in the Eastern Army at the Rio Grande. Julius' sister-in-law, Josephine Klier Ransleben, and her husband, Julius, were doing well.

Julius Schlickum describes his thoughts concerning secession from the Union. The Germans did not want to be instrumental in tearing up one of the most beautiful forms of government the world had ever seen, in order to build a new government founded solely on the principle of expansion of human slavery. When Schlickum refused to take an oath of allegiance to the Confederate States, he was arrested. He describes in detail the night that the 30 Confederate soldiers came for him in Boerne, Texas, and hauled him off to a San Antonio jail.

Julius Schlickum wrote the following letter from Mexico to his father-in-law, Friedrich Wilhelm Klier, in Muenster, Westphalia. At that time, his wife Therese and their children still lived in Boerne, Texas.

Letter #7

21. December 1862

Dear Father,

You probably are amazed to receive a letter from me, written on high seas, and after years of silence. I'm on my way to New York, from where I'll mail this letter off to you. I'm beginning to write now while having the time and leisure to report in detail. To begin with, the reassuring message that Therese and children are well and healthy in Boerne, under the protection of Holzapfel. Ranslebens[1] are doing well. Wilhelm is a soldier in the Eastern Army at the Rio Grande, and he only would need to swim across the river in order to be a free man. We haven't received any messages from you in a long time. We've gone through eventful times here, and I'll share our experiences with you as follows: We opened our business in Boerne during inauspicious times, when political disturbances[2] were arising, but nevertheless we were successful. We had many customers and made good money. Among the Germans in West Texas there were only few supporters for the disastrous Revolution. The free workers in West Texas were not supportive, or in favor of, a secession from the Union on behalf of the slave holders. They couldn't and wouldn't join the secessionist clamor of the South. They did not want to be instrumental in tearing up one of the most beautiful forms of government the world has ever seen, in order to build a new government founded solely on the principle of expansion of human slavery.

But the Union Party was clearly in the minority, and so we had no choice but to acquiesce. Meanwhile I had been elected Justice of the Peace of our district, and when the Texas Militia was organized, I was chosen to be Captain, and later Lieutenant Colonel. Our business was prospering, the prices of goods increased, gold and silver disappeared completely from circulation. Instead, banknotes of the "Confederate States" were circulated. Soon we had paid off our debts and built our own shop.

In January of (1862) Therese blessed me with a Heda II, a magnificent and healthy chap (Hugo), who is not as strong as Julius looks like him but is more restless; during the first months he was a little cry-baby. Meanwhile our dear Suze (Julius) has grown to be a stunning boy, he is as rotund as in the past, speaks very well, is in sound health, and ruling the entire house. Holzapfel is doting on him and utterly spoils him. Kathchen is still exactly the same, a little chatterbox, who has not forgotten anything of her long journey to Germany. She is vain as a peacock, likes to dress up and behaves properly. She remembers every word she hears and is a friendly and trusting child. She shares half of everything she has with Suze.

In spring the Military Draft Bill of the Confederate States was released, and at the same time the Northern Army and Fleet held exercises, making it appear as if Texas might become the theatre of war.

Fear of conscription[3] as well as the hopes that the Northern troops would soon restore the flag of the government of the States again, caused the Germans and

Americans in the Friedrichsburg [Fredericksburg] area to join a secret fratemization[4], primarily to counter attacks by the Party in favor the South, which was threatening to burn down settlements, as well as hangings. I was requested to join, and to become their leader. I had watched the formation of this association with anguish and worry and knew the situation well enough to know that such an undertaking was useless and dangerous. I was more than aware that a few backwoodsmen would not be able to successfully go into war with the State of Texas, with its more than 15,000 armed men.

What did we have? Hunting rifles, a little gun powder, and no line of retreat if we were going to fight. Despite all rumors, I believed that the Northern troops would soon arrive. The government of the United States was not able to send any troops to Texas as long as the outlook in Virginia and Tennessee was still unfavorable. I vehemently refused to join this venture and tried my best to explain to its leaders how foolish their undertaking was. I repeatedly showed to them that it would result in the ruin of the settlement, but in vain! At the same time, I received an offer to become a Captain of the Southern Army, and after I refused, a favorable offer as supplier for the Army. I did not want to have anything to do with that, and my refusal made me more suspect.

In March or April, Northwest Texas including the German settlements, were declared to be under siege, occupied by troops, and every inhabitant over the age of 16 was asked to take an oath of allegiance to the Confederate States. Many worried about their safety, left house, and farm, and retreated into the mountains. A terrible time began, as I had expected. Many a person was arrested and hauled off to San Antonio. I received trustworthy tips that I was going to be arrested for sure. But I felt that was not guilty of anything and believed that I had no need to worry. I was not a follower of the South, but had not violated any laws, nor committed any act that would prove otherwise.

Therese had become ill from an abdominal infection and was suffering from excruciating pain. With fear and worry I was awaiting the arrival of the doctor, who lived 12 miles away. Unfortunately, our maid had left a few days before, so we had no help. I had kept an eye on her all night and stepped outside the door towards daybreak. Our house is 500 feet from the store on a hill, surrounded by fields and gardens. About 30 Morgen[5] of land are enclosed by a wall. It was still twilight, and when I looked outside, two horsemen had stopped at the gate, and further away another one, then a third one. In short, 30 men had surrounded my house.

I knew why. I went back inside very quietly to prepare my deathly ill wife for what was to come and did it as gently as possible. Then I went to the gate where the Commander had just arrived, and whom I knew. He shook hands with me and said: " Mr. Schlickum, I'm very sorry, I have orders to take you prisoner." "I already expected you yesterday," I answered. — When he heard that my wife was sick, he gave me permission to stay in the house until the arrival of his Company, whose Captain was supposed to decide on everything else. He had the house occupied by his people. Towards noon the Company arrived. Through the help of rich friends, I offered a bail of 25,000 Dollar, if

I would be allowed to remain at home until Therese's condition would change. This was refused, and I was hauled off.

Permit me not to describe my feelings, as I left my sick wife and crying children.

---

[1]*Ransleben, an immigrant from Berlin, had married Josephine, the sister of Therese. They owned a farm near Fredericksburg.*

[2]*The Republicans, at that time the "progressive" party, won the Election of 1860. Thanks to a majority of votes Lincoln, a firm opponent of slavery, became President. Thereupon the South Caroline State Convention opted-out of the Union, a threat of secession had existed for 30 years, but now was acted upon in earnest.*

The atmosphere during this winter was tense, confused, accompanied by a general feeling of helplessness. Before the beginning of President Lincoln's term in the beginning of March 1861, six other states (Mississippi, Florida, Alabama, Georgia, Louisiana, and Texas) declared their independence from the Union and united as the "Confederate States of America." Four more states (Virginia, Arkansas, North Carolina, and Tennessee followed). Kentucky and Missouri were undecided but remained with the Union. Lincoln's most important goal was preservation of the Union. He explained in his inauguration speech that the secession of states was not permitted. But there would be no shedding of blood, unless the renegade states wanted it that way, and at any rate, he would not attack. He would however lay claim on the assets of the union in all states and collect moneys to the union everywhere. Although this assurance sounded peaceful, this claim inevitably had to lead to a civil war.

On 14 April 1861, the confederate troops shot at Fort Sumter located at Charleston Harbor and forced its surrender. Therewith the South had attacked, and the President called up 75.000 volunteers to suppress the "illegal alliance", and there with the Civil War had begun.

[3]*Compulsory military draft for all from 17- to 50-year-old.*

[4]*In his novel "Texas" based on historic events, (Droemer Knaur, Munich 1986) James A. Michener describes the situation as follows: "In the mountains staunch abolitionists went from one German settlement to another and tried to set people against slavery. In the beginning they only achieved little in Fredericksburg at the Allercamps, but they gained the energetic support of three other families, who brought them into contact with like-minded Germans in the South (Page 528).*

[5]*Translator's Note: A Morgen is a unit of measurement of land, varying in size from 1/2 to 2 1/2 acres, depending on each German state or area.*

On Christmas Day, December 25, 1862, Julius Schlickum arrived in Havana, Cuba after a very stormy seventeen-day passage. By late January 1863, the Confederate command reported to the Texas assistance adjutant-general that *"the Germans and others who had been in rebellion have all quietly submitted to the draft and all have come to the different rendezvous and been enrolled as soldiers. Those who were not drafted and are at home profess to be loyal and promise to submit cheerfully to the laws of the State and Confederacy."*

Julius Schlickum remained in Havana until January 2, 1863, and met Mr. Jenny there, a partner of Gustav Schmidt; Jenny was from Chur in Switzerland. Schlickum was guaranteed a part of the profit and he would work independently. From Havana, Julius Schlickum came to New York where he remained for 15 days and visited many businesses.

The following was a letter Julius Schlickum wrote to his father-in-law, Friedrich Wilhelm Klier, in Germany. Schlickum returned from New York via New Orleans to visit his brother, Ferdinand Schlickum. Schlickum finished the letter dated February 20, 1863, at his brother's home in Union held New Orleans. Julius Schlickum, age 38, wrote in great detail about his escape from the Confederate Prison in San Antonio. He included a drawing of the prison and stated that they even had whiskey for the guards, if needed. Jacob Kuechler had relayed (in October 1862) to Julius Schlickum what happened at the Battle of the Nueces, and Wilhelm Klier's participation in that event.

Letter #8

(Julius Schlickum to his father-in-law
Continuation while staying with his brother Ferdinand)
New Orleans,
February 20th, 1863

I was transported to San Antonio together with other prisoners and was permitted to ride my own horse. Once there, I was brought to a house that had been turned into a jail, where 17 fellow sufferers were staying. All of them were Germans, most of them educated and wealthy men. One of my friends, Mr. Braubach, the Sheriff of Gillespie County, was shackled with two balls and chains. Then there were Mr. Richarz from Duesseldorf [North Rhine-Westphalia, Germany], the Chief Judge from Medina County, as well as my friend Radeleff from Friedrichsburg [Fredericksburg], and others. We were heavily guarded and treated illiberally. Our meals were delivered from a hotel for 20 Dollar per month since we didn't want to eat soldiers' fare.

Already on the 2nd day Holzapfel wrote to me that Therese's health was improving, but that he had to wean the poor little one. It took six weeks until we were interrogated, although we complained nearly every day. I was accused of being generally disloyal. There were witnesses who testified that I was more sympathetic towards the North than the South; I supposedly recounted with satisfaction whenever newspapers reported on Southern defeats, and more such wishy-washy stuff. I took on my own defense and told the Military Commission that their witnesses had only voiced their opinions of myself but had not proven any facts; that I requested the right to my own opinion, and that a Military Court was no Revolutionary Tribunal, and therefore could not judge matters of faith.

Nevertheless, I was sentenced to imprisonment for the duration of the War, for lack of loyalty and antipathy towards the Southern States (disaffection of the Confederate Government). Two of my friends fared the same. Others were banished, and yet others sentenced to high fines. Texas was ruled by a sword-rattling militarist of the most loathsome kind. They suspended Civil Law completely. The slightest allegation by any boy was all it took to throw honorable men into jail, where they had to wait for months until someone made an effort to tell them the reason for their imprisonment. (To he hauled off into jail for the duration of the War was in affect about the same as going to be hanged from one of the first trees along the way; that was the fate of many).

I had prepared for a 'climate change' already before the sentence was passed down to me. At that moment I sent a message to my friends, telling them the time had arrived, and I decided on the night of July 18th to 19th. Braubach and Doebbler received the same sentence and wanted to accompany me. I received weapons and one bottle of nightcaps (whiskey for the guards), and the news that horses would be ready and waiting outside of town at 1 a.m. Our friends had been very busy. On the 18th in the afternoon, imagine my fright, Therese arrived, I could hardly believe my eyes.

She knew of my plans, and her worry, concern, and love, had prompted her to come see me one more time. I was quite worried and told her that she had gotten herself into grave danger and that I now would have to give up my plans so as not to compromise her safety. She adjured me not to pay any regard to her, and under no circumstance wanted me to give up my plan. She remained only a short time. — I haven't seen her since.

Our prison had 4 windows (No. 3, 4, 5, 6). There were guards posted outside of 3, 4, and 6. Door 2 is leading to the room where fire-equipment was kept, and door 1 to an open plaza, opposite to the main guard house. Door 2 was locked and bolted, but we had discovered a way to unlock it already a long time ago. *(see diagram on page 118)*

Night had fallen, and we had retired early, but no one could sleep. By 1 a.m. there was a changing of the guards. The moon lit up everything as brightly outside as if in daylight. One of the guards sat at the window, looking inside. We had no choice. We deliberated if we should offer him a drink mixed with strong whiskey. We always had liquor at our place since the soldiers never refused a drink. Then his comrade called out: "Let me have ... your ... ." He turned around, and — through the shadows, we slid out the door that was standing half open, while it was squeaking. — Door 1 in the fire house was opened quickly.

A few people passed by. In the shadows of the courthouse across the street there were two figures, with hats in hand. They were our friends. With loaded revolvers we slipped outside. The guard didn't see us and kept walking up and down. Their backs turned, we dared to jump. If the man would have seen us, he would never again open his eyes. Our friends were posted close, next to other houses, in dark doorways, in case there might have been an emergency and we might have needed their gun fire to cover us. We kept walking quietly. Finally. Outside of town we heard a whistle from thick underbrush. — We gave the counter sign, and six men on horseback, leading three saddled horses, rode up.

A short greeting, a deep breath, and an even deeper sip from our bottle of cognac which was making the rounds, and we dashed off through the prairie, avoiding all roads and bridges, until the horses had covered 22 miles in 2 hours. At daybreak we camped in a narrow and remote valley, in thick brush. "Over there in a dry riverbed in the middle of the woods is a cave, hide there! You will find food, goodbye!" and our friends chased on to hide the horses, which otherwise could easily have given us away.

We were free! — in this forest, probably the size of 100 Morgen, 2 miles from water, we spent about 6 weeks, until the pursuer's zeal had died down. We soon were told that all troops were patrolling along the frontier night and day in order to catch us, and that the Rio Grande, the river at the border between Texas and Mexico, was heavily guarded. They had orders to shoot or hang us, wherever they would come across us. The homes of our numerous friends were searched repeatedly.

Naturally, nobody believed that we would be staying so close to town, and so they kept searching us far away, as we had correctly figured beforehand. We were extremely vigilant in standing guard, never lit a fire, and got our water 6 miles from the spring at the farm of our friend Wilhelm Hester, who came every day in person to bring us groceries, bread, and salted meat. (Hester had helped rescue us, and he had done the same for others. Subsequently he was sentenced to death, but that was mainly based on the suspicion to having freed us. Pray for him!)

When our flight was discovered in the morning, my wife was asked to appear in front of a panel at the Military Commission, just as I had feared. She was accused of having helped me to flee, and they tried to intimidate her with threats, so she would tell them where I could be found. She remained firm and fearless. She was forbidden to leave town by a penalty of 5.000 Dollar. Therese rented an apartment and had the children brought to her. She had the message related to me that I should not worry, and that she was in good spirits.

After repeated questioning they realized that she wouldn't say anything and was permitted to move back to Boerne due to the mediation of acquaintances that were kindly disposed to her, while the General who was angry with her was absent for several days. Her bail was dismissed. — I heard from different people that Therese had conducted herself very discreetly, bravely, and with dignity throughout this affair. She was admired by friends and respected by enemies.

During my imprisonment, my friend Jakob Kuechler had retreated into the mountains with 20 men and decided to go to Mexico as the expected invasion of Northern troops failed to materialize. Sixty-eight of his companions, among them Wilhelm Klier, were ready to follow him. The others returned, took the Oath of Allegiance, and let themselves be drafted into the army. Kuechler is a fearless man who knows his way around the forests, and despite Cooper's Leatherstocking Tales a good hunter, while also educated in science.

But he is phlegm personified. 'Just don't push me!' He is a true jungle-drifter. He moved through the mountains with his people very slowly and was not in a hurry. They hunted deer, searched for honey, had barbecues and meals, and in the evening sang songs. Towards the end of July, while moving through the forests, they came upon the Western edge of Nueces springs, only a one-day journey or about 40 miles to the Rio Grande. They stopped at the spring, cooked dinner, and tied their horses in the grass. Two men stood guard, and the group camped under a few cedar trees at the edge of some brush.

Across from the camp was a huge, steep rock wall. The night was soft, southern, and warm, and there were bright stars in the deep, blue sky. Around three o'clock in the morning the guard called out: 'Wake up, we are betrayed! [1] To your weapons!' At that same moment there was crackling and flashing all around, and bullets whistling from all sides into the camp. Such was accompanied by screaming and shouting, as if 1000 Indians had been possessed by the devil. 'Don't stick your neck out! Keep your weapons ready! Don't shoot! Keep cool!' Kuechler shouted. The attacking troops had planned to chase the men outside the camp, and then to take them prisoner. Since no one moved this plan was thwarted. So, the enemies, 175 men, quietly occupied the cedar forest, the spring, and the road.

After the firing stopped, eight Americans sneaked out of the camp of the Union people. Others followed, and at daybreak Kuechler had 35 men left. This small number decided to fight by the sword[2] and die. They positioned themselves as well as possible and used the sparse trees as cover. Each had a six-shooter and a rifle. All of them Germans, and many of them had a wife and children at home, German youth of West Texas in their prime of life.

All were fearless hunters, sure shots who had been raised at the frontier, at home in pathless flatlands and wild forests, most of them intelligent, good-hearted boys, whom we had known when they grew up. At the break of daylight, the commando of the advancing troops sounded 'Forward, attack, the hell with them, kill them all!'— On the other hand, Kuechler shouted: 'Don't shoot your powder in vain! Whoever shoots, make sure to get your man!' They sent a hail of bullets into the camp of the Union followers, and then stormed towards it while howling like Indians. In silence they allowed them to approach up to 50 feet, and then shot into the rows of attackers with deadly precision, who retreated, shocked and under great losses. The Rangers [the Confederates] had them not only greatly outnumbered, but their terrain was also more advantageous, and they were armed with the best guns, and Sharps rifles that could be loaded with rounds from behind. The Germans on the other hand shot with taped bullets[3].

Brave Wilhelm had taken his position next to Kuechler, and as the latter assured me, he stood like a man, was undaunted, and held out to the very end. He was a credit to you, dear Father. He was one of the few who were not wounded. After the last attack had been repelled there were only seven fighters left, and in addition eight wounded who could still walk. Nineteen brave boys lay dead, or grievously wounded on the battlefield. Two sons of my old friend Degener from Sisterdale lay dead on the ground. They had been the joy and pride of their parents (their mother went mad because of this). They were famous bear hunters, and well liked everywhere.

Karl Besler lay there, their close friend, who had been as brave as they were. He had been shot at night while standing guard. And there lay Paul the Mexican, who had been bought from the Indians as a child and had been raised as a German. There lay my friend Wilhelm Telgmann from Braunschweig [Lower Saxony, Germany] who had been pierced by three bullets, still fighting with his sword while he was dying. — On the other hand, 44 rangers [the Confederates] had been shot, 18 of them mortally wounded, who have since died.

The Germans had shot with such deadly precision that there were only few rangers [the Confederates] who were lightly wounded. — But now their firepower was too weak, and they foresaw that they would not be able to withstand another attack. They decided to retreat, and in order to cover them, Telgmann and a few others who lay on the ground mortally wounded, opened fire powerfully with their still loaded revolvers. Thus protected, the survivors climbed the rocks on the opposite side at a passable place covered by wood and scattered in the thicket. [4]

From then on, my special account of Wilhelm, your dear oldest son, ends. I heard however that he was separated from the others and made his way alone through the wilderness for hundreds of miles, without food or clothes other than shirt and pants and a Colt .44 by his side. Half-starved and sick he arrived one night at his brother-in-law Ransleben's place, who thoughtlessly, shocked, like a fool, walked to town the next morning to ask for advice. He went from one place to another and didn't know what to do for fear. As a result, the news that Wilhelm had returned had already spread by afternoon.

The same evening the poor boy, who was sick in bed, was picked up by the Military, imprisoned and transported to San Antonio the next morning. Ransleben accompanied him and gave him a ride in his carriage. This was Wilhelm's luck, as the soldiers hung the three other prisoners not far from Boerne during that night. He was saved by the fact that Ransleben stood guard next to the sleeping Wilhelm. Wilhelm was kept in tight detention in San Antonio for several months. — A capable lawyer advocated his case, and there was no lack of intercessors since he was always well liked, and thus he was finally pardoned. Then he was put into a soldier's jacket, after he having given his oath of allegiance. He is no longer in any danger. Kuechler safely escaped with his people. Among greatest deprivation he was able to reach settlements again, together with those who had recovered after having been sick. Naturally, they had lost everything, horses, clothes, provisions. After the Rangers [the Confederates] had plundered the camp, they murdered all of the living in cold blood. A great number of those who had left before the fight were taken prisoner by them and hanged without due process. Enclosed letter will relate to you how that gang operated in Friedrichsburg [Fredericksburg] later on. It was written by a woman whose husband was one of the victims. She is asking me to find out information about him; alas, she won't be seeing him again despite her good hopes. His corpse was prey to vultures and wolves.

In September we made preparations to leave Texas. Two acquaintances, who had taken part in the fight at the Nueces, had meanwhile been brought into our camp by friends, and then a third joined us. One evening, after horses, provisions, and weapons had been procured for everyone we left on horseback.

This story of our escape, the account on how we were betrayed, how we avoided settlements and sentries; and how we had to be on the alert at all times not to leave any traces, much like Indians; and the means we used to trick the keen eyes of roaming hunters, — it would fill pages if I described in detail. — Finally, we arrived at the border. — We came upon the Rio Grande when it was high and impassable. We were at the river three times, in places at a distance of a day's journey. Once we found ourselves in the middle of a Ranger's camp [Confederates' Camp] in the light of day, but nevertheless got away unnoticed.

Finally, we had nothing left to eat, our powder was drenched and unusable, and we had to return back to a settlement again. Indeed, on this trip we spent once three entire days without enjoying one bite of food. Those were difficult days, though not as unbearable as one day in agonizing heat without as much as one sip to quench the dreadful, and torturous thirst. After we had managed to buy provisions without getting recognized, and were rested again and our horses had recovered, and I had bought powder, we set out again and finally crossed the still torrential river at night, close to the stockades of the Confederate Fort Duncan [near the town of Eagle Pass, Texas], on a small boat sent there to us by friends from Mexico. We greeted Mexican soil at 1 AM.

For the first time in quite a while we were able to breath freely, without any danger of showing our faces in public! But our adventures had not yet come to an end. We had left our horses on the other side in Texas, and as soon as we had arrived in Piedras Negras (the latter is a Mexican border town), they hired a Mexican who swam across that same night to get them. He found the horses at the place we had described and brought them to the river at daybreak. About to swim them across, he was stopped by Americans, taken prisoner, and led to the

Provost Marshall in the little town of Eagle Pass, naked as he was. But he already found an opportunity in town to get away on one of the horses. He was not hit by the shots fired after him.

Piedras Negras is located across from Eagle Pass and Fort Duncan, separated by the Rio Grande flowing in between them. We soon heard that our horses had been given into the care of the same man who had stopped the Mexican, and since we heard that not more than three men were staying at that farm 9 miles away, we decided to retrieve our horses again. We sent a reliable Mexican across who reported that the horses were tied down not far from the house. Four of us went, unnoticed, to the place at the river across from the farm. We built a small raft from dry tree trunks.

When nighttime fell, we set it into the water, packed our weapons and clothes in covers, tied them to it, and pulled and pushed the raft with the help of a Mexican, while swimming across the rapidly flowing stream, about 750 feet wide. We made it across safely, and after getting dressed and our weapons in order we approached the farm carefully. But — no horses were to be found there. Then the moon was setting, but the night was lit brightly by stars. To begin with we approached the buildings. Braubach and myself crawled closer on hands and feet, carefully making sure that the dogs did not notice us. We soon discovered that horses were tied up between the house and the barn.

We cautiously retreated approximately 50 feet from the house, behind a few low bushes where our companions lay hidden. But the dogs had become restive and were barking. While we were still contemplating what should be done, the door of the suddenly brightly lit house opened, and lots of armed men came outside. I just about believed in magic when people came from all sides. We were nearly surrounded, and therefore had no time to lose. Those guys were so close to us. We aimed our guns, and when it barely cracked, downright pellet-fire started on all sides. We had laid down close to the ground, protected behind the dense, low brush and undergrowth. They did not see us, and the bullets kept flying over us without causing us any harm. We did not owe the attackers an answer, and all of them soon retrieved to the house, cursing and moaning, while carrying a soldier hit by 9 bullets who died that same night. A number of others were wounded. As soon as the firing began the Mexican had disappeared. Then I looked around for my comrades, but to my astonishment found none. I didn't feel like running after them and did not want to leave without any of the horses. Carefully I sneaked around the farm, circling it from a distance, as I heard the sound of horses, and right thereafter saw how a man led two horses.

Before he knew I was there, took hold of him with one hand and with the other held my revolver to his head. 'Don't move, or you're a dead man!' I said to him in English. 'Oh, Don Julio, don't kill me, it's me!' he answered in Spanish. It was our faithful Mexican, who used the confusion of the battle to cut the horses loose and had brought them out. loose and had brought them out. 'Where are the missing horses?' I asked. 'Only three were there, and I brought them outside the fence; the third did not want to be led, so I was happy to get these out.'

I thought for a moment, went back to the fence where I found the third one, wound the rope around its nose, jumped on its back and followed the Mexican through the bushes. No one followed us, the people were afraid. At the Rio Grande we met up with our guys, who didn't believe their eyes when they saw the horses. These were then driven into the water, the raft was made ready, and soon we arrived at the other bank. Apparently, this must have been trap. The horses were probably brought to the farm so we would try to get them, and that is why 30 military men had been sent there quietly at night. Why they were so easily intimidated remains inexplicable to us.

Only after having arrived at the other side, we discovered to our amazement that we were in possession of completely different horses. Well, that wasn't our mistake, and I sent them away that very night to Monterrey [Mexico], together with three of our people. Braubach and I stayed in Piedras Negras, where Kuechler, W. Hester, and 15 others traversed the river several days later, 15 miles further up. While they were crossing, they were attacked by Rangers [the Confederates], lost their horses, and only 11 of 17 reached the free shore. Among them were two friends of Wilhelm, the Weiss brothers, as well as Mr. Felsing. He is the husband of the lady who came from Germany accompanied by Mrs. Oswald and Therese.

Then we traveled for 280 miles to Monterey. There I met many acquaintances who treated me kindly. Regrettably, I soon discovered that there was little opportunity for me to establish a livelihood. I did not wish to live off the support of acquaintances. Just when I had made the decision to go deeper into Mexico, Gustav Schmidt from Houston who is originally from Hagen [North Rhine-Westphalia, Germany], arrived in Monterrey. He offered me to travel to New York for him, and naturally I snatched up that offer. Three weeks later we traveled to Matamoros together. From there I sailed to Havana [Cuba], where I arrived on Christmas Day after a very stormy 17-day passage.

I began writing your letter during this journey, but meanwhile have sent a letter to you via Mr. Leye, and to my sisters as well. I remained in Havana until January 2nd, and met Mr. Jenny there, a partner of G. Schmidt, who is from Chur in Switzerland. I have been guaranteed a part of the profit, and I work independently. I came to New York where I remained for 15 days and visited many businesses, then returned via ... to New Orleans to my brother Ferdinand, from where I'm writing now.

I have bought a schooner here from my own money, that can traverse the shallow waters of the barrier reef of Matamoros. I'm going to load it with grain and goods we bought and am about to sail there. As soon as my livelihood is assured, I will do everything in my power, so wife and children can move out of that miserable Texas and come there. I hear from my family often through acquaintances, and all are well. I don't receive any letters, although I often use safe opportunities to send letters through friends.

I don't wish to say anything, about the local politics. Once I got to see the North in person, I was very disappointed. It appears as if the intended purpose of this war was only to enrich suppliers[5][6] Should I be able to make some money, return to Germany. Ferdinand is doing quite well. He earns 90 Dollar a month as a customs inspector. He is well liked at work due to his rare, incorruptible integrity, loyalty, and punctuality: His wife and children are healthy and content. I'm awaiting letters from you with longing. My family is taken care of for one year. When I left Texas, I had 7000 pounds of flour in storage. I had protected my assets from confiscation by signing them over to Holzapfel, who is our most faithful friend. You can easily understand how things are in Texas, by the fact that 100 pounds of flour cost 40 Dollar by 1.

---

[1]*Compare Michener: On 1 August 1862, 65 Germans moved westwards and then to the south, to escape the War. Yancey Quimper ... had infiltrated a spy by the name of Henry Steward (into the Fredericksburg area). Steward reported to the General: "Fifteen hundred heavily armed Germans have secretly met up at a place in the mountains near Fredericksburg. The place is called Lion Creek. They don't speak a word of English. I know the plans of these men: They want to drive fear and terror into towns such as Austin and San Antonio through acts of violence, and then cross the Rio Grande into Mexico and thereafter travel to New Orleans, to join the Northern Army."*

Quimper wanted to march off immediately after reading the report in order to fight against the Germans before they had reached the Rio Grande. He submitted his plan to Major Reuben Cobb, who refused. "This is an agent's report, and as I have heard this man is not reliable." Three days later Agent Steward was found with his throat cut.

Upset about this crime, Cobb was now even more eager than Quimper to punish the Germans. Together they hurried southward, where they put themselves under the command of a certain Captain Duff who had been dismissed from the Army during peace times as unworthy to bear arms. Now he had been readmitted due to the War, Duffs 94 horsemen saw the 65 Germans while they were about to flee across the Nueces River on foot.However, in the afternoon of 9 August 1862, with refuge in Mexico within grasp, Ludwig Allerkamp felt uneasy, when the men who lead the German refugees decided to rather spend a quiet evening under the stars, instead of pushing onwards to the Rio Grande. "We have to leave Texas as quickly as possible," Ludwig suggested, but the leader lulled him with the assertion that Confederate Troops would assuredly not bother them.

[2]Translator's Note: literally "to fence." [3]Translator's Note: unsure how to name these bullets.

In Germany they are described as "replaster Kugeln." These bullets treated with wet or oiled cotton on linen tapes.

[4]Compared to Michener again:

At three a.m. Ludwig Allerkamp awoke disquieted, when Emil (Wahrmund) did not answer his call. He began to search for him, but even before he had found him, he walked into a hiding place of soldiers. They missed him but killed his son who had followed after he had heard the shots. Now there was shooting everywhere. under the greatest confusion. The Confederates fired deadly bullets directly into the crowd of horrified Germans, who tried to form a line of defense from where they could respond to the firing. A few fell dead to the ground, others fled across the Nueces back North; but most of them held out and fought against the attackers who greatly outnumbered them. Allerkamp, outraged about the death of his son in such a senseless slaughter, belonged to the those who fought. Three soldiers in grey uniforms descended on Allerkamp and killed him with their bayonets. Once the deadly fight ended shortly before daybreak, nineteen Germans and two Confederates lay killed in this unjustified action of War. Nine wounded Germans who could no longer flee, capitulated. It was their fate that aroused so many bitter memories of the battle at the Nueces later on. When they lay helplessly in the morning sun, Captain Duff asked Quimper to help him move all of them to one side. "Oh God," Major Cobb called out when he heard of it, but he arrived too late to intervene. While he was rushing there to stop any excesses, he heard shots. When Duff and Quimper returned, they were grinning. "What the hell did you do?" Cobb roared; Duff answered: "We're not taking any prisoners." When Reuben inspected the battlefield, he discovered that twenty-eight Germans had been murdered, and thirty-seven had fled. Eight of them were about to he killed once they crossed the Rio Grande, and another nine elsewhere. One of them sneaked back to Fredericksburg (that was Wilhelm Klier, the brother of Therese, two letters of whom are printed here. H.D.), and the rest fled to Mexico and California.

 [5]Translator's Note: manufacturers or suppliers
 [6]Transcriber's Note:

Gol Mann in Propylen World History. Volume 8, 1960, Page 19:"When slavery went under it was a destructive and creative chaos. Destructive - after the Thirty Years War up to the wars in our Century, no war in Europe was as destructive as this one. Burnt towns, ruined fields, planned destruction of railway lines; homeless refugees wandering around, among them many freed slaves, a ratio of inflation of I to 20 and more, and finally erasure of the entire Confederate government's debt ... such were the facts in the South. Completely different the North: Here Americans experienced, as they would again later on, that a destructive war that impoverishes, may also enrich."

"Incidentally, the North ... could also turn to their peaceful interests, and now did so without any hindrance by those, who had thwarted them for many years before that. The creation of huge territories in the West   a   law assuring settlers in these areas that public lands were made available for a nominal fee; a tightening of currency that only served the interests of the wealthy, such as the old Jackson would never have permitted protective tariffs that in the end amounted to about half of the value of goods — those were easily and quietly implemented in the midst of turmoil of war. The innovations appeared to prove the view of those who saw in it above all a battle between two economic systems. Capitalists, farmers, and free workers were no longer impeded by the system of slavery, and their wishes from time immemorial fulfilled they grabbed what they could — the workers admittedly the least."

Julius Schlickum wrote letters to his father-in-law (Father Klier) in Germany while staying with his brother, Ferdinand Schlickum, in New Orleans. (Julius started the letter in January 1863 and continued the letter on March 2, 1863). Julius' trusted friend, Hermann Holzapfel, was turning his assets into cash. After Schlickum's imprisonment and escape, he is contemplating his return to Germany.

Letter #9

January 1863

Continued on 2 March 1863

Yesterday Ferdinand received your letters. You are all well, may God be thanked! Yes, we will soon be with you again, according to your wish, dear father, but I really don't want to return empty-handed, and want to try with all of my power to make money, while Holzapfel is turning our property in Texas into cash. I don't wish to be a burden to you. You shouldn't forget that I no longer fit in well over there, and now have a difficult time adjusting to unfamiliar employment that doesn't allow for independence. If you'd like to help me, please ask his Excellency the Chief President to procure for me a local, large Consulate. That would be of value to me. 1000 regards to dear Mother and brothers and sisters. I am, and am remaining your faithful and devoted son.

Julius Schlickum

The following was a letter that Julius Schlickum, living in Mexico, wrote to his younger brother, Otto Schlickum, in Germany. Schlickum was separated from his family in Boerne.

Letter #10

(Extract from a letter to Otto Schlickum, his youngest brother, a merchant in Gelsenkirchen, North Rhine-Westphalia, Germany). Presumed to have been written after Julius Schlickum' letter to Papa Klier dated March/April 1863

I have gone through hard times, and now that the worst is over, I'm still separated from my family and don't know when, and where, I will see them again. I'm deeply pained because of it, and have an insurmountable longing for them, and am continually worried about them. I did what I had to do as a man, and if I was in the same situation, I'd do the same all over again the same. That is why I don't feel unhappy. Fate has hit me hard, and I have learned to face life, and suffering, and joy, with a little more equanimity. In the manuscript sent to Father Klier which is also for you, you can see how I was imprisoned, escaped, and how I fought. The story of my flight from Texas could fill many more pages.

How often did we escape from greatest danger through a miracle! I only got to know hunger and thirst then, but also discovered that my strength and energy can surmount all obstacles. I never trembled, never lost my head, never complained, and never gave up hope. Physically I also feel well, and able to cope with exertion and privation: heat, cold, hunger, thirst, night- and day-marches, lack of sleep, and dangers all around! At the same time, I remained in good spirits. Once we rode 250 miles within 3 days and nights, on the same horse and without halt, on Spanish ponies.

In Mexico I made good friends and now have comfortable employment. People have put great trust in me, and therefore I'm the more obligated to justify their trust. I'm hoping to officially be made partner upon my return. I'm also hoping to then find letters of my dear ones. You can imagine how anxious I am to get there, and to hear from them.

Julius

Meanwhile in Texas, Hermann Holzapfel was turning Julius Schlickum's property in Boerne into cash on March 2, 1863. Peter Bonnet dies from his wounds in Mexico on March 12, 1863, from those wounds he received at the Rio Grande on October 18, 1862. He was interred at the *Treue Der Union* in Comfort, Texas.

The following was written from Germany by Otto Schlickum and Minna Schlickum, dated July 24, 1863, to their brother, Julius, in Mexico.

Letter #11

(Letter dated 24 July 1863. Minna 's addendum is the continuation of her letter dated 22 August 1863)

Continued'[1]

July 24th, 1863

My dear Julius,

Enclosed letter was returned twice by the post office since the specified address didn't seem correct enough to the postal authorities. Now we have been offered a safe opportunity that we had anticipated already for a while, and have accepted it with joy, to send the message via Mr. Groos to let you know how pleased we are that you have safely escaped the perils of war. May God grant that you may spend happy days in your family circle again very soon. The War over there is getting more and more alarming, and we are worried that you might have to struggle with it for several more years.

The situation in Texas must be awfully oppressive now. Holzapfel's brother recently sent a report to his Mother, saying that agriculture isn't doing very well at all. Here in Anti ... ?[2] things appear even worse since I have written the enclosed letter. Every business is slow, and confidence in businesses is completely lost. Our House of Parliament has adjourned, and the King is surrounded by incompetent Ministers[3] as formerly in the year 45 the ... ?[4] King under von Brandenburg and Manteuffel. Freedom of the press has been abolished, and public assemblies are being dispersed. All associations are about to be closed down, such as the Gymnastic club, Gun club, and so on. We have a Secret Police like in France. May God grant us another 48[5], then things will turn out differently.

Meanwhile I left my position in Duisburg [North Rhine-Westphalia, Germany] for another one in Erwitte [North Rhine-Westphalia, Germany], with the Kute[6] Brothers, and hopefully I'll like it here. As soon as times change somewhat for the better, I'll start up my own business.

Minna is very happy that I am living with her, she is already getting sickly. Her foot is bothering her a lot, although it is not grave. and she is suffering from asthma. Other than that chipper, and not droopy as you were suspecting.

Kathinka wrote quite a cheery letter yesterday from Brussels [Belgium]. I'm pretty sure you know that Mr. von Savigny is now an Ambassador in Brussels. I'm sincerely happy that she finally is pretty content with life and with her employment. Things are looking bleak with Mrs. Vollmer, the teacher. The poor woman recently gave birth to a child, after the death of Vollmer. Her son-in-law Kolkenbeck returned from America not very long ago without any means, and they ended up being very destitute and poor. Now he has taken Mrs. Vollmer to court over his wife Clementine's inheritance and would have turned his mother-in-law into a beggar if Eduard from California had not pledged to support his Mother with 400 Thaler[7] per year.

Toni Klier wants to join the Monastery of the Poor Clares Sisters no matter what, and is not to be dissuaded, despite the wishes of her Father. She is displaying such resolute obstinacy and stubbornness; it is hard to believe anyone could be that crazy. Maria Klier is staying in Paris [France] with a cousin[7], to help out his wife with housekeeping.

At Kliers everyone is sickly. Uncle and Maria were in Pyrmont [Lower Saxony, Germany] at the Spa. Uncle has grown quite weak and suffers from dizziness, Maria has a weak back, and Aunt has a liver disease.

But for now, goodbye. Kindest Regards to Therese and the children. Kisses from

Your brother Otto who faithfully loves you

---

[1] *said letter is missing*

[2] *transcriber was not able to decipher*

[3] *transcriber was not able to decipher*

[4] *transcriber was not able to decipher*

[5] *Translator's Note: the uprising of 1848 is meant*

[4] *transcriber was unsure of this surname*

[6] *Transcriber was unsure of this surname*

[7] *transcriber was unsure if he deciphered correctly (he added a question mark).*

The following was from Minna Schlickum in Germany to her brother, Julius Schlickum. Minna is writing about all the news from back home in Germany in regard to their relatives and friends. Julius Schlickum was free and safe living in Mexico awaiting the arrival of his wife, Therese, and children, from Boerne, Texas. Minna Schlickum sent 300 Thaler for her brother, Ferdinand, to buy a substitute during the Civil War. Under the Confederate conscription law, a draftee could evade service by hiring someone who was exempt from the draft to replace him-someone under or over the mandatory conscription age, one whose trade or profession exempted him, or a foreign national.

Letter #12

(Letter from Minna Schlickum to her brother Julius.) Remark: Otto Schlickum had written a letter on 24 July 1863 to his brother Julius. It appears that this letter was refused at the post office, as it had been addressed to two different addresses (to make sure it would arrive). Minna opened it, and enclosed her own letter dated 22 August 1863, and added the sequel on the back of a page previously unused, as well as in the margin of Otto 's letter, so that the dates of Minna's 2-part letters are reversed)

Erwitte 22 August 1863

My dearly beloved Julius,

I am so very happy to know that after so much suffering you are free and safe, to the point that I may be completely underestimating your difficult situation and privations. Thank you, thank you so much for your long letter! It gives us a glimpse into your circumstances, into the secrets of the country, and into your heart and your life. I copied it twice from beginning to end, the last one this week, and read it aloud countless times, and therewith urgently reminding myself to answer you immediately; how you might be angry at us for not having done so thus far. Otto might be telling you how he traveled around with his letter, but no post office wanted to accept it because of the two addresses.

Your last letter to Father Klier arrived with the 2nd address, and I sent it immediately to Kath(inka) [1] in compensation, since she'll only receive the account of your travel by tomorrow. But she isn't returning it, imagine how upset Father Klier is with me. Antonie asked for it repeatedly; and because of this I don't know the address yet. I sent the copy of your travel report to Cologne [North Rhine, Westphalia, Germany] as Kath(inka) spent 8 days there while on her way to Brussels. But it missed her and first made the rounds among our relatives there, thereafter, was sent on to Mettmann and then to Otto who took it on his trip to Hamm [North Rhine, Westphalia, Germany] and Ibbenbüren [North Rhine, Westphalia, Germany] and forgot it there. Kath(inka), somewhat irritated, asked for it, and three letters[2] were not able to deter the guys in Ibbenbüren from their laziness; now Father Klier has sent me his original once more, which I copied. It was finally accepted by the Belgian[3] [Belgium is a country in Northeast Europe; Germany is to the East] post after it had been sent back 3 times.

So please don't be upset about Kathinka's neglect. All relatives, without exception, sent me assurances of their deepest sympathy in writing. Heinrich and Ferdinand Ohm, Uncle and Aunt Ohm, Pokornys, Pfleiderers, all of them were in tears about your suffering and requested to relate to them further news. I have asked Kathinka repeatedly to arouse the minister's interest in you and have attached your urgent plea for an endorsement to the

Consulate in Matamoros to the report. May it find its way into willing and powerful hands!

Your regards were reciprocated with sincere love by those to whom they were addressed, and also by those to whom they were not. Please, always add the words Mettmann and Ibbenbüren, in your letters, they are quite touchy, and all of them are very faithful and dear relatives. I wrote to Mrs. Holzapfel immediately and added your regards and instructions verbatim. Their answer was rather sad. They had recently received a letter from their son, after having waited for news for such a long time, and he also confirmed that all were doing well, but recounted bleak news of hunger and sorrow, poverty and privation, bad harvests and of legs shot to pieces. Their son was praising the faithfulness of her Hermann, who however had to give up his business. (Wasn't he your partner? That means that your share was lost as well). She thinks Mr. Groos might take a package from her along, but he cannot do so. She is thanking you and sending kind regards. — So, you haven't turned grey.

Oh, dear Julius, I was so teary-eyed and happy about your little photo. I'm not growing tired of looking at you, although at the first moment I was startled about your dark facial expression, which does not fit the picture in my memory. Looking at the photo I can see what they have done to you — but, I'm hoping to God, that the time will soon come when a cheery smile will lighten up your face again and reflect the peace and contentment of having regained possession of your children and of your Therese, and you will be happy again. This will be my hope for as long as I can pray. God hears and answers, may he praised and extolled, and thanked! You were led miraculously and saved from such great dangers.

Oh dear, faithful Julius, have you thanked him as well? Think of your God as the giver of good and love him, and he will enrich you in this and in the next life. Mr. Groos said to his Aunt that you had made such a nice impression on him, and that you are such a brave and honorable man. I never knew you to be any different, and probably was more aware of it than a thousand others, but it's still nice to hear. When will I see you again? — But I would forego it in this life with the heaviest of hearts and a soul filled with greatest sorrow, if only this would buy you a happy reunion with your children and Therese as soon as possible!

This excruciating and bitter uncertainty, this when and how! I don't want to think of the children, nor talk about them, it so pains me; how you must be aching! My dear sweetheart Kathchen and my dear sweet Manneken[4] . And poor little Hugo, he doesn't even know you! God is going to strengthen my dear Therese — otherwise she wouldn't be able to bear it. One thing I know however: she is up to her task! She is intelligent and steadfast, courageous, and strong, faithful, and loving. Misfortune makes great souls greater, they don't break during storms, but instead grow deeper and stronger roots. I'm not worried about those who have learned to pray and trust. May God help her and bless her, together with her dear, dear, little ones, and you as well!

It soon will be a year since all of that misfortune befell us. Ferdinand's bleak situation and your terrible imprisonment, "and I thought I'd never be able to carry it;

nevertheless, I did, but don't even ask me how I did?" I can add that as well. Thanks to your many and dear letters, we were delivered from this fear soon as well[5]. Ferdinand was especially faithful when it came to writing. Only lately he remained silent for a long time. He kept silent after he collected the 300 Thaler I had deposited for him in New York in order to buy a substitute, and I'm frightened that he might have had to join anyway.

If he really has become an Inspector? Imagine this, Emma[6] has never written one word to us, except for a greeting when she was engaged. She appears to be a kind and good wife to Ferdinand. Ferdinand always is very proud of his Ida[7]. You did well in staying with him for some time, and that you have buried all of the former disagreements. All of us love each other so much, a fact that can never be darkened, even though waves might be crashing on the surface. But they don't last longer than a second, and we shake them off next thing, and keep loving each other.

When is there going to be peace? Aren't there any prospects yet after all of those decisive victories by the North? Texas remains under blockade? And Matamoros? Does France still want to occupy the harbor? The newspapers reported of 15 miles below? I don't understand that. Would French, or the Austrian Archdukes rule, improve the situation soon, and quickly create a strong police force? Would trade be hindered, and speculation be impeded for now? What is your position and what are you working? Are you transporting goods from sea to land or land to see with your own schooner, or are you still working independently in the service of G. Schmidt's company?

Klier was very happy that you mentioned Wilhelm. He wants to send a letter to Mr. Groos, so he can deliver it was well. He is doing well, and Mother also. Otto was there for one week in spring, but Father must have been quite unfriendly since Otto's progressive views clashed with his loyalty as a civil servant. Otto wasn't able to put up with it, and I'm seriously worried that he may have offended him. But Father wrote to me soon thereafter that his fatherly love and heartfelt affection was remaining the same towards all of us. Antonie went on a trip for four weeks in order to distract herself. She keeps insisting on her idea of joining the strictest religious order there is, although her clergy, acquaintances, and relatives are advising her against it, and her parents are grieved about it. I don't understand her, and truly wished she'd rather get married.

In the beginning Maria (?) had a difficult time getting accustomed at Ferd. Petersen's in Paris, but now that she understands the language better and is becoming so fond of her sister-in-law, she is doing fine. Gustav (?) is doing well at the business where he is employed. Mr. Delius in Versmold [North Rhine, Westphalia, Germany] is very happy with him. — But it is still a pity that Klier took him out of grammar school two weeks before his university-entrance exam[8], for which he had all the qualifications, as all of the professors were saying. I enjoyed the week I spent there at Easter time; there I feel as if at our parents' house. I'm always the one who has to pack, and so I packed Gustav's (?) suitcase.

Three years ago, I had celebrated the arrival of my dear Therese there, and the baptism of my sweet little, precious godchild. And since I'm in the process of talking about myself for once, I'm adding that I'm doing well. I'm treading the old beaten path year after year, in the same environment, working the same job, only letters bring news to me. They always bring love, and therewith good things, but often also sorrow which I tend to transmit to everything and everywhere else; nevertheless, my sphere of action completely engrosses me in body and soul and helps me to regain composure more easily. I'm learning to conquer myself. My foot has recently been hurting again, due to pains caused by cramps. The Doctor prescribed 12 saline baths to me. I traveled daily to the Westernkotten [North Rhine, Westphalia, Germany], 1/2 hour from here, where there is a nicely furnished saltwater bath. It did me good, and I'm hoping that these ... glands[9] will diminish completely.

No one should worry about me because of this, as I'm not worried either. One week from now I'll be going to Pfleiderers on vacation, and I truly like it there the most. While not much of anything goes on, there is lots of love. Aunt has much to tell and to complain, perhaps I'm more of a confidante to her than Uncle is a confidant. She always feels miserable, her lump is growing, and everyone believes that water would be a cure [10], only the doctor disputes it. She was at home alone for 5 weeks, while Uncle and Maria(?) stayed at the Spa. Meanwhile she did not feel well, and the oldest child ... very dangerous ... to Pyrmont[11] masons were in the entire house, and a new large addition was built in back, with a kitchen and so on.

In short, Aunt has a difficult life. When Uncle and Maria returned, I traveled from Lippstadt [North Rhine, Westphalia, Germany] to Soest [North Rhine, Westphalia, Germany] with them which was enjoyable, then came back the next day, and they continued on. Maria has quite a happy life with Herzog, but she is the ruler of the house.

Uncle Ferdinand (?), my dear little Uncle, is currently visiting in Mettmann. I'll be meeting him there as well and am looking forward to it. Friederichs has recently lost a little son. Pauline is always feeling quite miserable, her three boys are growing and lively. But now I should first turn my attention to Kathinka. I don't know where our dear little sister is at this time, I suspect she is spending two months with the family in Ostende [North Rhine, Westphalia, Germany]. She is feeling a lot better than formerly and is much more content. She has to toil in utter dependence from early until late, and for her, who was used to independence, that is a difficult task; especially so since she is not passionate about dealing with children, although she is developing an unrivaled talent for it. She is always being treated nicely and politely, at times as a confidante; they always tell her how grateful and appreciative they are of her efforts. She often goes for walks with the children to the park and teaches them nearly all by herself. The oldest boy's age is eight or nine years.

Towards evening she spends time with the children in the family room where they play raffle, tell stories, dance, or read. Recently the Minister read the new trade law to her and showed her all ... [12] of divers ministers who were involved. She is interested in that. Recently, at the baptism, she had to go along to church, with the Minister and the godparents who are of high social standing. When they left the church, the Minister handed her a beautiful bouquet, and Mrs. Minister a precious gown. You may be sneering that people in such high positions, and the fact that their actions and goings-on are of such great importance to us, but consider our point of view and our outlook, then you can share our feelings of contentment.

Kathinka gets to see many new and beautiful places. First magnificent Dresden (Saxony or Sachsen, Germany), then she was 6 weeks in Berlin [Germany] and saw everything there. Thereafter 8 days in Cologne, and since Easter in Brussels. She goes on many trips and gets to see all kinds of curiosities and things of scientific interest. That is especially important for Kathinka.

(On the last page, written diagonally)

Continued in Otto's letter, which I will break open, since Mr. Groos is not taking sealed letters along with him.

(4. page of Otto Schlickum's letter dated 24 July 1863, covered by writing in single-space, then continued in the margins of pages 1, 2 and 3.)

Our Fatty[13] is currently high up in the world. He would like it best if he could attend the Frankfurt Furstentag [14]. What might he be thinking of the fact that solely our Prussian Royal Highness has excluded himself from attending! Our Otto is a dignified brother; it is only annoying that our dear late Father hasn't passed on his love for the Fatherland to any of his children, not even to his daughters, although the latter have at least a more accurate understanding of what a subject's duties entail, besides their fear of revolution, which necessarily overthrows everything that is good at the same time with everything that is bad. The current extremes might make a Unification[15] possible. — Otto was here for two weeks. He lives life in the fast lane and doesn't worry about money or time. I seriously wished that he'd acquire his own proper little business, and besides that a respectable housewife. In regard to the latter, he once had a bad experience, and now is afraid of trying a second time. After he's done with work his mind is set on amusing himself at the inn, and chances are that he'll have a difficult time getting used to a simple family life and working a hard and petty job, and limitations. He is loyalty, respectability, and good-naturedness impersonated, and everyone loves him. He was here while the Shooting Competition and Fair was going on, and invited cousin Wilhelm Lang from Cologne, who came and had a magnificent time here for 4 days.

Otto is continuing on to Munich [Bavaria, Germany] and Vienna [Austria], and his next trip will be to Poland, that unfortunate country, which is receiving much sympathy, but hardly any help. I met Uncle and Aunt Ohm two weeks ago in Lippstadt. They needed treatment at the health resort and spent 5 weeks with Johannes who owns a saline spa; they only spent 1 day in Lippstadt since Uncle wanted to go to Norderney [Island off North Sea Coast of Germany] as well, where Ferdinand and Anna go to the spa. Heinrich is afflicted as well and goes to the spa in Pyrmont. As you can see, everything according to proper fashion! I spent the day in Lippstadt and was excited to see these dear old people in such a good mood. They are still the same!

Ohms' children are so lucky to have their parents for such a long time; I felt like asking: why were we already completely orphaned 17 years ago? — Only God knows the answer, and presumably this was a good thing for us. On the 14th of this month 24 years ago our dear Mother left us already. Did you receive the letters dated 24 August 1862 via Mr. Groos? They were addressed partially to Ferdinand, and partially to you. But Ferdinand had already left Monterrey before it arrived there. I subsequently sent a letter to which Mrs. Groos kindly enclosed for me in a letter to her cousin who lives there and asked him to send the letters to you in case they might still be located there.

It contained the photographs of our parents. Mother's photograph is for you, and Father's for Ferdinand. That is to say, Kliers had held on to both photos of our parents for you, so I had to split them up. I would prefer if you had them, but otherwise write to Father Klier and ask him to send you the little photographs of our parents, and perhaps he'll part with the ones he still has. Otherwise, I'll send the passport photos to Muenster again and have them reproduced one more time.

Other than that, everything is still the same in the family. Heinrich Ohm pesters me to come visit him for an extended time; at every opportunity he assures me that no one is as close to you as he is, and vice versa. He is in high repute but claims to be suffering from green-sickness [16]. Kath. .. .[17] and Elisabeth are living at home, are going on many trips, and Uncle complained that wherever they are, they like to be number one. Emma's engagement was cancelled. Heinrich Pokorny is working as administrator at a pharmacy. Otto is in the service for three years or longer and is brave. Hermann works as a merchant's clerk in Berlin, Gustav is apprenticing at a pharmacy in Wesel [North Rhine, Westphalia, Germany], the two youngest ones are living at home. Aunt has a successful business, but Uncle has kept true to his old habits, and is lacking perseverance. Carolin is still their faithful help, and everyone is healthy. Aunt Doris is fine. Louis is doing well, and his boss will certainly look out for him, just as he does for the entire family, he ... [18]. Albert learned the baker's trade in Bruhl [North Rhine Westphalia, Germany] and is making good money; Robert is once again totally partial to Cousin Lang, and is apprenticing in his business, and the little girls are with their mother. — I had to leave Agnes at home again; I can't make a case based on the kind of salary I have, and the child was always sick here.

Now you're well informed on the family. I don't know anything to write about your friends. I already told you earlier that one of the Babbecks[19] lives in Prague [Czech Republic] and sent for a former housekeeper to become his wife; I think Bremer is deceased, and his parents are still alive. Dr, Weber[20] is still practicing in Driburg [North Rhine, Westphalia, Germany] and Lippspringe [North Rhine, Westphalia, Germany] as formerly, and told me that a patient who is known to me, was engaged to Director Fritzchen Gipping[21], and suddenly it became clear that her professor was engaged with a chambermaid in Laer [municipality of Steinfurt, North Rhine, Westphalia, Germany] at the same time. Now she is living at a cousin's, a Pastor Frede, in Marienfeld [12 miles Southwest of Cologne, Germany] together with her parents.[22] Hermine is ... [23] came to visit last week and told me many a story about Stadtberg.

Chaplain Schneppendahl is once again a good and popular vicar and isn't drinking any more. Much has changed in our dear Institution. Director Kastner and his wife (one of Rhoden's nieces) are very interested in their patients, they arrange dances, shooting matches, picnics, concerts, teas, and such, for the ladies and gentlemen, and the townspeople are invited to attend those occasions as well. A second, capable doctor may not ... Since Loeffler was discharged the Inspector's post was put away with and replaced by an economist's and an accountant's position.

Klier was so upset that Loeffler had been dropped like that. The latter implicated himself, although no one had known about the cash deficit, in an amount he could have covered himself. Klier would have gladly procured the money for him if he had been informed and could have secured it through yearly deductions from his salary. But now Loeffler will likely also be imprisoned. Everything was sold and the Institute did not have any losses, although others did. The family lost their livelihood, and their good name ... [24]. Hermann Knabbe, of whom I had previously told you, ... [25] is nowhere to be seen. Nabe left behind so much debt that his children's clothes have been sold, and that was the end of Hermann's academic studies. The police brought him to Stadtberg, where Schmidt took interest in his case. Thereafter he received employment in construction?[26], but to no avail, now he was sent to ... [27].

The old Ruer's practice in Hamm is pretty busy again. Louise and Dorotha Knabbe have endurance.[28] Supervisor

Duff is a pensioner and childish, but newly married. His lovable little Fritz Durr is currently substituting for the State Attorney in Lippstadt. He is supposedly engaged to Maria Schmidt, the daughter of Ju ... [29]. Bertha Schmidt is ... [30] sister in Warburg [Thuringia, Germany]. They say Antonia would like to do that as well, as her stepmother Emilie is treating her so nasty. Nolte from uptown is still a supervisor, Heide the Mayor was demoted, and his children are causing him lots of worries. Master Rische keeps complaining that the old times are gone. His wife stopped by weeks ago on her way to Coblenz, where her son works as conductor[31]. Theodor Rath is a judge in Warstein [District in Soest, North Rhine, Westphalia, Germany]. The oldest son of young ... [32] came back from America this summer, where he was shot by two bullets: he died soon thereafter. Strickler, formerly a chief supervisor, is now a rich doctor in Dortmund. After this difficult year Vollmers are doing so-so now. In the beginning she wrote to me often, but when I did not respond to her request to take in her daughter and to train her to be a teacher, she is remaining silent; I cannot accomplish[33] because I have nearly no assets left. Eduard is sending her 100 Thaler every 4 months. (Kolkenbecks?[34]) have cause him much worry and sorrow. Last thing Eduard sent 100 Thaler to Clementine, so they would return again. Poor Vollmer suffered from terrible headaches for 1 year, and thereafter soon died from softening of the brain. The letter arrived last fall, at the same time as all the disastrous news from you. Otto was so attached to Vollmer, whom he had visited 4 times in the past, and he was not able to console himself.

Now I would like to end this letter. Don't make any fun of me because of my frugality in regard to the paper, I don't want to importune Mr. Groos too much. Please write to us often, dear, precious Julius — and your exact address as well. Please send 1000 regards 1000 times to dear, poor Therese, and to your dear children, whose suffering I can only dimly imagine. I don't have to tell you how much I'm wishing and praying from all of my heart for your happiness and joy, reunion, and a worry-free life. I cannot help but to repeat how much I'm worried that you might not recognize or search for God's hand and might thus miss out on his blessing. Once again, my dear brother, please write soon, and of good things!

I nearly forgot to relate everyone's thank you to you for your photos. Pfleiderers were besides themselves about it; and Kathinka and Otto, and I, even more so. It means twice as much to us, as we are looking to find everything in your facial expression we learned in your letters. We'll always be interested to hear of the fate of your friends as well. May God bless all of those who take care of you, 1000 times over. And now, goodbye my dearest Julius! Be as happy as I'm most ardently wishing you to be, Your Minna Schlickum. Beckers, my second home, as you have heard through Therese, are sending regards to you. Kathinka writes only every 6 weeks............[35].

---

[1]*Possibly Katherina Schlickum (born 3 August 1827), Julius' sister, age 36.*

[2]*Translator's Note: 3 reminders to return the letter.*

[3]*Kathinka worked there as a governess at a diplomat's house.*

[4] *Translator's Note: "little Kathe" and "little man."*

[5] *Translator's Note: Referring to the poem quoted above.*

[6] *Emma Wueste, Ferdinand's wife, married June 1, 1858. She was the daughter of a doctor in Gummersbach (North Rhine, Westphalia, Germany).*

[7] *Ida, his daughter who was born in 1859, and died 1875 in Brownsville.*

[8] *Translator's Note: "Abitur:" there is no equivalent in the English/American school system. It is a school leaving exam and university-entrance exam at the same time but equal to the associate degree at college.*

[9] *Transcriber's Note: transcriber clearly mis-deciphered to the point where the true meaning is lost and can no longer be guessed.*

[10] *Translator's Note: context is unclear, it could also mean that everyone believes the growth is due to water retention.*

[11] *Transcriber was not able to decipher, and clearly must have mis-deciphered some words.*

[12] *Transcriber was unsure.*

[13] *Otto, Julius' brother, and writer of the letter, continued here by Minna.*

[14] *Translator's Note: the Frankfurt Furstentag was an assembly of German princes, who were supposed to decide on a reformed German federal constitution. They met from 16 or 17 August to 1 September 1863.*

[15] *Translator's Note: The Unification of German States headed by the Prussian Monarch.*

[16] *Chlorosis, anemia.*

[17] *Transcriber could not decipher.*

[18] *Transcriber could not decipher.*

[19] *Transcriber was unsure of this surname.*

[20] *Dr. Weber who was famous as author of the epic in verse "Dreizenlinden."*

[21] *Transcriber's Note: I've tried to guess the meaning, as transcriber obviously mis-deciphered several words.*

[22] *See 72.*

[23] *Transcriber could not decipher.*

[24] *Transcriber could not decipher.*

[25] *Transcriber could partially not decipher and the rest is incorrect and makes no sense.*

[26] *Transcriber was unsure.*

[27] *Transcriber could not decipher.*

[28] *Meaning unclear/unsure.*

[29] *Transcriber was unsure and may have mis-deciphered (Justin?).*

[30] *Transcriber could not decipher.*

[31] *Transcriber as unsure of the profession.*

[32] *Transcriber could not decipher.*

[33] *Transcriber could not decipher.*

[34] *In brackets — transcriber was either unsure or added the name in retrospect.*

[35] *transcriber could not decipher*

The next letter was the last one Julius Schlickum wrote from Bora del Rio, Mexico, to Therese Klier Schlickum, in which he sends her good advice how to get to him in Matamoros, Mexico (from Boerne, Texas). Therese Klier Schlickum planned to leave October 1, 1863, for the 270-mile trip to Brownsville. Julius Schlickum had purchased a new boat from Captain Schwibbe which was constructed in Bremen. Schlickum was working long hours and had three boats that sailed on his behalf. One of his lighters was named *San Roman,* the other one is called *Teutonia,* and the third one is *Wester.* Schlickum had arranged for an apartment for his wife and children.

Letter #13(This letter is, as I suppose, the last one Julius wrote to Therese. He died on the day she crossed the Rio Grande. HD.)

Bora del Rio, August 26, 63[1]

Dear Therese,

It has been about one week since I received your letter No. 11, dated August 2nd, and three days ago your letter No. 10 arrived, dated in July. I wasn't able to answer any earlier as I'm extremely busy. I'm working so much that I wasn't able to go to bed at night before 1 or 2 o'clock. I had work in excess, having to unload ships and load cotton, receive and send goods, measure the size of loads, write invoices, take care of business correspondence every day from 5 - 10 o'clock, and thereafter, at night, had to make out bills of lading for goods shipped during the day.

I bought another boat for myself, a.....brand new. It was imported by Captain Schwaben and constructed in Bremen. I only paid $400 for it and it earned me $201.00 within about ... days, and that is good[2] money. I'm now earning lots of money with my own business, and my relationship with Jenny is as before. I'm making much money, but that is also accompanied by a lot of risk; I have lost already quite a bit and have to work hard for it. Three boats sail on behalf of my own account, and on some days, I earn an unencumbered profit of 50 - 100 Dollar. Each workday I have up to 100 Dollar in expenses that have to be paid out, but often on we cannot work. The boats could be shipwrecked any day, and loads might be lost. Yesterday someone stole $100 worth of goods from me, and it looks as if I'll have to come up for that amount.

Imagine the potential mankind has? I would never have believed that I'd once be dealing with ships, and now all I hear and see is ships. One of my lighters is named *San Roman*, and I earn 1/3 net off it, the other one is called *Teutonia*, and I get half from its profit. The name of the third one is *Wester*, and I get its entire profit.

I have already made preparations to add on to the apartment, and as soon as I hear of your departure the construction will begin. I suppose we'll have lunch brought in from a restaurant, as helpers aren't available here. I already have furniture, a beautiful table, a washstand with a marble top, and a graceful ... chair, a rocking chair, several bedsteads, and also the chairs we need. As we don't have many things, we won't be needing any large armoires. We'll stay here for the duration of the War, and if it continues past next summer, we'll figure out what to do at that time.

Take care of all preparations now for your departure from there in the beginning of October, then you should be arriving here by the middle of October. As soon as you arrive in Brownsville[3], make inquiry as to where Mr. Weston resides, or if he is not there, ask for Mr. Jac. Rosenfield. Both gentlemen, the latter a Jew, are partners in our business (C. F. Jenny), and their store is a branch of ours in Matamoros.

These gentlemen will be instructed by me and get everything ready to send you over here. In Matamoros you'll stop off at the Hotel Matamoros with Seunier, and then have Mr. L. called, and talk to him. The following day you'll sail from there to here on the Diligence, a 4-hour trip. If you have your own vehicle and animals, bring them along, and send word to me by first available stage that you have arrived, and I'll set out to meet you. In case you should be delayed in Brownsville for any amount of time, and you either are prevented from passing the river, or any difficulties might be put in your way, Weston will be instructed to help you cross over from Texas to here. Mr. Clark, one of my American acquaintances, and his family live across the river. Formerly he was a Provost Marshall, and he will assuredly take good care of you.

Here the river can be crossed with no problems whatsoever. I wished I could plan your journey through Texas ahead somewhat as well. It would be best if Mrs. Bosshardt would instruct you as needed, and if you could travel with her. So far there haven't been any occurrences of Yellow Fever here, and since its already September, chances are that it won't appear here either. It the climate would stay this healthy I naturally would love to have you here, the sooner, the better. But you better wait until October 1st to be on the safe side and leave San Antonio that day.

The distance from there to Brownsville is 270 miles; the road is partially sandy, but safe from Indians and Rangers [the Confederates]. The trip to Brownsville will take you 10 days with good animals, therefore I expect you here around, or before mid-October. Get your provisions and whatever you need while in San Antonio, as you can't buy much along the way. I cannot determine from here if it would be best to travel with your own wagon. If you can find a dependable female to accompany you, bring her along. In any case, Herm. will search for a dependable driver and should rather pay a few Dollar more.

Sell what can be replaced, and if you can only get a somewhat adequate price of it, sell it as well. And why not? Only have it sent here in lieu of selling it dirt-cheap, and only then. Don't be afraid of the journey, you can and will be able to handle it. It will be exhausting, and you'll have to make use of all your physical and mental strength. Watch out for your children, whom you have to keep and guard, and think of the end of the journey, and that I'm awaiting you lovingly with longing, and your strength will recover. Send an answer immediately, two or three different letters by different routes via Borchard Co ... Matamoros, via Brownsville.

I'll write again in 8-12 days, hopefully the last letter before seeing you again. I cannot determine and advice you from here if Andree's partner ... will be in San Antonio on time to bring you along according to our former plan, of if you can ride in Mrs. Bosshardt's vehicle against appropriate payment, or if you would be more independent and it might be better to come with your own, or a rented vehicle. I'm prepared to pay whatever needs to be paid either here, or in Matamoros. If Hermann would like to have goods from here, tell him to write up a business-order, and buy the goods for him and pay for them. I'm waiting for more detailed reports with longing. If Mr. Stakes, who'll bring this letter, wants to take something along, send wine for the journey, preserves, shoes, etc., also a coat, and things for Otto and Werner. I am very worried about the children's eye diseases. Thousand regards to all of you. Kiss my sweet little ones from their Papa.

I feel so sorry for poor little Kathchen with her weak eyes.

(Writing in margin, 1. page)

Peterson says hello to his family. I'm very happy with him. He earns 50 Dollar per month. I don't hear anything from Wilhelm. We haven't received any political news in a long time. The ships arriving here from Havana don't know of any news. The climate is still healthy here. I'm not hearing anything from New Orleans either. We expect to be conquered by the French soon, which doesn't make a difference.

(Writing on third page on top) B.d.R. August 29, 63 (here the date is correct.)

Best regards to Brotze, Uncle Werner, Schluter, and those friends and acquaintances who still kindly remember me. No letter from Germany. — Please write soon.

(Writing on fourth page, side margin)

Keep your strength and come healthy and in good spirits into my arms.

Your faithful Julius

---

[1] *The correct date should be August 16, 1863.*

[2] *Translator's note: this word is my guess. The transcriber was unable to decipher a number of words in this sentence and from the context it is clear that the original word must have said "good" or "excellent."*

[3] *Brownsville is located at the Rio Grande in Texas, across from Matamoros, where Julius Schlickum had his*

business. The distance from there to the coast is about 40 kilometers.

The following letter was from Minna Schlickum in Germany to Therese Klier Schlickum in Boerne. Minna Schlickum was Julius's oldest sister. She was a teacher and lived at Erwitte/Westfalia, Southwest of Muenster, Germany. She copied part of Julius' letters and his poems and so kept them for later times. She was Therese's sister-in-law as well as her admiring friend. She sent the letter after having received the news that Julius had escaped persecution and now lived in Mexico but was still separated from Therese.

Letter #14

Erwitte, September 1st, 1863

My beloved sister!

It is already 10 p.m. - tomorrow I will travel to Mettmann (a town in the Rhineland not far from Dusseldorf) to begin my holidays there and Mr. Austin to Texas what I did not hear before this evening, and so I can virtually write only a short greeting to you. Even if it is not much, I lay all my heart into it and I confirm that there is neither rest nor pleasure in us as long as you are still separated from Julius and in such manifold dangers and emergency with your dear little children.

Before short Julius enclosed us a letter from you, at the greatest consolation of your parents, in which you speak in such a harmless manner of your little ones as if nothing had changed. But your letter was from February, and since that time a lot of water flew down the Rhine (German saving meaning a lot of things happened since)

204

perhaps many sorrows across your course of life. Hunger and sorrows, privation and want is the daily bread in your country, as here one tells the other, and it as usually happens in war anyway.

My beloved Therese, who could have thought this three years ago! *(when Therese had visited her German relatives)*. Tonight, I still got a letter from Kathinka from Brussels, the answer to Julius' five pages letter with that flood of bitterness, which had experienced in the last year. So many hot tears we have wept, the wonderful guidance of the merciful God has made us trust that he will give you peace, and you were physically saved, and you are bewared and will be with him forever. I do know you'll have taken his hand in prayer and that in this only source of hail you have searched and found help, strength and protection for yourself and your children and for Jul. and your brother and sister.

Why don't you ever write to us, as we would like so much to have a letter from you! Whether our letters reached you or not, I do not know. We sent them via Ferdinand and via Monterrey. We are happy about the opportunity to send you things which you lack most, but nobody will take it with him because of customs and law. We know nothing of your way of life. Could you keep the shop with all the lack of money and goods? Is Herr Holzapfel still with you? Have you already colored the last mattresses and tablecloths blue for the most necessary clothing?

Alas, how often did I gratefully remember the strength of your soul, your heroic courage, your powerful spirit! You more talented than a hundred others are strong enough to withstand the beating of the waves and the power of the tempest, when others sink. Could I add ... You in the power of faith," - then I would know you were invincible, and I would not fear."

Oh, dear Therese, may God help and sonn give peace! I hardly dare ask how the children are doing, my Kathchen and our Heda - your Suze (Pet name of Julius) - and the unknown darling, your Hugo, alas, if we had them here, we would never again let them go!! Be God with them and give us a merry reunion. When I was just going to write tonight the whole house of the Beckers shouted their greetings to you and the children and Kathrina added with her eyes wet: "I 'm praying all days for my youngster!"

Also (?) send greetings and all relatives and all friends, letter after letter with 1000 wishes for your well-being. Among, them there is Frau Holzapfel, too. I tell her about every word of her sons in Julius' and Ferdinand's letters, and even if it is not more than a sign of life it calms her and gives her peace. When I heard that H. Gross from Monterrey went back again, asked for letters for your friend. She sent the enclosure (sealed but I opened it I beg your pardon for it was necessary) H. Gross, however, told me that H. Austin's voyage was more certain. Jul. before long wrote her something, because one of her sons had visited him in Mat(amoros).

We thank H. Holzapfel forever for his faithful friendship and his helpfulness towards you. God reward him in this life and in eternity! His mother wrote that his brother was quite proud of him and praised his sacrifice and honest goodness. But I forget that you do want to hear of your dear parents. Your father will write you via Herren

Gross if he only doesn't miss the right time. He sends me Jul.'s letter from July and added himself that the thought of his hard-pressed children never left him.

He and mother are doing well. Life in your dear house is much calmer and more comfortable than in the old times. All are fair and everybody bears for himself what makes him problems. On Easter I was there for a week. Antonie (called Toni, Therese's sister) causes the parents great sorrow because she tenaciously clings to her idea of becoming a Clarisse (a catholic nun in a very strict cloister). Kaal (a catholic priest at the main church of Muenster) has influenced her in an eccentric and extreme way.

The parents keep to their refusal - with good reasons - but Antonie does not give in. She wanted to visit me during the summer and had announced it already from Elberfeld and Dahlem (towns in w-Germany), but then she was called back. Marie (sister of Therese) was taken to Paris by Petersen, where she will as I suppose stay for a long time, because now that she understands the language and conditions she feels well with the friendly cousin.

Gustav (Therese's youngest brother. He, too, emigrated to America, and letters from him are among the Klier-papers) since Easter has been with Delius in Versmold who is very content with him. But a pity that he could not pass his Abitur (final examination of a grammar-school, enables for studies at a University) although he had been very successful at school. All professors (Teachers at grammar-schools in Prussia at that time had the title of Professor) were angry with your father because the date of the examination was only four weeks after Gustav had to leave school.

Your good dear little mother hasn't changed at all. Of your friends I know nothing. (?) is at a teacher's training college as he could not develop because he lacked talent. I visited Pastor (title of a catholic priest) Muller; you know his warm compassion. Gustav Fellinger has happily landed in Calcutta [India]. Your uncle and your aunt, the charming Lina visited the parents in Munster. In Mettmann things are as they always were. Tante is weak and suffering, Uncle and Maria have taken a cure in Pyrmont for five weeks.

Tomorrow I will go to them and there I will also meet 0. Ferdinand. I am pleased to meet him. All there wish you the best with great love. Otto (Julius' youngest brother) is well. He is now a representant of a tobacco firm here at Erwitte, H. Kruse, and at the moment is in Munich or Vienna. Last week he sent two letters to Julius, and in it that his heart is always moved when he thinks of you and the children. Kathinka is in Brussels and very content. She has a quite comfortable job as a `gouvernante' with the Prussian Ambassador von Savigny. Before she had been one year at Dresden, 6 weeks in Berlin, d.W. (three weeks) in Köln, six months in Brussels and before short at Ostende she has collected a lot of knowledge . She is treated with great respect and introduced to many important persons . I enclosed her really interesting letter and a little picture to Julius. She hopes that she can do something for Julius when the Minister returns. He wishes so much to become Consul at Matamoros.

I myself have the same old life which you know. The fear for you beloved always is a permanent depression, I do not believe any more to have the right of free breathing. Besides this summer I had much pain with my foot and took brine baths for some weeks at Westernkotten. Tomorrow recreation begins, and then it will all be easier. Not tomorrow, but this day, because it is already midnight and I have still a lot to do. Therefore Adieu, my dear Therese with all your sufferings and long and anxious separation. Keep courageous as long as God will, and because God will and let this way of suffering, the narrow path to eternal life, rich of merits for a world beyond and a (?) full of grace and blessing for you your family become a peaceful and calm life here in our world. I kiss you 1000 times and my beloved beloved Kathchen and my dear Heda I and II.

In most faithful sisterly love, your
Sister Minna

On October 1, 1863, Julius Schlickum sent for Therese Klier Schlickum and his three children living in Boerne. He had an apartment in Bocca Bagdad, and he was looking forward to their arrival. Bagdad, Tamaulipas, Mexico was a town established in 1848 on the south bank of the mouth of the Río Grande. This town is also known as the Port of Bagdad or the Port of Matamoros, since it is inside the municipality of Matamoros, Tamaulipas. Officially declared non-existent in 1880, it is now invisible, covered by the shifting sands of time.

Since there had not been any occurrences of Yellow Fever in Matamoros, Julius Schlickum thought that

October 1, 1863, would be a safe date to depart for the trip to the Rio Grande. Therese Klier Schlickum left Boerne on October 1, 1863, for the three-week trip with her three children to Brownsville and Matamoros, Mexico. The distance from Boerne to Brownsville was 270 miles; the road was partially sandy, but safe from Indians and Texas Rangers. Therese had to keep her travel plans secret since she was not free to leave, and the police kept an eye on her at all times. After Therese had finally been able to put everything in order and her friend, Hermann Holzapfel, had managed to remove all obstacles, they packed, and procured provisions for three to four weeks, canteens, etc. Richard Brotze from Boerne, a friend of Julius Schlickum, accompanied Therese Klier Schlickum on her trip to Brownsville with her three children.

Therese Klier Schlickum traveled in a covered wagon pulled by six mules, and they traveled long distances across sandy flatlands, without any water except for puddles along the way, which was filtered and used for cooking. There was constant worry that they might be discovered and attacked by Indians, roving bands of thugs, revolting Negroes, or the military. They traveled surrounded by howling wolf packs, lonely roads, never passing through towns, and never meeting any people

In the evening, Mr. Brotze sat under the wagon with a loaded gun, and the mules searched for food in the distance. The next morning, they had to search for the mules for hours and round them up, while bread was baking, coffee brewing, and they washed up at the wagon. At one time, the covered wagon broke, and Mr. Brotze was gone for three days with the front part in search for people who could help him repair it. Meanwhile, Therese was alone with three children, in mortal fear in this endless desert.

On October 19, 1863, after almost three exhausting weeks, through danger and distress, they reached the border. Brownsville is located at the Rio Grande in Texas, across from Matamoras, where Julius Schlickum had his business. Another stopover was required as the Rio Grande River was swollen, and the trip was delayed. Julius Schlickum had hurried to Matamoros to welcome his family, but they failed to appear. He caught a cold, returned home, felt sick, and contracted yellow fever.*

Eight days later, Therese and her children crossed the Rio Grande and arrived in Matamoros on October 27, 1863. On the same day that Therese arrived at their apartment in Bocca Bagdad, she found the apartment vacant. She found Julius dead in a back room. While waiting for his wife to arrive, Julius had become very ill and died, October 27, 1863, on his 38th birthday.

Therese and her family were left alone in a strange place and without any means. The doctor requested $300 for the eight-day treatment, but Schlickum's records, papers, money, clothes, assets, equipment had been stolen and had disappeared! She then packed up their belongings and the three children and eventually made her way back to the family in Germany.

In the fall and winter of 1863, the fear and trepidation in Gillespie County became even worse. Camp Davis had been set up on the Pedernales River and William Banta (1827-1897) was named the new commander. He was persuaded that a "bushwhacker" insurrection was at hand. The partisan rangers (the Confederates) rode up in the night, burned homes, snatched young men from their homes, and harassed their parents for avoiding

Yellow fever is a serious, potentially deadly flu-like disease spread by mosquitoes. It's characterized by a high fever and jaundice. Jaundice is yellowing of the skin and eyes, which is why this disease is called yellow fever.

conscription. Pendleton Murrah became the Governor of Texas on November 5, 1863. On November 6, 1863, the last entry was made by Hermann Holzapfel as Kendall County Clerk. In Volume 1, Page 196, 197, 198, dated November 23, 1863, Hermann Holzapfel gives power of attorney to Max Falkenstein (to collect Holzapfel's debts and sell his real estate, etc.). This document mentions the Merchant's Firm known as "Schlickum & Holzapfel."

196

....of said county, by the powers vested in me by law, and in accordance with the laws of said State for such case made and provided, have this day appointed Erastus Reed Deputy County Clerk, to continue in office during my pleasure.

(Seal) Given under my hand and official seal at office in Boerne this 23nd day of November 1863.

H. Holzapfel

C.C.K.C

****

197

State of Texas   }
County of Kendall   }

I, Erastus Reed, do hereby solemnly swear that I will faithfully discharge and perform all the duties incumbent on me as deputy county clerk in and for said county, according to the best of my skill and ability and agreeable to the Constitution and laws of said State, and also to the Constitution and laws of Confederate States of America so long as the State of Texas shall remain a member of that Confederacy. And I further solemnly swear that since the 2nd day of March 1861 being a citizen of said State have not fought a duel with deadly weapons within this State nor out of it, nor have I tendered or accepted a challenge to fight a duel with deadly weapons, nor have I acted as second in carrying a challenge or aided, advised, or assisted any person thus offending – so help me God.

Erastus Reed

Sworn to and subscribed before me this 23rd day of November 1863.

(Seal) Witness my hand and official seal at office in Boerne this same date.

Hermann Holzapfel

C.C.K.C.

Filed for record at my office in Boerne the 23rd day of November 1863 at nine o'clock A.M.

Herman Holzapfel

Erastus Reed

Deputy Clerk C.C.K.C.

****

197

State of Texas   }

Kendall County }

Know all men by these present that I, Hermann Holzapfel, of the county and state aforesaid, have constituted, made, and appointed and by those presents do constitute, make and appoint Max Falkenstein, of the same County and State, to be my true and lawful Attorney for me and in my name and stead and to my use, to ask, demand, sue for, levy, recover, and deliver, all such sum or sums of money, debts, rents, goods, amount due, accounts, and other demands whatsoever which are or shall be due, payable and belonging to me, or detained from me, in any manner of ways or means whatsoever, by all those, their heirs, executors, and administrators or any of them, which are named in the Ledger. I hereby submit to my Attorney and are in debt to me, according to said Ledger conducted for and by me for the Merchants Store, named and known as the firm and co-partnership "Schlickum and Holzapfel" in the town of Boerne, County and State aforesaid --- giving and granting unto my said Attorney by these present my full and whole power, strength, and authority to sue and take all lawful steps for the recovery of said debts, dues, or sums of money, and upon the receipt of any such debts, dues or sums of money act acquittance or other sufficient discharges for me and in my name to make, deliver satisfying, allowing or holding for firm and effectual, allow whatsoever my said Attorney shall lawfully do in and about the provisions, by virtue hereof and further I hereby constitute, make, and appoint said Max Falkenstein to be my lawful attorney to enter into and take possession of all such measures, land, tenements, hereditability, and real estate which govern in the State of Texas, whereof I am and may be in any way entitled, and to grant, bargain and sell the same, or any part or parcel thereof for such sum or price and on such terms as to him shall seem much ----and for me and in my name make, execute, acknowledge and deliver good and sufficient dee conveyances for the same, either with or without conveyance warranty and until the sale thereof to let a demise the said estate for the best amount that can be procured for the same and to ask, demand and secure all sums of money which shall become due and owing to me by means of such bargain, sale, or lease and take all lawful ways and means for the securing thereof to compound and agree for the same.

198

Execute and deliver sufficient discharges and acquittances therefore with the power of substitution giving and granting unto my said attorney full power and authority to do and perform all act and whatsoever and necessary to be done in and about premises as fully to all intents and purposes as I might or could do if personally present, with full power of substitution, hereby satisfying and confirming all that my said attorney or substitute shall dutifully do or cause to be done by virtue thereof.

In testimony whereof I hereinto subscribe my name in the town of Boerne this 19th day of November 1863.

Subscribed in presence
A.H. Bantis
Hermann Holzapfel
Adam Vogt

****

State of Texas   }
County of Kendall   }

Before me Erastus Reed deputy clerk of the county court of said county this day personally appeared Hermann Holzapfel to me and known who stated that he did execute the instrument of writing on this same paper to which this is attached for the consideration and purposes therein expressed.

(Seal) Given under my hand and official seal this 23rd day of November 1863.

Erastus Reed
Deputy Clerk C.C.K.C

Filed for record at this office in Boerne this 23rd day of November 1863 at half past nine o'clock A.M.

Erastus Reed
Deputy Clerk C.C.K.C.

****

In December 1863, in the midst of this terrible situation, Hermann Holzapfel arrived in Matamoros, as a friend and protector for Therese Klier Schlickum. Several bales of cotton were turned into money, but no Union ship was yet to arrive. In January 1864, Therese Klier Schlickum and her family were still stranded in Matamoros, Mexico.

Ernst Schaper was elected sheriff of Gillespie County in 1864. Max Falkenstein (as attorney in fact for Hermann Holzapfel) sold the four lots to Albert Schlueter for $500 on January 25, 1864 (recorded in Volume 1, Pages 201-202 of the Kendall County Deed Records).

Finally, in February 1864, Therese Klier Schlickum and her family saw passage to New York. Gustav Schmidt, a business partner of Julius Schlickum in Matamoros, paid for Therese's passage to New York. They remained in New York for two weeks since Kathchen contracted typhoid* fever. In March 1864, Therese and her family returned to their family in Muenster, Germany. On her return, Therese battled insurmountable grief for her beloved husband, Julius Schlickum.

In 1864, outlaw James Waldrip; desperado William Banta; and the border ruffians, Quantrill's raiders; went on a deadly rampage throughout the Texas Hill Country. Waldrip led a group of 60-odd men who claimed to be Confederate soldiers, but they were really rustlers, bandits, and murderers. They committed murder without thought or remorse and stole anything that was not tied down. They made up the dreaded *Haengerbande* (hanging band), a lynch mob that targeted anyone they suspected of being Union sympathizers, pulling them from their homes and hanging them from the nearest oak without a trial or proof. On February 24, 1864, Louis Schuetze, a teacher at Live Oak was dragged out of his house and hung by the *haengerbande*. (*Phillip Braubach, Gillespie County Sheriff, was the fiancé of Louise, the daughter of the murdered schoolteacher.*) A band of outlaws, believed to be Waldrip's gang, surrounded the Schuetze home. The outlaws ransacked the house, stole $400 cash and lynched Schuetze from a live oak tree. Authorities arrested James Waldrip on suspicion of the Schuetze robbery and murder and placed him in the Gillespie County Jail. A grand jury indicted Waldrip and 25 other men for crimes committed during the war, but Waldrip was not prosecuted, possibly for fear of retribution.

Typhoid fever is an acute infectious disease characterized by high fever, rose-colored spots on the chest or abdomen, abdominal pain, and occasionally intestinal bleeding. It is caused by the bacillus Salmonella typhosa ingested with food or water.

James Waldrip left Gillespie County for a while. The deadly rampage culminated in the hanging of four men who lived on Grape Creek on March 9, 1864. The four men executed were: John Blank, Peter Burg, Wilhelm Feller, and a Mr. Kirchner. Blank is buried in the Grape Creek Catholic cemetery under the oak tree in the forefront. It is said that the ground underneath the tree from which Blank was hung never allowed any vegetation. In the Hill County alone some 20 men were executed, mostly by hanging.

In March 1864, Therese Klier Schlickum returned to her family in Germany. The following was a postscript by Aunt Minna Schlickum to her four-year-old nephew, Julius Schlickum *(son of Therese and Julius Schlickum)*. Aunt Minna detailed in this postscript the three week and 270-mile trip to Brownsville that Therese Klier Schlickum and her three children made on the way to Matamoros, Mexico.

<u>Letter #15</u>

(Postscript by Aunt Minna, sent to her four-year old nephew Julius Schlickum after March 1864.)

Finally, your dear Father had secured his livelihood, and was able to send for you. His friend Brotze offered to pick you up in Boerne, and to transport you safely over there. Your father showed his business records to a friend, according to which he had already made 12.000 Dollar.

He had built a new house for you in Bocca Bagdad[1], and he was looking forward to your arrival so impatiently.

Your Mother however had to keep her travel plans secret since she was not free to leave, and the police kept an eye on her at all times. After she had finally been able to put everything in order and her friend Holzapfel had managed to remove all obstacles, they packed, and procured provisions for 3 -4 weeks, canteens, etc.

You were accommodated in a covered wagon pulled by 6 mules, and you traveled long distances across sandy flatlands, without -any water except for puddles along the way, which was filtered and used for cooking. There was constant worry you might be discovered and attacked by Indians, roving 'bands of thugs, revolting Negroes, or the military. Surrounded by howling wolf packs, on lonely roads, never passing through towns, and never meeting any people. In the evening Mr. Brotze sat under the wagon with a loaded gun, and the mules searched for food in the distance. The next morning, they had to search for the mules for hours and round them up, while bread was baking, and coffee brewing and they washed up at the wagon. Once the wagon broke, and Mr. Brotze was gone for three days with the front part in search for people who could help him repair it. Meanwhile your Mother was all alone with three children, in mortal fear in this endless desert. Finally, after three exhausting weeks, through danger and distress, you reached the border. Another stopover was required as the river was swollen (Rio Grande).

Your Father hurried to Matamoros to welcome you, but you failed to appear. He caught a cold, returned home, felt sick, and came down from Yellow Fever. Eight days later you arrived, and with that came the news that Father was dying. The next day, on his birthday, he was dead, — and he hadn't been able to press any of you to his heart. — How much sorrow that was for your poor Mother! Left alone in a strange place — and without any means. The doctor requested 300 Dollar for the eight-day treatment, but Father's records and papers, all of his money, clothes, assets, equipment, completely everything had been stolen — had disappeared! Mr. Jenny behaved innocently, and God only knows if he was the one. Soon, in the midst of this terrible situation Mr. Holzapfel arrived, as your friend and protector. Several bales of cotton were turned into money, but no Union ship was yet about to arrive. Instead, you experienced 3 revolutions in Matamoros, and disease, and adversity of all kind. Finally, Mr. G. Schmidt saw to your passage, to New York to begin with. Since Kathchen contracted typhoid fever, you were forced to remain in N.Y. for two weeks. We were glad to see you again in March of 1864. Oh, repay your Mother with gratitude for the long, difficult years she suffered, fought, and cared, and how she brought 1000 sacrifices and pains for you in love.

Your Aunt *Minna Schlickum*

The next letter was written by Mrs. M. Staudt and Richard Brotze, friends from Texas to Therese Klier Schlickum in Germany. Mrs. Staudt, Richard Brotze, Ferd. Schutz, Boerner, Staffels, Mrs. Schuckhart, Mrs. Gartz, and Mrs. Schentz were all acquaintances of Therese

---

[1]*Bagdad, Tamaulipas, Mexico was a town established in 1848 on the south bank of the mouth of the Río Grande.*

This town is also known as the Port of Bagdad or the Port of Matamoros, since it is inside the municipality of Matamoros, Tamaulipas. Officially declared non-existent in 1880, it is now invisible, covered by the shifting sands of time.

Klier Schlickum in Texas. Richard Brotze had accompanied Therese Klier Schlickum on her journey from Boerne to Matamoros, Mexico. Therese Klier Schlickum and her children (*Hugo, Julius, and Katchen*) were living with Father and Mother Klier in Germany after the death of her husband, Julius Schlickum, in Matamoros, Mexico, October 27, 1863.

Letter #16

(Letter by Mrs. Al Staudt and Richard Brotze to Therese Schlickum)

April 29th, 1864

Dear Mrs. Schlickum,

I have received the letter you sent via Mr. Brotze. I was very happy to finally hear from you, but I became very sad when imagining your sad days. Believe me, dear Mrs. Schlickum, I felt the entire misery together with you, although not as much as you did. I know what it means to be alone, and still vividly remember the time when we lost our Father.

However, don't think back to the sad situation in Matamoros, and to the times when you lived here, but think of your dear children, whose presence will raise you up again with time. Such wounds can only be healed by time, so don't give yourself completely over to grief, poor Mrs. Schlickum. You have now arrived safely and sound in Germany at your parents. Be very happy to be there, as they will undertake the greatest effort to help you learn to forget your grief and loss. Your children are safer there, and will enjoy a better education, and attend better schools than you could have provided for them here under these circumstances here.

Think of all this, dear Mrs. Schlickum, and you will become calmer. Times here are quite sad, and chances are that they will get still worse. Later you will find out about the disaster that befell Ferd. Schutz, and several other people who are possibly acquaintances of yours, it is too horrible.

Now I would like to also tell you something about myself. I'm still at my brother's farm, my Mother has been in San Antonio for three months at my sister's, who has had a little daughter. The Burners are still the same, or rather worse. Mrs. Schuckhart is playing a big show with Staffels now, as well as towards others, and in their eyes, she is a good woman; and you had thought much better of Mrs. Gartz than she deserves, since you thought to find a certain sympathy, as would have been normal. But keep silent about that.

You are now among better people, and I wished I'd be able to leave here as well. I'll probably report other news to you later on. My best thanks for the armoire, should I be able to find an opportunity if perhaps my brother-in-law is going to Germany in the next years, try to return the favor to your children.

Please write soon again and tell me how you and your dear children are, and how they like it there, if they are healthy and in good spirits, and especially how little Hugo

is doing, and grown-up Julius and Katchen [Catharine].
Now I would like to end, otherwise I'll only bore you.

Awaiting your answer and kind regards,

Your girlfriend *M. Staudt*

Many regards from Mrs. Schentz.

(Addendum by Richard Brotze)

I was permitted to fill in the still empty spaces; I'm
gladly doing so. Have you now arrived at a frame of mind
that allows you to live your days more contented? I'm
hoping and wishing that you'll make the effort and work
towards this goal. Make sure to do so! As far as I know
you, you are abandoning yourself too easily to your grief,
that's why I have made this remark. Fight against it with
all your might (and you have enough of that if only you
wish to make use of it), and your body will recover again
as well.

What are your children doing? Are all of them doing
quite well? Chances are that Katchen will like it in her new
surroundings and has forgotten about us poor Texans
already a long time ago. And Julius and Hugo will become
good Prussians, but that won't, hurt, as they can build a
happy life in that capacity as well. We cannot fathom at all
what the future might bring to us.

Goodbye, and don't completely forget a friend,

Richard Brotze

This next letter was written by Maria Klier and by
Father Klier in Muenster, Germany, to Therese Klier
Schlickum, then staying in Oerlinghausen (North Rhine,
Westphalia, Germany) at the Spa. It is not dated, but
probably from early summer of 1864. Father Klier
mentioned Holzapfel in his letter below as "our friend,

Holzapfel." Holzapfel's date and location of death is not known but he may have returned to Germany after the Civil War.

Letter #17

(Letter by Maria, Therese's sister, and by her Father Wilhelm Klier. It is not dated, but probably from early summer of 1864.)

Dear Therese,

We received your 1st letter on Sunday and were pleased to hear that you are quite liking it in Oerlinghausen, and hopefully the same is still the case at this time. Chances are that you're longing to hear something about your dear boys. They are of best of health, God be thanked, and aren't missing their Morn much, or not at all — and are rarely mentioning you, although at times, while talking among themselves, or when they receive tiny slap, they say: I'll tell that to Mom.

By the way, they are quite well behaved and are fun. You should have seen them on Pentecost, they behaved so nice and refined like little dolls. Since yesterday they have been parading around in light colored summer clothes. Mother bought them quite nice *(black and white)* straw hats that look very good on them, and she, bought each of them new shoes *(little fabric boots for Julius)*. He was happy about it, after all, he has little fabric boots with rosettes on it, and he said to Mother: Grandma, you are really very good, you take even better care of us than Mom!

Yesterday, on Tuesday, we were at the castle garden with the children - Hugo kept wanting to play with children he didn't know, but Julius absolutely wouldn't stand for, as if they were deadly enemies. You should have seen it; we were laughing about it heartily. Last week, on Tuesday evening, Chaplain R. returned, and I went there for a short visit and took Julius along. Julius behaved silly again, he didn't want to go upstairs as he believed that this was to the way to Heaven, but finally gave up after lots of crying. R. kissed him numerous times but was rather short as visitors kept arriving constantly.

Today Toni took Hugo to the Kaal. The little fellow ingratiated himself quite a bit with the Sisters there, and prayed, sung, etc. But when Toni took him upstairs in the Kaal he was supposed to pray, but he said: No, can't do so, and then kept saying: Hugo has to go pooh. You can imagine Toni's embarrassment. Luckily, we're done cleaning, but there is still some more work left; Aunt Therese and little Therese will arrive here tomorrow, and so there should be more work for a few days. Aunt will be very fond of the children. She thought you might be at the Spa but wanted to take advantage of little Therese's school vacation on Pentecost. I'm enclosing Minna's and dear ... letter. Minna's ... is not finished yet, therefore I was at Beckers last week ... [1]. Are the baths doing you good? ... ?

Goodbye, more soon, write again soon, and every now and then think of your faithful sister *Maria.*

---

[1] *Transcriber could not decipher. Translator's Note: Possibly Maria was staying at "Beckers?"*

(Addendum by Father Wilhelm Klier to Therese)
My dear Therese,
This time please contend yourself with only a few lines from me. It is past 11 p.m., and oh, how I'm tired. So,

Oerlinghausen it is anyway! May it entirely fulfill its purpose — was this a good idea?! Whatever may be, I suspected it would be, and God knows what it was connected to. But in each case, it was so strong and insistent, that I just about feel the urge to go there myself, but not to take baths, bur!!! I'm getting goosebumps from fear of the cold water, and of wet packs, ... etc. Moreover, I have such an inexplicable longing, only work and homelife are keeping me. Our Assessor Hefte is on vacation, Winkler (Haverkamps successor) went on a business trip after 14 days, and now I finally have matters together to ... the Institute and am busily working to prepare the invoices so they can still be submitted in August at the meeting of the Parliament. And on top of that I have a number of special projects at work that threaten to disturb my peace in my old age — how could I even think of traveling, and even to Oerlinghausen at that!? Besides, that wouldn't help you either, since I would surely be an impediment to the perseverance you need to accomplish the continually increasing bath treatments.

And so, keep it easy and follow the good advice of our friend Holzapfel with a frivolous disposition, but not with frivolousness. Get rid of your low spirits, and return to us in good spirits, completely healed and strengthened! We are expecting my sister here tomorrow afternoon, together with her little daughter Therese. They would like to enjoy themselves here for a few days during the Pentecost holidays.

Let us hear more soon, on how and what you are doing, and your experiences there, but don't let it cause you any trouble. Two newspapers from New York arrived again, if you'd like I'll send them to you soon, and other reading material as well if you have time and are in the mood for it. I don't know anything new to report that would be of importance, therefore I'm only adding heartfelt fatherly regards.

Klier

On June 22, 1864, two-year old Hugo Schlickum was baptized at Sankt Laurentius *Roemisch-Katholische*, Erwitte, Westfalen, Germany after Therese Klier Schlickum returned to Germany to live.

In April 1865, Ernst Schaper was elected sheriff of Gillespie County. On April 9, 1865, Confederate General Robert E. Lee surrendered his army to Union Lieutenant General Ulysses S. Grant at Appomattox Court House in Virginia. The official news did not reach Texas for weeks. It arrived on June 19, 1865 – a day now celebrated as Juneteenth – when General Gordon Granger and Union forces landed in Galveston. After the Civil War, Ferdinand Schlickum moved to Austin and became a member of the Texas Legislature.

On the night of April 14, 1865, well-known stage actor John Wilkes Booth slipped into the presidential box at Ford's Theatre in Washington, D.C., and shot President Abraham Lincoln in the head, mortally wounding him. John Wilkes Booth died at about sunrise on Wednesday, April 26, 1865, on the porch of Richard Garrett's house near Port Royal, Virginia. Andrew Johnson became the President of the United States of America in 1865.

After 32 months of being conscripted into the Confederate Army, Wilhelm Klier was mustered out of the 3rd Infantry Regiment Texas on May 26, 1865, in

Galveston, Texas. After the war, Wilhelm Klier returned to Gillespie County, and again worked for Johan F.G. Striegler, by whom he was held in high esteem. He had a pleasing personality, being well liked by all his friends.

It is not known where Wilhelm Klier lived after the Civil War, but he continued to own 160-acres (*one-half of the acreage*) on River Road. This land had been sold previously to Wilhelm and his sister, Josephine Klier Ransleben, by Julius and Therese Klier Schlickum on June 28, 1856. It is known from letters that he had cows on this property after the Civil War. *(Wilhelm's half of this property was sold later to Julius Ransleben on November 2, 1872.)* Fletcher Summerfield Stockdale was elected Governor of Texas on June 11, 1865. Andrew Jackson was elected Governor of Texas on June 16, 1865. H.P. Garrison was elected sheriff of Gillespie County in August 1865.

Chapter XI - Reconstruction in Gillespie County (1865-1877)

The Reconstruction in Gillespie County began in 1865. There were no celebrations by the German; it was time to get back to the task of making a living. Now that the war was over, it would soon become busy with cattle drives, ox carts, and wagons freighting throughout the Hill Country. Farmers raised their own vegetables, meats, and used the barter system where work was exchanged for food and clothing.

Ernst Schaper became the sheriff of Gillespie County in April 1865. Fletcher Summerfield Stockdale became the Governor of Texas for a few days on June 11, 1865, after Governor Pendleton Murrah fled following the collapse of the Confederacy. On June 16, 1865, Andrew Jackson Hamilton became the Governor of Texas. On July 7, 1865, four people were hung in Washington, D.C. for conspiring with John Wilkes Booth to assassinate President Abraham Lincoln: Lewis Powell (aka Lewis Payne), David Herold, George Atzerodt, and Mary Surratt, the first woman to be executed by the federal government. H. P. Garrison became the sheriff of Gillespie County in August 1865.

Citizens of the Comfort area discussed how to honor their dead from the Nueces massacre. It was decided that a common grave topped by a monument would memorialize their sacrifices. In the summer of 1865, a delegation led by Henry Schwethelm *(1840-1924)* returned to the battle site on the Nueces River. There they collected the bleached bones and returned them to Comfort for proper burial. Maria Klier, sister of Wilhelm Klier, married Heinrich Neuhaus on January 11, 1866, in Muenster, Germany. In June 1866, Ferdinand Ohlenburger was elected sheriff of Gillespie County. Thereafter, W. Wittnebe was elected sheriff of Gillespie County in 1866.

The following was a letter to Wilhelm Klier in Fredericksburg from Father Klier in Muenster, Germany, regarding Wilhelm's engagement to Ida Striegler. Father Klier had hoped that his son would return to Germany.

Letter #18

Muenster, July 30, 1866

Dear Wilhelm,

The enclosed letter to all of you, I will address to you so you can read it first and then together with Ranslebens and Josephine. I especially wanted to answer your letter of June 5 which I received a few days ago about your wedding plans. As I remarked in the enclosure, I cannot say much because I don't know any particulars. I want to talk in a well-meaning way. If you based your plans on the expectance that I would send you money for it, you can see from your letter to all of you that you would be completely wrong. However, if you can get along without my help, you will know what you have to do. If your engagement is at a point where you can't turn back, then I cannot and would not try to stop it in the hopes that your chosen one is brave and friendly and will stand with you in good times and bad and that you will be able to make a decent life for yourself. If that is not the case then I would have to regret your engagement all the more because, from the beginning, when I heard about it, it disturbed me. All of us and I, mostly, have been counting on your returning here soon. Even though there is unrest and the possibility of an uncertain future here, a nice opportunity for you has opened up here. Something suited to your ability and interests and the possibility of building a promising future. You could have had a completely suitable position with Maria, as her husband, Heinrich Neuhaus, is the son of the Major of Warendorf and who is ____? of the House Goldschmieding[1], not far from Dortmund. He is an outstanding agriculturist and businessman who could have trained you, possibly in a year's time to be a good German agriculturist. Furthermore, you would have had a good opportunity in that area to have the help and guidance of your brother-in-law Neuhaus. Also, if you wanted to get married you would easily have found a suitable bride of some means. Otto Schlickum has settled in Gelsenkirchen [North Rhine, Westphalia, Germany], not far from there, a town on the Cöln-Mindener Railroad[2], as a tradesman in cigars and groceries. He has found a suitable bride and is already doing so well that he wants to get married soon. He wanted to have Therese and the children with him but the children have the whooping cough so that wasn't possible.

I am writing this letter separately to you so it would not get to your bride-to-be and make her think bad of us. So, if you think it best, you can burn this letter without the others reading it, or you can share it with them. I have told you what I think, wanting what is best for you. God grant that my advice is not too late. If you decide to marry and remain in America, I wish you well. You know both there and here and are in a better position to make a decision than I.

Gustav, who has a bad cough, and who may have caught whooping cough[3], will sail on the ship *Bremen* on August 4th for New York. He is packed and ready to go. I will give him duplicate of both letters to be mailed in New York. So, you should surely get it even if the ones I mail here should get lost. However, if he is too sick to sail then, he will sail from Bremen on August 11th on the ship *America,* or even later on another ship. And now, stay well. May God protect and sustain you, from all of us (Mother and siblings). They want to write some family news for Gustav to mail.

With hearty greetings, your true
Father Klier

---

[1] *The House Goldschmieding is a former noble residence. Its origins lie in a manor from the 13th century. In the last quarter of the 16th century, the former house in the style of the Lippe Renaissance was completely redesigned by its owners and presents itself today as a simple plaster building which is used as a restaurant. From the interior, the ballroom with a beam ceiling has been preserved, which has a special Renaissance chimney made of Baumberger sandstone was a special showpiece.*

[2] *The Cologne-Minden Railway Company (German, old spelling: Cöln-Mindener Eisenmann-Gesellschaft, CME) was along with the Markiece Railway Company and the Rhenish Railway Company one of the railway companies that in the mid-19th century built the first railways in the Ruhr and large parts of today's North Rhine-Westphalia.*

[3] *Whooping cough, also known as pertussis, is a highly contagious disease affecting the lungs. This cough starts out small with bacteria called Bordetella pertussis. Anyone exposed to the bacteria can get sick.*

Left: Treue der Union, Comfort, Texas ("Loyalty to the Union")

On August 9, 1866, James W. Throckmorton was elected as Governor of the State of Texas. The remains of those Unionists who died for their ideas were interred in a common grave underneath the *Treue der Union* monument on August 10, 1866.

"This German language monument, erected 1866, honors the memory of 68 men (mostly Germans) from this region who were loyal to the Union during the Civil War. Trying desperately to reach U.S. Federal troops by way of Mexico, about 40 of the men were killed by vengeful Confederates bent on annihilating them, in the Battle of the Nueces (on Aug. 10, 1862) and a later fight (Oct. 18). The bodies of the slain and those who drowned swimming the Rio Grande were left unburied. A group of Germans gathered the bones of their friends and buried them at this site in 1865."

Entered in the National Register of Historic Places (1976) Official Texas State Archeological Landmark (1996)

The following was a letter written to Wilhelm Klier in Fredericksburg, from his cousin, Carl Wolters, in Alexandria, Virginia.

Letter #19

Alexandria, VA, January 21st, 1867

My dear cousin Wilhelm,

I'm not sure if you know already that I have made America my future home. I arrived here not quite as inexperienced as most others, as I had already made all bitter experiences of a new immigrant in London, where I had lived before for 1 year. I also learned the language quite well there. I did very badly there, England is no country for Germans. That is why I decided to come here, and arrived safely in New York on August 8th, where I stayed at the Hotel Taegel.

I received your address from your sister Therese when she sent me a letter to London. I wrote to you 1 month before my departure from London and was hoping to receive a letter from you either there, or at my arrival in New York in care of the post-office, but it appears that this letter has not come into your possession. I had to remain in New York for one month as I continually felt unwell, probably due to the change in climate. I had planned to go further out West, to the States· of Illinois, Iowa, and Wisconsin, but man proposes, and fate disposes.

The first day after my recovery I saw an advertisement in the newspaper for a brewery manager. I applied at said place in New York, where I met the owner of the brewery, Robert Portner from Alexandria, Virginia. He took me along to this place without any prior conditions, and so I ended up in the South despite all my intentions. I arrived here on September 10th and took over management of the brewery. It is twice the size of my father's brewery, and everything is run by an 8-pound steam-engine. Thus far they had only brewed lager, but I added English ale, which immediately enjoyed a high reputation.

My boss is a young, unmarried man, who treats me like a friend. He, his brother, and I, live together in the same place, which is run by a young German housekeeper, and thus we live quite cheerfully. My boss is very happy with my work, and I'm going to get a big 6 caliber revolver for New Years, and he agreed on a salary at 1000 Dollars per year, with the promise to take me in as a business partner later on. Thus, I am contented for now with my livelihood, and have enough to send 500 Dollars per year to my family in Germany, that is, to my wife and three magnificent boys, who want to stay there until they have completed their education.

In all likelihood we will be investing into a vinegar factory very shortly, and I'm hoping to be able to become a partner then, besides earning my salary. And so, I immediately had a good start in America, and was more lucky than I could ever have hoped for, and only regret not to have come here earlier.

However, I have not experienced any of the nice hunting excursions, lush fields, or beautiful primeval forests, I had dreamed of. Around here everything is uncultivated and barren. The only game around here are little rabbits the size of rats, and partridges the size of sparrows, and also a few squirrels so that it isn't worth the effort of hunting them. It is very hot here in summer, and on the other hand also quite cold in winter; indeed, it is much colder compared to back home at the Rhine.

The Potomac River has been frozen already for more than 6 weeks, and we've had snow since then as well, and at times it was as cold as 15 degrees below 0, according to Beauvier.

In letters from Dahlen *[Saxony, Germany]* I have learned that your brother Gustav has arrived in New York already as well, and that my brother-in-law Ewald Tilges is supposed to be on his way. Thus, everyone is slowly moving over here, but still, we're not finding each other over here. The cost of privations are either too great, or on the other hand again too small, if only sacrifices of money are involved. Should I once be doing very well to the point of not having to worry about the cost of travel, I'm hoping to be able to visit you once in Texas so we can talk about everything one cannot write about; meanwhile I'd be very pleased to receive a letter from there.

Please let me know, dear Wilhelm, how you have fared so far, what you are doing, and what your plans are for the future? Are you married or still single? How is your dear sister Josephine doing, whom I can still remember from my younger days? How many children does she have, how is her husband, and what kind of business is he in?

Please send my kindest regards to everyone. Tell me everything that might be useful to know about the circumstances there. Could any trade be set up between here and there? As you know, I am always enterprising, and the same goes for my boss. We are planning to also import Rhine wine. Let me know what goods are produced in Texas and what is being imported from here or from other states. Please let me know in case you might not have a profitable livelihood yet.

Write to me in detail and soon, and my most heartfelt regards and kisses to you and to everyone from Your faithful cousin, Carl Wolters ... In care of Mr. Robert Portner, Alexandria, Virginia.

The following was a letter from Heinrich and Maria Klier Neuhaus, living in Germany, to Wilhelm Klier, living in Fredericksburg. Maria Klier married Heinrich Neuhaus in1866. Maria was against the engagement of Wilhelm Klier and Ida Striegler because he had promised to return to Germany. Maria inquired if the bride-to-be were Catholic, hoping that their children would be raised in the Catholic faith.

Letter #20

January 30, 1867

Dear, kind Wilhelm,

Since we are visiting in Muenster right now, and you haven't received a letter from me in a long time, we shall add a few lines, as there are letters to be sent to you and to Gustav right now.

I have been married to my dear Heinrich now for more than one year, and I regret nothing more than the fact that you haven't gotten to know your new brother yet in person. If you only had kept your promise and would have returned to us, then Heinrich would certainly have helped you establish a new livelihood, and thus you would have also been close to the entire family. However now you are not giving us much hope — and are founding your new family home over there ! !! Heartfelt wishes for happiness to you and to your dear bride. May the good Lord grant for your chosen one to be a good and kind wife, and that you will be very happy with each other, then I will gladly call her my dear sister. She makes a nice impression on me on the photo, and I'm sorry that I can't get to know her in person. Dear Wilhelm, give her my heartfelt regards, and assure her of my sisterly love, and I'm also sending heartfelt wishes for happiness to you.

You're not saying anything in your letter about religion, is Ida catholic? Hopefully you will remain faithful to the religion wherein you felt so happy again a few years ago, and in case the good Lord will once give you little children, you will raise them in the catholic faith!! Mother will likely write to you about that, and may you accommodate her pleas and wishes that are rooted in her sense of duty. I am extremely happy that we agree also in religious matters, as with everything else. If one does not abandon God and religion, then the good Lord won't abandon us either. In the year since we've been married, I have been sick quite often, and our children as well. But now we are doing well again, thank goodness. The three children are giving us much joy, Gottfried is 6 years[1], Anna 4 1/2 years, and Ernst 3 years old. In the beginning I was not used to life on the countryside and farming, but I have quite gotten used to it. This summer, Father, Mother and Therese came to visit with the children and with Gustav, and thereafter Fellingers.

See, dear Wilhelm, this is one of the pleasures of having parents and relatives rather close, and one can visit quite often. I feel very sorry for our dear Josephine, chances are that she would like to come here sometimes but can't. All that work she has with her turkeys. Give my best to Josephine from me. And now, dear Wilhelm, be well and take care, and once again I'm sincerely wishing you happiness and God's blessings. And now Adieu, my dear, kind Wilhelm, and remember your faithful sister in love,

Maria

My dear brother Wilhelm,

Although presenting my most cordial, brotherly congratulations to your engagement, and although still unacquainted but yet a faithful brother, am asking that you send my regards to your bride, but nevertheless have to protest emphatically against this marriage as it prevents me from getting to know you, regretfully you won't be minding my protest. From the depth of my heart, I'm wishing to you and to your future wife as much happiness, as the good Lord is granting to me with your dear, kind, and faithful sister, my wife.

And hopefully the opportunity will arise, and you will visit your old homeland once again, so that have the opportunity to get to know you in person. With this expectation I'm wishing you my goodbye, dear Wilhelm, and may we once meet. I'm remaining your faithful brother-in-law.

Heinrich Neuhaus
January 30th, 1867

As soon as you visit with Josephine or Ransleben, relate to them my most cordial regards.[2]

(Most of the writing in the margin is no longer legible as much of the paper is torn and missing. Writing in top and side margins, rear).

Since there is still room in the margin, I'll add a few lines, and as everyone is writing to you, I shouldn't be remiss either. Along with the others I also am wishing you ... to your choice and am hoping that you will be quite happy with your dear ... once you have your own home ... that the distance from here to there is so great, otherwise you could introduce your bride to us. But if God ... Since last year, our family has increased, and 2 more members.

Heinrich and Ida ... rr[3]

Writing inside margin, front:

I'd be happy if I could get to know her very soon ... that you will fulfill your religious duties ... catholic ... and with God you shall receive ...   Hopefully, you and Gustav are writing much and often to each other in America and will exchange news soon again.

---

[1]*this number is unclear/unsure.*

[2]*Translator's remark: part of this sentence is missing (page torn), and some or the words are just a good guess on my part.*

[3]*Paper is torn right at this place. The name might be something like Stir or M.rr.*

The following was a letter from Gustav Klier in Central, Missouri to his brother, Wilhelm Klier, and sister, Josephine Ransleben Klier, in Fredericksburg. It mentioned the discord between Wilhelm Klier and his brother-in-law, Julius Ransleben. Father and Mother Klier blamed Wilhelm Klier for the discord......the discord that happened when Wilhelm returned to hide out at his sister and brother-in-law's farm after the Battle of Nueces in 1862. Julius Ransleben went to town to inquire what to do about his brother-in-law hiding out and, subsequently, Wilhelm was arrested by Confederate soldiers and hauled off to prison in San Antonio, Texas. Letters from Gustav Klier in St. Louis, Missouri began on March 9, 1867.

<u>*Letter #21*</u>
Central, Missouri, March 9th, 1867
My dear, precious brother and sister,

I received your dear letter already 5 weeks ago. I had been looking out for it carefully, and would have answered it a long time ago, had I not been prevented from doing so by those divers new experiences I already had to go through in this country since writing my last letter to you, as well as the fact that I had been expecting a letter from Germany to arrive beforehand, and which I had wanted to enclose for you right away.

I received Wilhelm's letter already in the beginning of December but waited just as long before responding to it. Yesterday I already received his second letter. He is quite worried as I haven't answered yet, and also because he hasn't received a letter from Germany either so far. Since I have finally received the long-expected letters from Germany, I won't keep you waiting for another moment. [1]

Despite having been separated for such a long time now, my love for you is so cordial and sincere, just as if we had always lived together in greatest harmony. After all, there is nothing more beautiful than brothers and sisters who love each other faithfully, who conciliate in love with the one who might have failed and try to win him over with love; although Wilhelm alone is to blame for the discord between you, and he forgot how many worries, troubles, and fears you had suffered for his sake. Father and Mother also blame him for this, as you will see in the enclosed letters.

Please forward them to Wilhelm after you have read them. I have also urgently pleaded with Wilhelm in the enclosed letter to reconciliate with you. Please hold your loving hand forth to him in reconciliation as well. I'm much too sentimental to believe that there might exist disunity between us brothers and sisters. The account of your situation in Texas has also touched me deeply. This miserable country has caused us already many a worry and grief. Therefore, our most ardent wish had always been that you might leave this calamitous country the sooner, the better, in order to try your luck again in another part of America.

Now that I'm living here in America as well, I'd be overjoyed if you would also reside here in Missouri. Try to make a special effort to sell your land and cattle there at a good price, and thereafter to move here. To begin with you can rent a farm here that produces well, and if you're successful you can buy one later on. The farmers on the countryside here are very prosperous. A good and hard-working farmer in this place can not only make a good living, but also acquire quite a fortune within a few years. Supposedly business in St. Louis is currently very sluggish, and the merchants are complaining about bad times in general. It should be quite difficult at this time, while money is tight, to open up a new business.

However, a good opportunity might eventually come up to buy an existing, good business at a low price; — in the end, taking it over and running it shouldn't be too difficult. St. Louis is a very beautiful town, which extends over an extremely large area. It is built along the Mississippi River. St. Louis is one of the most populated American cities, with some of the heaviest traffic, and at the same time it is also the Portal to the American West.

Hopefully, you and the children are doing well again. I'm already looking forward to seeing you again, if only on a picture. Please write again very soon! — From the enclosed letters you'll be able to see the news from Germany for yourself. Our cousins Gustav Fellinger and Carl Wolters are behaving quite nicely, don't you agree?

Already a few days after I am sending my last letter, Mr. Wissmann procured good employment for me as a bookkeeper in a German Currency Exchange and Bank. Regrettably, I had to give up this job again after 10 days, as I was laid up with malaria for 3 weeks. Once I was cured, they had already given the job to someone else. Thereafter Mr. Wissmann found employment for me at a retail grocery store. This position was nothing special, but it was too difficult to find something else. During these bad times in St. Louis many young people are pounding the pavement who cannot find work.

During the first month I earned 8.— besides free room and board, and laundry, and in the second month 10.—. As my boss was very happy with me, he gave the job as a storekeeper in his store on the countryside, 9 miles from St. Louis. I've been in this place since February 5th. I'm taking care of the store here all on my own and am therefore my own boss. We are selling groceries, dry goods, hardware, and so on. I can already manage pretty well when it comes to the English language. Although I haven't made an agreement to this regard with my boss, I am counting on receiving 15 — 25 Dollar per month, and free board. I rather like it here, but at times things get somewhat too rough for my taste.

A few days ago, an American smashed a number of different things at the store without any provocation, and the matter will likely go to court. That is why I went back to town yesterday. I have an excellent chance of getting good employment as a bookkeeper in a wholesale grocery store, one of the best companies in St. Louis. The company's name is Meyer & Meister. Chances are that Meister, who was born in Versmold, would like to give the position to me, if his partner agrees with it as well. be notified within 1, or 2 months at the most. Mr. Wissmann told me that the current bookkeeper is earning $2500 per year. To begin with I'd probably receive $700, until I have acquainted myself better with this work. This would be a magnificent chance for me, may God grant that I get the position. remain at my current job as long as I have no assurance.

And now I'm wishing you, my dear brother and sister, goodbye, and am sending my most heartfelt and best regards to you and to my dear nephews, and to little Josephine. Please send all enclosures to Wilhelm as soon as possible, so that he should no longer be worried.

I'm remaining yours in true love.

Your faithful brother

Klier

Mr. Gustave Klier Care of Messrs. Wissmann & Senden, North Second Street

Old No. 182

St. Louis, Mo.

Carl Eichle is sending his best regards. He is working at a wholesale grocery store in St. Louis, earning $40 a month. Whenever you are writing letters to Germany, it might be best if you send them to me, as chances of arrival there would be better. Lately several of your letters were lost!

[1]*Page break, line missing.*

In the spring of 1867, J. P. Waldrip rode into Fredericksburg two years after the Civil War. Many German anti-secessionists had been killed by Waldrip's *Haengerbande,* the hanging bandits. Waldrip left his hideout and rode into town; he either thought he would not be recognized, or the end of the war constituted amnesty. An unknown party in Fredericksburg wired by telegraph, Captain Phillip Braubach in San Antonio; the son-in-law of Louis Schuetze, schoolteacher, whom Waldrip was accused of murdering.

The telegram brought Braubach, riding as fast as a horse could carry him, to Fredericksburg. Waldrip was soon recognized in Fredericksburg and fled towards the Nimitz Hotel. Braubach took a shot at him and winged him in the shoulder. Waldrip then came vaulting over the hotel's high stone fence. Henry Langerhans, standing in the second-story window of his boot and saddle shop, kitty-corner from the Nimitz Hotel, reached for his rifle. Langerhans saw Waldrip take refuge behind a great oak tree near the fence. Taking careful aim with the long rifle, Langerhans fired. Waldrip was dead! Mrs. Langerhans kept the secret from her [eight] children until her husband, the man who had got the drop on Waldrip, died of natural causes.

The following was a letter from Gustav Klier, in Central, Missouri, to his brother, Wilhelm Klier, living in Fredericksburg. Wilhelm Klier was engaged to Ida Striegler.

Letter #22

Central, Mo. March 11, 1867

My dear, precious brother,

I received both of your dear letters dated November 14th & February 20th. The reason for not answering the first letter is to blame on all the adventures I have experienced already since my arrival in this country on one hand, as I did not find the time to write. On the other hand, I wanted to wait for a letter from Germany, so I would be able to enclose it right away. Four days ago, I finally received news from Germany, and am making haste to forward them to you immediately.

I was very happy to hear more details from you about your dear bride. I'm wishing you good luck from all of my heart to your choice, and may you feel as happy with Ida as Maria is with her Heinrich! Please extend most heartfelt regards and wishes from me to my dear new sister. I would call myself very happy if I'd be able to get to know her already at this time. But since that won't be possible, would you please do me a big favor and send me a picture of her, as well as one of you.

With deep sorrow I'm learning from your and Ransleben's letters, that you have been at odds with each other already for quite a while. Dear Wilhelm, please remember how much worry and anguish Julius, and especially Josephine, have suffered for your sake during that miserable war — and how much Josephine, who loves you and is attached to you so much, is suffering as a result of this discord! For my sake, please offer your hand in reconciliation to your sister and your brother-in-law and enter everything that has happened in the past into the book of oblivion. Josephine & Ransleben would certainly not refuse the hand offered to them in reconciliation, and thereafter you will feel twice as happy next to your dear bride. Hopefully, you won't ignore or misunderstand my plea, which is coming from a heart filled with true, brotherly love! I'm quite suffering at the thought that we, as siblings here in this country, should not living together in accord & peace!

I won't have to write any details or news from Germany, as you'll be able to read them yourself in the enclosed letters. Hopefully, you haven't answered Carl Wolters letter yet, and I'd advise you not to answer it at all. He doesn't deserve it, after what he has done in England, and it would be best to stay away from him.

As mentioned above, I have already experienced quite a lot here, since the last letter I wrote to you. A few days after I had sent my letter to you, I was offered very good employments as a German correspondent and bookkeeper at a German bank, thanks to Mr. Wissmann who had procured it for me. But I had to quit this job after 10 days since I became ill. I came down with malaria, which kept me in bed for 3 entire weeks. I spent 14 terrible days at a hospital, the remaining 8 days at a boarding house. I requested for the closest doctor, who happened to be Dr. Nagel. He had traveled with Therese from Mexico to New York back then and had cured Kathchen on the way from typhoid fever. You may possibly know him, as he lived formerly in Texas. He was very happy to get to know me. After my recovery, Mr. Wissmann procured another job for me at a retail grocery store, where I was making $8 the first month, plus free room and board, and $10 the second month. My boss was very happy with me and gave me a job as a storekeeper in his store on the countryside in Central, 9 miles from St. Louis. I have been here since February 5th, and am running the business all on my own, and am therefore my own boss. We are selling groceries, dry goods, hardware, and so on. I don't know yet how much I will we making here but am expecting $15— to $25 per month. I rather like it here, but at times. things get somewhat too rough for my taste; many bad people live around here. A few days ago, an American smashed a number of different things at the store, without any provocation. That is why I went back to town yesterday. The matter will certainly be dealt with in court. In town I discovered your letter. At the same time, I was told by Mr. Wissmann that he has a chance of getting employment for me as a bookkeeper in one of the best companies in St. Louis, a wholesale grocery store. The company's name is Meyer & Meister. Chances are that the latter, who was born in Versmold, might want to give the position to me, if his partner, who had suggested another young man, agrees with it. I'll be notified within 1 or 2 months. The current bookkeeper is earning $2500 per year. To begin with I'd probably be receiving $700, until I have familiarized myself with this work — a magnificent chance for me! May God grant that I get this position!

I have to end now, dear Wilhelm. Please write to me again very soon. Please give my best regards to your dear bride & to your future parents-in-law, and special regards & kisses to you from your brother who loves you sincerely.

Klier

Please address letters as before to:

Gustave Klier

Care of Messrs. Wissmann & Senden North second street, Old No. 182

Please let me know your address in your next letter. I cannot send mail to you directly at this time since you didn't specify it for me. Forward the letter to me next time you write to Germany, as chances of it getting there would be better. Lately many of your letters did not arrive there!

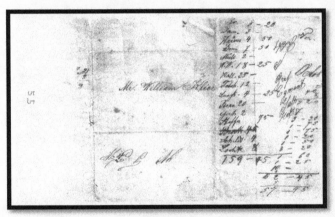

Page 4 of letter 5 appears to be a list of purchases. Some words ore abbreviated so much that their meaning is completely unclear. This empty page may have been used by Wilhelm for his own bookkeeping purposes, but it might also be possible that Gustav used note paper, from the store for his letter. Some of the handwriting may be Gustav 's:

"43 P, Graf Egmont, ... " (*referring to the literary work "Graf Egmont," either by Goethe or Schiller*).

On May 26, 1867, Franz Jung was elected sheriff of Gillespie County. The following was a letter from Gustav Klier in Central, Missouri to his brother, Wilhelm Klier, in Fredericksburg.

Letter #23

Central, MO

May 17th, 1867

Dear Wilhelm,

I received your dear letter and photograph already about 3 weeks ago. I was extremely pleased that I was able to get to know your dear bride, if only through a photograph. Hopefully have the pleasure to make her valued and personal acquaintance quite soon. I waited before answering your letter until now, in order to fulfill Ida's wish to send the enclosed photograph of myself. I wrote to Germany on March 11, however, haven't received any news from there yet, and Ranslebens haven't answered so far either.

You appear to have misunderstood my last letter completely; in no way did I blame you in it for the discord between you and Ranslebens. Such a thing wouldn't occur to me in the least, since there was no way for me to judge from your letters what the discord between you was all about, and who might have caused it. But the thought of us siblings not being able to live together in harmony in this country was just so unpleasant, that I not only asked you, but also the Ranslebens to conciliate with one another, and to forget what has happened.

The last time I was in St. Louis I asked Mr. Wissmann about the cost of land, as he knows this area quite well. Around here it is already quite expensive, both unimproved and farmland goes for $100 to $200 per acre. But Mr. Wissmann told me that currently the best opportunities to buy cheap land are in the State of Kansas, and supposedly they have a company there that is actively seeking to populate and cultivate the land. He also owns shares in that company, and he heard from different sides that the land there is very good. It is being sold at 5 to 8 Dollar per acre. A farm in that area would not only produce enough for subsistence, but also make a profit, as there is a very good market for grain and such, high prices are being paid for it, and the railroad is not far from there. Therefore, he feels that he can recommend it to you, but you should probably travel there in person to look at everything. He wouldn't mind giving me more details should you be interested. Please let me know in your next letter.

How are things going with the brewery, are you no longer interested in it? Perhaps you might find a good opportunity to this regard. This just came to my mind when reading your letter. Mr. Kampmann from Quincy, Illinois, and his wife, who is the sister of Mrs. Moersch, were visiting in Germany last year and returned 3 weeks after I left for America. They spent several weeks in St. Louis, and I visited them a number of times. Mr. Kampmann told me that he owns a beer brewery in Quincy, Illinois, which he had rented to a certain Wichmann from Munster prior to his departure to Germany, but that the latter was in arrears with his rent.

He had returned as quickly as possible from Germany in case matters might be going badly, and to repossess the brewery. Wichmann left Germany due to bad debts, and fraud. Mr. Kampmann might possibly be inclined to rent his brewery to you. I'm upset with myself for not having thought of this while he was here in St. Louis. Mr. Kampmann started out with nothing, so to speak, and made a fortune of about 40000 Thaler within a few years. If you feel up to it, I'd gladly write to Mr. Kampmann regarding this matter. They are very nice people, and I have taken quite a liking to them.

Regrettably, I did not get the job at the wholesale company, as one of the bosses gave it to his own son, and Mr. Wissmann couldn't raise any objections against that. On the other hand, I have prospects, although not right away, to rent a retail grocery and feed store with a bar in St. Louis, possibly within half a year. The owner suffers from rheumatism and can't run the business by himself. The current renter has leased it for three years but doesn't have the know-how and may give it up. I'll remain at my current employment for the present and will wait patiently.

My original plan had been to remain in this country for several years and to continue training as a merchant, and thereafter to return. If I should like it as much in the long run as did in the beginning, it is doubtful that I would return to Germany as quickly. In Germany it looks like there might be another war, Prussia against France, as both of them are fighting over Luxembourg. Although the most recent telegrams sound as if things have calmed down somewhat, and both powers supposedly have stopped arming for war. If it should in fact come to war, all of Europe would be become embroiled in it, and no end would be in sight.

And finally, dear Wilhelm, I'm sending my most sincere and best regards to your dear bride and your parents-in-law to be. Please write again very soon, and most heartfelt regards and kisses to you from your brother who loves you sincerely,

Klier

I have heard horrible things from Eichles about postmaster Brekenkamp in Versmold. He kept fake books and declared bankruptcy in the amount of 14 — 15 thousand Thaler, and then hung himself in the cellar. Isn't that dreadful?

On August 8, 1867, Elisha M. Pease was appointed Governor of the State of Texas. Gen. Philip H. Sheridan, Federal military commander of Texas, removed Governor Throckmorton in 1867. General Sheridan appointed Pease as provisional Governor to enforce Reconstruction policies.

The following was a letter from Gustav Klier in Missouri to his brother, Wilhelm Klier, in Fredericksburg. He mentioned the passing of their dear sister, Maria Klier Neuhaus, wife of Heinrich Neuhaus, on July 1, 1867, at the age of 26 years old.

Letter #24

St. Louis, Mo. October 8th, 1867

My precious and dear brother,

I have received your letters dated June 18th and August 27th and would have answered the first one a very long time ago if I hadn't waited in vain for letters from

Germany. But this time I alone am to blame for expecting a letter which did not arrive, as I had solely replied directly to Maria in Goldschmieding after receiving the last letters from Germany which I had forwarded to you and had mentioned in my letter that I would be writing home shortly. But I forgot about that completely, and upon my letter to Goldschmieding was therefore expecting an answer from home. Until now it was impossible for me to fulfill your request to answer your last letter right away, as I had come down with a deadly disease when I received it. At first, I had typhoid fever, of which I was successfully cured again after 2 1/2 weeks, but thereafter was faced with a much more-nasty condition, namely a lump on my right side. The doctor immediately declared it to be an ulcer of the liver and recommended that I go to the hospital since I was in need of very good care, and I naturally did so at once. After 2 weeks the lump had developed to where the doctor had to perform surgery on it. It contained such an enormous amount of pus, that even the doctor was amazed about it. You can imagine how much of my energy was consumed by that. One week later I was well enough to leave the hospital again, but I was still so week that I barely was able to walk 20 steps and had become so thin that even Dr. Nagel did not recognize me when I went to see him several days later. He then told me that he had only sent me to the hospital as he had not believed that my health would be restored again, since these ulcers of the liver often tend to burst internally, and the patient then is past any help. He also said that I should also be happy that I had been cured so quickly, as this normally takes 5 - 6 months. I have been staying in the countryside now for 14 days to recuperate and will remain here for another 2 weeks as the air on the countryside is doing me good.

I'm very sorry that you had to wait so long for news from me, however there is nothing I could do about it. But I'm not so sensitive as to take jokes the wrong way, especially not from my brother. I received the enclosed letters from Germany just about the same time as yours. Unfortunately, they only contain very sad news, namely the premature passing of our dear, kind, sister Maria. For us who remain behind this blow of fate is a very hard one. But Maria is doing well, she no longer suffers, and may have been lucky to escape many a severe suffering. This knowledge has to empower us in our bitter sorrow about her death, which took her way too early. May she rest in peace!

I quit my job in Central at the end of June, as things became too rough for me there at times, and I went back to my old employment at the grocery store in town at $15 per month and free lodging. However as soon as times are better here and a good job will be available, I shall accept it at once, as I don't feel at home at my current position. I discovered that my boss is a miser when it comes to money matters. Mr. Wissmann continually keeps making efforts on my behalf but hasn't been able to find any placement for me yet. I have to insist on finding employment at a wholesale company, as I'm too weak to keep working in a retail business in the long run. I am absolutely convinced that my last disease was only caused by overexertion. Sorry to say, naturally I can't accept your kind invitation to attend your wedding, but will be there in spirit, and am pronouncing my most cordial congratulations to you for your marriage. I sent a letter to Germany yesterday, and promised to write another one within about 4 weeks. If you would like to send letters along with it, please send them to me immediately.

Meanwhile, have you definitely made up your mind to move to the springs of the San Saba River, or have you decided otherwise? I haven't heard back from Josephine since I sent my last letter to her through you in mid-May, which I cannot understand at all. Have you perhaps heard something from the Ranslebens meanwhile? You will be so kind to send them the enclosed letter, including the ones from Germany?

To conclude, I'm sending my best regards to your dear bride and to your future parents-in-law, and kindest regards, especially to you, from your brother who sincerely loves you.

Klier

Address on last page is mostly illegible:

Fred

Texas

Agate Pet ...

W St.

The following was a letter from Mother Josepha Klier in Muenster, Germany, to her son, Gustav Klier, in Missouri. She mentioned the passing of her daughter, Maria Klier Neuhaus.

Letter #25

Muenster, October 27th, 1867

My dear, kind, Gustav,

We received your letter yesterday in the morning when all of us were having coffee together. Aunt Theresa and Richart were here, visiting with us for the day, and they were happy for all of us to have received news from you. The good Lord may be thanked a thousand times that you, poor son, have survived the danger well, and we shall hope and pray to God that he will completely bestow your health unto you again, and you will be able to conduct your business in good cheer. You cannot imagine how much I have worried about you.

Now that we heard that you have an ulcer in your side, I immediately had to think of our Karl, as he had an ulcer of the liver as well. The dear Lord and Mother Mary have heard my prayer, and have kept you for our sakes, and I will also keep praying for your health and healing since a Mother's prayer pierces the clouds, and the thought that you, dear Gustav, will return back home to us comforts me.

We have gone through much suffering and worry in the past two years, and I cannot accept the loss of my dear Maria yet, although I'm not begrudging her of her eternal peace. She is well, she has overcome, and who knows what else she would have had to suffer through. The dear Lord loved her more than that[1] and took her to herself. She is praying for all of us, and we want to pray for her, so that we shall once all find together again up there.

This is a difficult fate also for Heinrich, he has to resign himself to God's holy will as well and look for comfort in prayer. After the year of mourning has passed, he certainly will remarry again, since the household can't be run like that if he doesn't contribute. Therese will tell you quite a bit about it. He moans about his Maria very much, but there won't be anything one can do about it. In time, once he has a wife, calm and peace will console him again. We have promised not to leave him during his time of mourning and to support him.

And oh, Frieda Petersen wants me to send you a thousand regards as well, she was very worried about you as well. Supposedly Julius inquired with her why cousin hadn't talked to him, and asked for employment, as he gladly would have taken you in. This is however just talk, as we had told her about it often enough, and Aunt now said that Julius still has too many people and that he couldn't employ any more, and that Petersen's customer service was still good. Petersen's father-in-law also died shortly after Maria's death. Both his in-laws were visiting Ferdinand for 4 weeks, he got sick during the first week, and died there. Ferdinand wanted to visit us this summer, but he didn't come because of this death. Other than that, everything is well.

And now, dear Gustav, I would also like to know in detail how things are in regard to your piety, did you celebrate Easter, and haven't you found a confessor yet, and are you able to go to church on Sundays. Tell me soon about this and how you are doing with this, you might be able to imagine that I'm quite worried.

Give kindest regards from all of us to Paul Eichla, we were all very pleased that he was thinking of us as well and added on a few lines. Paul's Aunt is often getting letters from him, she is attached to him like a mother. We don't know anything more about Breckenkamps terrible demise than what you have already heard from Eichla[2].

Recently Nick Stulle was here and told us that Commerce Councilor Delius borrowed eight hundred Thaler lately, ... to allow to go to college ... [3] if the children know what to do with it, who knows, we are puzzled what he did with all that money, who would have thought things would turn out like that.

Last week I received letters from Lilli Walters, and took them with me to Aunt's name day[4], she writes that her Mother missed me so much, if I might want to treat her by surprising her. She is doing well there, Uncle Peter did good selling his lease and lands there, Heinrich was able to take over and pay on his own, and Fritz is supposed to get the beer brewery from him. Juliane Pauline is working in Dusseldorf [North Rhine, Westphalia, Germany] in a linen goods store.

And little Josephine, who used to call herself an old damsel to amuse us, is in Gottesberg [North Rhine, Westphalia, Germany] at a boarding-school to learn English and French. Lilli is keeping house, and subsequently Aunt and Uncle's days should be quiet. She doesn't talk about Peter and Paul in her letters. Jetchen had another son, 8 are still alive, and she is generally doing well.

Now, dear Gustav, I'll have to end this letter for now, more will follow soon. A thousand kind regards from all of us, also regards to all acquaintances, from your Mother who loves you with all her heart and is in mourning.

J. Klier

---

[1] *"than that:" than to let her suffer through more.*

²*Here the spelling appears to be Eichle, earlier it was
Eichla.*

³ *... missing words and lines due to the poor condition
of the letter of this place.*

⁴*Saint's Day*

The following was a letter from Toni Klier in Muenster,
Germany to her brother, Wilhelm Klier, in Fredericksburg.
Wilhelm Klier had set the wedding date and mention was
made about the discord between Wilhelm, Julius, and
Josephine Ransleben.

Letter #26
Muenster, October 29, 1867
Dear Wilhelm!
From your last letter of September 27, we saw that you
had set your wedding date for four or five weeks from than.
May God bestow his blessings on your union and make
you happy forever. By now you have probably received our
letters through Gustav in which we wrote about the
passing of our dear Maria. This loss will probably shock
you as much as it did us, as you had no warning at all.
Even though she lived not far from here, nobody except
Therese saw her in her last days. Her married happiness
lasted only a short while. She was very happy with her
Heinrich, but she went through some hard and
unpleasant times. There is no true happiness here on
earth; it is all interwoven with thorns. She has gone and
we must all follow her sooner or later.

Hopefully, dear Wilhelm, you will be very happy with
your Ida and that you both will overcome all hardships
and differences through your love.

I would never have thought that you would be against me; we so often sang together in times past. We both found out what false love is. Those were different times; we learned a lot when we were all together in our parents' home.

There is something else I want to say. You wrote about some difficulties between you and Ransleben. Be friendly and don't take everything so seriously. Josephine has always done so much for you and now when she didn't rush to help you in your undertaking, you regard her as your enemy. Start with God. Though you don't have much, man doesn't need much to be happy. If there is no other way, start with what you have, and God will bless you.

Now, in closing, I want to repeat my best wishes for your marriage. Greetings to your Ida, her parents and the Ranslebens.

Remember your loving sister, Toni.

The following was a letter from Mother Klier in Germany to her son, Wilhelm Klier, in Fredericksburg. This was in regard to the wedding invitation to Wilhelm Klier and Ida Striegler's wedding, and Wilhelm's estrangement from Josephine Klier Ransleben.

Letter #27
Muenster
October 29th, 1867
Dear Wilhelm,

We received your dear letter about two weeks ago, and the following day we also received a few lines from Gustav, after we hadn't heard from him in 8 months. The poor fellow was doing quite badly during that time and turns out our worries that he might be sick were not ill-founded. Chances are that Gustav has written to you by now as well and notified you and Josephine of the death of our dear Maria. She has been resting in the cool earth now for already 4 months. This was a difficult blow for all of us, but we have to submit ourselves to God's holy will. He took her to Himself as he loved her more, and she is well, and has successfully overcome; and who knows how much suffering she has escaped. Her marriage was only of short duration, barely 1 1/2 years. This is a hard blow for poor Heinrich as well, he keeps lamenting for his dear Maria, but nevertheless he will have to look for comfort in prayer, just as we have to. My heart is broken and cannot be completely mended.

May our good Lord[1] only preserve our dear Gustav, so that he'll recover and be completely healed very soon. This is causing us much worry. Isn't human life nothing but ... [2] suffering, and mercy and fate ... but still ... As hard as the struggle may be ... then we have fought a good fight, and we shall receive a good reward as well.

Dear Wilhelm, there is a hitch to the wedding invitation, if there only was no ocean, and if you wouldn't be living so far from us. Thus, we want to pray to the dear Lord to bestow rich blessings on your marriage and endow you with things that are presently and eternally beneficial for body and soul, and may He keep you from all danger. Give your dear bride a kiss from me, and extend many regards from me to her, and to her family. I'm going to pray for your well-being daily, but also don't forget to pray for your old parents every now and then.

And, dear Wilhelm, I would like to especially enjoin you not to estrange yourself from Josephine. Hasn't she always taken care of you like a mother, and has shared many a worry with you? Make sure to hold on to your brotherly and sisterly love. Don't heed to the gossip of other people, and don't make enemies over little matters, but rather, support each other in deed and in counsel and love each other, this is my deepest wish. Father will likely write to you about this as well and consider means or ways on how you should approach this.

Why don't you mail the enclosed death notice to Josephine? Aunt Petersen asked me to give both of you her most heartfelt regards and best wedding wishes. I have to end now as the letters are supposed to be leaving, and I have to apologize for my bad handwriting, and also the fact that I'm not able to write a nice letter at this time, and you'll have to be content with this, Wilhelm. I'll write more soon, and once again give my kindest regards to your bride and her entire family from afar, Your Mother who loves you, and who is in mourning.

J. Klier

---

[1]*According to the original "may the good only preserve" - the word "Lord" was forgotten, but clearly was part of the original thought.*

[2] *... words are missing or completely illegible due to tear or missing paper.*

The following was a letter from Father Klier, in Germany, to Wilhelm Klier living in Fredericksburg. Father Klier had sent a dowry in the amount of $350 on the condition that Wilhelm reconcile with Julius and Josephine Ransleben.

Letter #28

Muenster,

October 30th, 1867

My dear Wilhelm,

I won't have to report about family news, that has already been taken care of, and therefore will get directly to the matters at hand. My most heartfelt congratulations to your wedding, which may have already taken place by now, and the blessings of your Father!

To satisfy your request for a dowry I have asked Gustav to send you 500 Prussian Kr[1] (here about 350 Dollar) as soon as possible, under the condition and the expectance[2] that you reconcile and make friends again with Josephine, and with the entire Ransleben family in general. I have forwarded money to him via the Councilor of Commerce Delius in Detmold [North Rhine-Westphalia, Germany] and on to Bremen, and he will be receiving it shortly. I can't write anything else as this letter has to leave today together with the other letters. Regards and kisses to your dear wife or bride, as well as her entire family, and keep loving your faithful Papa.

Klier

---

[1] *Currency is somewhat unclear/unsure but appears to be Kreuzer (Prussian).*

[2] *Word is just a good guess and unsure, as the paper is torn at this place and much of this word is cut off.*

Left: Wilhelm Friedrich Klier (1834-1907)

The following was a letter from Therese Klier Schlickum, living in Germany, to her brother, Wilhelm Klier, written on the day of Wilhelm's marriage to Ida Striegler in Fredericksburg. Wilhelm Klier married Ida Striegler on November 6, 1867, at the age of 33 years.

Letter #29

November 6, 1867

My dear Wilhelm!

For your still upcoming or already accomplished wedding with dear Ida, our sister, it presses me to send my deepest sisterly wishes for your happiness. So, out of the depth of my heart, I wish for you all the best from Heaven and Earth. May the Heavens bless your union and the Earth yield its fruit a thousand-fold. You will have a difficult beginning as you are totally dependent on your own strength. But if you stay healthy, love one another and the heavens provide good harvests for your work, it will all work out. It pleases me, dear Wilhelm, that your spirits are so high and that you are so trustful of the future. You have been through hard times especially in the last years when you have had to face the serious side of life. Therefore, it is wished that you will now see a higher side. You have made a good beginning in that you now have dear Ida as a helpmate for life.

One thing I would ask of you: keep peace with Josephine and Ransleben; no matter what differences you may have had. Forgive past quarrels and think of the many years when, as true siblings, you lived together in harmony. Even if there has been talk over there, no one has ever written about it over here. Think of poor Josephine who has worked so hard, who with so many children must have many worries. It is too hard on parents to have you as enemies to each other.

Again, I want to wish you blessings and luck. Especially greet your dear Ida, also your parents-in-law and relatives. When you see R. and F. give them greetings from all of us. In the other letters and in the letters to G. you will find more about what we are doing. For today, sisterly greetings.

Think sometimes of your,
Therese

Twelve years later from the time Ida Agathe Petrino Striegler emigrated to Texas and after the Civil War, she was married to Wilhelm Friedrich Eduard Klier, on November 6, 1867, by Julius Schuchard, who was county judge at that time.

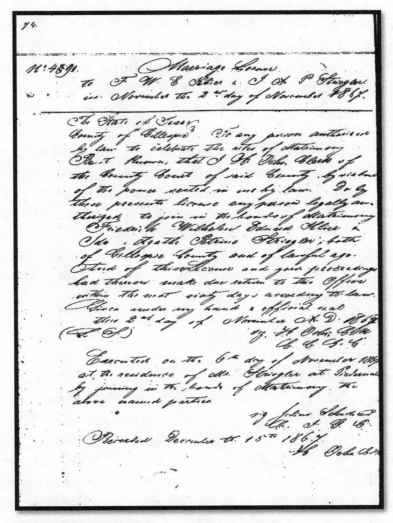

<u>November 2, 1867</u>
Date Marriage License was issued.

To F. W. E. Klier & I. P. Striegler issued November the 2nd day of November 1867.

The State of Texas }
County of Gillespie}

To any person authorized by law to celebrate the rites of Matrimony. Be it known that I, J.B. Ochs, Clerk of the County Court of said county by my hand and the power vested in me by law. Do by these presence license any person legally authorized to join in the bonds of Matrimony.

Friedrich Wilhelm Eduard Klier and Ida Agathe Petrino Striegler; both of Gillespie County and of lawful age stood of this cause and your proceedings had thereon make due return to the Office everything that meet 60 days according to law.

Executed on the 6th day of November 1867 at the residence of Mr. Striegler at by joining in the hands of Matrimony to above name parties.

Signature Julius Schuchard

Recorded December the 15th of 1867.

****

Wilhelm and Ida Striegler Klier, as a young married couple, moved to the Bonn place at Meusebach Creek *(present day Bonn Place at Meusebach Creek, 356 Kuhlmann Road, Fredericksburg)*. The Bonn Place consisted of Mathias and Maria Bonn. Their son, Peter Bonn, had built a charming stone home for his wife, Caroline Lochte Bonn, on the Bonn Place, shortly after their marriage in October 1859. In 1867 (during the time Wilhelm and Ida Striegler Klier lived on the Bonn Place), Peter and Caroline Bonn had three children: Wilhelm, age six; Henry, age four; and Bertha, age two.

Friedrich Klier, first son of Wilhelm and Ida Klier Striegler, was born in 1868, on the Bonn Place in the Meusebach Creek community, Gillespie County, Texas.

The date of birth is unknown. After a few years, they purchased a farm and ranch adjoining the Friedrich "Fritz" Lochte place in the same community *(present day in the area of 777 Lochte Road, Fredericksburg, Texas)*

The following was a letter from Gustav Klier living in St. Louis, Missouri, to his brother, Wilhelm Klier, regarding the arrival of Wilhelm and Ida Klier's first-born son, Friedrich Klier born in Gillespie County in 1868 (exact date of birth is unknown). The discord between Wilhelm Klier and his brother-in-law, Julius Ransleben was mentioned again.

Letter #30

St. Louis,

August 19th, 1868

Dear Wilhelm,

I was just about to answer your dear letter dated April 19th, when your letter from August 1st arrived with the joyous news of your dear wife's successful delivery of a healthy boy, and so I'm making haste to present my most sincere congratulations to you and to your dear wife. Hopefully, she and your first-born are feeling well and in good spirits when this letter arrives! I will relate this happy, news still today to those back home, although I assume that you have already done so. I can only apologize for my lengthy silence and blame it on my 'avid passion for writing', which has still increased due to the terrible summer heat in this country. Although, I was not lacking the time to write, as you will be able to see from the following.

Since April 1st I have resigned from my former job and exchanged it for a better one ($150.00 per month), but quit the latter already again after 2 months, as it was too much of a challenge for me, and I would have lost my health again within a rather short time. Thereafter I was without employment from the beginning of June until the end of July, since I was not able to find any appropriate work. Since August 1st I have a very pleasant job in a grocery store, which is founded on stock, or on shares, as they call it in this country. Its name is "St. Louis Consumers Cooperative Association." I was hired there as a manager at 65.00 per month, and in this position am in charge of the entire business, that is, of purchases and sales. Good things come to those who wait! Mr. Wissmann has guaranteed the security collateral of $1500 for me.

I received the last letter from Germany in the beginning. of May with a deposit for Ranslebens, and the order to send $240 in currency to them, which I took care of yesterday. Father wrote in his last letter that he was going to send me a letter for you, and I'm waiting for it to arrive daily. The discord between both of you is causing our parents much grief and worry. I therefore wrote to Ranslebens in all earnest, and asked them to reconcile with you, however they replied to me that they were not to blame for the strife between you. Supposedly Ransleben and his Carl came across you a while ago, when you were looking for your cows. He said he had greeted you whereupon you looked at him but did not respond to him. Shortly thereafter they came across your cows and Ransleben sent Carl after you, to let you know of the whereabouts of your cows, but that you hadn't thank him either. Naturally, I don't know how much of the story is true, and I really can't make a judgement on who of you is to blame for the discord. But as your brother I'm asking and conjuring you to reconciliate yourself again with Ranslebens, for the sake of my and your poor parents. Even if the latter are truly in the wrong, forgive the past. I am confident that you can overcome your personal feelings. Our dear Mother is pining away because of your discord.

In case my renewed and sincere request should be in vain—then I'd have to acquiesce and be patient, and suffer bitter grief in my heart, along with our parents. Please don't be angry with me for having raised this subject again. I only did it from love to all of my sibling, and to our parents. I'll write again as soon as I hear more details from Germany, and meanwhile am expecting your kind letters.

Best regard from me to your dear wife, and parents-in-law, and kindest regards to you as well as from your brother who loves you sincerely,

Gustav

Send letters to:

Gustav Klier

Manager of the St. Louis Consumers Cooperative Association

South 2nd Street No 420, St. Louis, MO

The following was a letter from the widowed Therese Klier Schlickum after she returned to live with her parents in Germany to Wilhelm Klier and his now wife, Ida Striegler Klier in Fredericksburg. Katchen (Catharine) Schlickum was 13 years old and was to receive first communion the next year.

Letter #31

Muenster,

29 October 1868

Dear Wilhelm, dear Ida!

We are late sending you the heartiest congratulations from all of us on the occasion of the happy and important event, the birth of your first child, and, therefore, you have a just cause to be angry with us. But don't think that indifference or anything like that is the reason. If you said that, you would do us bitterly wrong, because I can swear that all of us without exception are heartily glad about your happiness. Minna was just here, and we made several toasts (*cheers?*) to the Kliers' son and heir.

You, dear William, have punished us severely by the shortness of your letter, and the new relative will remain nameless for us for a longer time. I hope Ida and the little prince are doing well. We hear only good things about all of you. Be convinced that we all tenderly take part in your living, and never think again that we hold anything against you. The letters to America are different from others. Everyone wants to write something, so it is easily postponed from one week to the next. One day there are visitors, another day someone is ill, and before you know it a long time has passed, which you suddenly realize with no little consternation. If you, dear Wilhelm, think back, you will remember that the house of the Kliers always has been a very restless house and many friends called it "Hotel Klier." That was not incorrect and, these days, it is not much better, and the mentioned enterprise still has the same name.

I am going to travel to take Katchen who spent her holidays here, back to Erwitte (*the village where Minna*

Schlickum was a teacher). The trunks have already been packed, and tomorrow morning we will start very early. Next year Katchen (*Therese 's daughter*) will have her holy communion, after which she will come back here. She is thirteen years old now and is very tall and strong for her years. She is already taller than Tony and very proud of it.

Julius and Hugo (*Schlickum, Therese 's sons*) are growing up very nicely and have become rather wild fellows, but both learn very well and therefore give us a lot of joy. Julius already attends the Realschule (*grammar school*) where he is the youngest of all pupils in the Sexta (*first class*) as he has been the best since the beginning. Learning is very easy and a joy for him. Hugo, too, learns easily and is already in the first department with Specht (*probably a primary schoolteacher*).

But I have a lot to do with them, and in my old days I still have to learn Latin to help them with their work. May God will that someday they will be competent, useful men.

Surely you hear from Gustave from now and then and have heard what we are doing all the days. Since we wrote him the last time nothing of importance has happened. Father, mother, and Toni will tell you themselves how they are. Aunt Peterson, who had her eightieth birthday recently, is doing rather well, except she is growing very weak, but she still looks very nice. Just yesterday she was here all day. Julius with his wife and children are doing well, also Ferdinand, who lives in Basel [Switzerland] now. His business is excellent. He now has carriage and horses and generally lives well. Last spring, he was here with his wife for a day.

Fellingers, who now live at Dusseldorf (as you perhaps already know), are doing well. Richard D. has a good position in Elberfeld at a salary of 500 (*denomination?*).

From Erwitte I will go round to Gelsenkirchen, Dusseldorf and Mettmann, and then can report to you next time what is new.

Eduard Certain [sometimes spelled Cortain] sends best wishes and congratulates you. He is building his "nest," a house at Wolbeck [*North Rhine, Westphalia, Germany*] to settle down where he has the license for a Chemist's shop. Next Easter he will take home his bride, a Therese Bugge from *Uberwasser* [church in Muenster]. The Certains [Cortains] so far are doing well. I have nothing to report from your other acquaintances, dear William.

So, for the end I will once more repeat my hearty and sincere congratulations. May the little Nameless one grows

up and bring you joy and may all of you live happy and contented lives.

Send greetings also to Ida's parents and other relatives. Think sometimes in love of your sister.

Theresa

Caroline Therese Klier

10/12/1826-
5/16/1905

The following was a letter from Gustav Klier in St. Louis, Missouri to his brother. Wilhelm Klier, in Fredericksburg.

Letter #32

St. Louis,

November 25th, 1868

My dear Wilhelm,

Hopefully, you have received my last letter by now, which I mailed to you several weeks ago. Yesterday I received letters from Germany addressed to you, which I have enclosed for you immediately. As I had already feared in my last letter, my worries have unfortunately come true, and the St. Louis Cons. Coop has dissolved. The store was sold out 1 week ago today, and since then I have been unemployed again. But hopefully I'll find another employment soon. I won't report about it to Germany before I have found another job either.

I'm sending you my most heartfelt and sincere wishes to your upcoming birthday! Please say my kindest regards to your dear wife, who is hopefully doing very well, and the same goes for your firstborn. Please write me again you very soon. I'm remaining your sincerely loving and faithful brother,

Gustav Klier

In 1869, Ulysses S. Grant became the President of the United States of America.

The following was a letter from Gustav Klier in St. Louis, Missouri, to his brother, Wilhelm Klier in Fredericksburg. Gustav had sent regards for the recent born. Father Klier was planning to retire at the end of the year (1869) and wanted to take up residence along the Rhine, likely in Coblenz, Germany.

Letter #33

St. Louis,

March 14th, 1869

My dear Wilhelm,

I have received your last, dear, letter dated December 28th about 8 weeks ago, and am herewith returning your heartfelt good wishes for the New Year, although a little bit belated! May it be filled with contentment and many blessings for us all! At the same time, I'm also adding my belated and most sincere wishes to your birthday which has long past, hoping that you may have celebrated this happy day healthy, and will continue to celebrate it many more times in your family circle!

As I had hinted to you already in my last letter in October, the business where I had been employed back then was sold out on November 18th and I had been unemployed ever since, until February 20th. Businesses here are doing so miserably, so that I wasn't able to find a job despite my greatest efforts. Even now things are pretty piteous, and thousands are walking around without finding any work. I expect things to get better as soon as the weather is going to turn a little warmer.

We have had a really weird winter this year, with rather cold weather for 2 weeks in the beginning of December, but from the middle of December until the beginning of March there was constant spring-like weather. Subsequently the beer brewers and innkeepers no longer expected to get some ice for the summer. But about 2 weeks ago we were taught otherwise, instead of the arrival of spring in the beginning of March we've had uninterrupted, and strong frost for 2 weeks. Everyone had hoped that sales would pick up for spring, and times would finally get better, but we were bitterly disappointed.

I'm therefore very happy to have found a job again. I've been employed as a clerk in a grocery store again since February 20th at $50.00 per month. So far, I like it a lot, however I wished business was better. I'm planning to keep this job only until I can find a better one at a wholesale business. I would like to have a position as a bookkeeper, as that kind of work would suit me better, and it pays more as well.

A few days ago, for the first time in about 6 months, I also wrote a letter to Germany again. I'm very happy that everyone there is doing well. Father is planning to retire at the end of this year, and then wants to take up residence somewhere along the Rhine, likely in Coblenz. I was very happy to see in your letter that you and your dear wife, and the little Klier, are still quite healthy, and I'm hoping that such will be the case for a very long time to come.

Hopefully, you have successfully ... [1] your house and have settled there nicely together with your family? I have enclosed another photograph of myself which turned out better than the previous one; that one had been taken when I was already feeling sickly. Nowadays I'm feeling very well and am gaining weight daily. Apparently, I have finally acclimatized myself. I have to end now, my dear Wilhelm. Most heartfelt regards from me to your dear wife, and to your recent-born, and most heartfelt regards to you as well from your brother who faithfully loves you,

Gustav Klier

Write to me again soon!

¹*Page is torn at this place, and words are missing.*

On May 24, 1869, Sylvester Kleck was elected sheriff of Gillespie County. The following was a letter from Gustav Klier in St. Louis, Missouri to Wilhelm Klier in Fredericksburg. Their sister, Therese Klier Schlickum, moved to *Frauenstrasse* [a street in Muenster] away from Father and Mother Klier.

Letter #34

St. Louis

September 23rd, 1869

My dear Wilhelm,

Your last letter has been in my possession already for several months, and you may have already felt distressed while waiting for my answer. I would gladly have carried out your request pertaining to the bread-wheat if I could have done so. But the new wheat has only come to market 2 - 3 weeks ago around here, and I have made great efforts to get a very good variety for you. Hopefully, I was also able to accomplish this task. That is to say, I turned to a man who lived in Texas for many years, and who knows the local climate there and soil conditions thoroughly. He procured a bag of the best bread-wheat that is available here, and he asserts that it should be excellent for your local area. Around here wheat is sown beginning in mid-October to mid-November. I'm hoping that this bag of wheat will arrive there on time. As you can see from the enclosed bill of lading, I have⁻ sent the bag 1 week ago today via New Orleans and Indianola to W. Westhoff + Co. and have given notification to the latter immediately about it. It would probably be best if you would write to W.W. + Co. right away after receipt of this letter and ask them to forward the wheat as soon as possible.

I received news from Germany about 2 months ago, and everyone is doing well. Therese moved away from our parents to *Frauenstrasse* since they can no longer handle well the commotion with the children anymore. Other than that, everything has remained the same.

Please forgive my hasty letter this time, as I am very busy with work. I'm planning to enter into a partnership with my current employer, if Father gives his consent to do so. If yes, we would like to open a business branch which would be managed by my employer, while I will continue to run the old business. As soon as I have sorted out this matter, I shall report to you about it in more detail. Meanwhile please let me know soon if you have come into possession of the wheat. Times are very bad around here, and money very scarce! I will close for today, until soon, and best regards to you, to your dear wife, and to the young Klier. I'm remaining,

Gustav.

Edmund Davis takes office as Governor of the State of Texas on January 8, 1870. Sylvester Kleck was elected sheriff of Gillespie County in 1870. The population of Gillespie County, Texas in 1870 was 3,566. The 1870 Census of Gillespie County, Texas consisted of the following: Wilhelm, farmer, age 35; Ida, age 25; and Friedrich, age two. The new Legislature convened and ratified the 13th, 14th and 15th Amendments to the U.S. Constitution, the final requirements for readmission to the Union. President Grant signed the act to readmit Texas to Congressional representation on March 30, 1870.

Later that summer on August 1, 1870, Wilhelm, and Ida Striegler Klier purchased 150-acres of land in the Meusebach Creek community from Friedrich and Charlotte Lochte (part of Lochte's 700 acres). They paid $150.00 for Property #2. Wilhelm and Ida Striegler Klier lived in the Meusebach community for about 29 years and most of their 14 fourteen children were born and reared here. *(Wilhelm Klier was 35 years old when he purchased property #2.)*

Vol. K. Pg. 325 – August 1, 1870

<u>Friedrich Lochte & wife</u>

<u>to Wilhelm Klier</u>

State of Texas   }
County of Gillespie }

Know all men by these presents that we, Friedrich Lochte & Charlotte Lochte wife of Fr. Lochte of the County of Gillespie State of Texas for and in consideration of one hundred & fifty coin Dollars to us paid Wilhelm Klier of the County of Gillespie State of Texas, the receipt whereof is hereby acknowledged, have sold and conveyed, and by these presents do sell, convey and deliver, unto said Wilhelm Klier his heirs and assigns, all that tract or parcel of land lying and being in the County of Gillespie and State aforesaid, being part of survey No. 37 south of the Pedernales river and said parcel or tract of land is to include all that part of land situated on the east side of Meusebach Creek, & containing about one hundred and fifty acres of land, more or less. To have and to hold, all and singular the premises above mentioned, with the rights, members, hereditaments, and appurtenances to the same belonging, or in anywise incident or appertaining, unto the said Wilhelm Klier his heirs and assigns forever. And we hereby bind ourselves, our heirs, executors, and administrators, to warrant and forever defend all and singular the said premises unto the said Wilhelm Klier his heirs and assigns, forever against every person whomsoever, lawfully claiming or to claim the same, or any part thereof.

In testimony whereof, we have hereunto set our names in Fredericksburg the 1st. day of August A. D. 1870.

In presence of
(sig.) *Fr. Lochte*

H. Bierschwale
   Charlotte Lochte

R. Stamp
$50
F & S. L. August 1, 1870
****

State of Texas   }
County of Gillespie }

Before me H. Bierschwale Clerk of the District Court of said county personally appeared Friedrich Lochte a citizen of said county and state and to me well known, who acknowledged to me that he had signed and delivered the foregoing instrument of writing and he declared the same to be his act and deed for the purposes and considerations therein state. To certify which, I hereunto sign my name and affix the (L. S.) impress of the county seal, at office in Fredericksburg the the 1ˢᵗ day of August A. D. 1870

H. Bierschwale Clk D. C. G. G.

Also personally appeared Charlotte Lochte wife of Friedrich Lochte, parties to the foregoing instrument of writing dated the 1ˢᵗ. day of August A. D. 1870 and having been examined by me privily and apart from her husband and having the same fully explained to her the said Charlotte Lochte acknowledged the same to be her act and deed and declared that she had willingly signed and delivered the same and wished not to retract it.

To certify which, I hereunto sign my name and affix the seal.

****

leftt: East End of Old Klier House (Meusebach Creek)

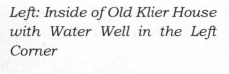

Left: Inside of Old Klier House with Water Well in the Left Corner

Right: Northeast Corner of Old Klier House.

In 1871, 1872, and 1873, Alfred Hunter was elected sheriff of Gillespie County. Gustav Klier, second son of Wilhelm and Ida Striegler Klier was born March 15, 1871, in the Meusebach Creek community, Gillespie County Texas. In May 1871, Fredericksburg celebrates its 25th anniversary. Signe Klier, first daughter of Wilhelm and Ida Striegler Klier, was born on June 17, 1872, in the Meusebach Creek Community, Gillespie County, Texas. On November 2, 1872, Wilhelm Klier sells one-half of

Property #1 (160 acres) to his sister's husband, Julius Ransleben for $300.00.

<u>Vol. L, Page 420, November 2, 1872</u>

State of Texas   }

County of Gillespie }

Know all men by there Presents, That I Wilhelm Klier of the County of Gillespie State of Texas for and in consideration of Three Hundred coin dollars to me paid by Julius Ransleben of the County of Gillespie State of Texas the receipt whereof is hereby acknowledged, have granted, bargained, sold and released, and by these presents do grant, bargain, sell and release unto said Julius Ransleben his heirs and assigns, all that tract or parcel of land lying and being in the County of Gillespie on the south side of the Pedernales River being part of survey No. forty five (45) containing one hundred and sixty acres of land and being one half of the three hundred and twenty acre tract conveyed to Julius Schlickum by Jno. Twohig by deed dated the twenty-eight day of August One thousand eight hundred and fifty and recorded in the Clerk's Office of Gillespie County in Book B, fol 125 which said deed is hereby made part and parcel to these presents and reference made thereto for further description, as well as to the transfer from Schlickum to me together with all and singular the rights, members, hereditaments, and appurtenances to the same belonging or in anywise incident or appertaining.

To have and to hold all and singular the premises above mentioned unto the said Julius Ransleben his heirs and assigns forever.

And I do hereby bind myself my heirs, executors, and administrators to warrant and force defend all and singular said the premises unto the said Julius Ransleben his heirs and assign against every person whomsoever, lawfully claiming or to claim the same, or any part thereof.

In testimony whereof, I have hereunto set my name in Fredericksburg the 2nd, day of November A. D. 1872.

****

The State of Texas }
County of Gillespie }

Before me H. Bierschwale District Clerk of said County personally appeared Wm. Klier a resident of said county and State to me well known, who in my presence executed signed and delivered the foregoing instrument of writing and he declared the same to be his act and deed for the purposes and considerations therein stated.

To certify which I hereunto sign my name and affix the impress of my official seal at office in Fredericksburg this 2nd day of November A.D. 1872.

H. Bierschwale
Clk. D. C. C. C.

I do hereby certify that the foregoing instrument of writing was filed in my office for record the 2nd day of November 1872 at 4 o'clock P. M. and duly recorded the 11th day of November 1872 at 9 o'clock A. M. in present book I fol. 420 & c.

H. Bierschwale
Clk. D. C. C. C.

****

The following was a letter from Mother Klier (Josepha), and Therese Klier Schlickum in Muenster, Germany to Wilhelm Klier, living in Fredericksburg. Condolences were extended to Ida Striegler Klier upon the death of her father, Johan Striegler, who died on November 13, 1872. Inquiry was made as to whether they have found a church of God close to where they live and referred to the children--Frederick, Gustav, and Signe Klier.

Letter #35

January 3rd, 1873

Dear· Wilhelm,

My most sincere wishes to all of you for the upcoming New Year, and Happy New Year. We shall and should continually ask and thank the good Lord that it will also remain a Happy one for all of us. Are you going to have another holiday as well, perhaps on ... [1], so we can all share our condolences; with your dear Ida, and mother-in-law, God disposes, we ... the good fight.

We were very pleased with both of your letters, you are writing quite jovial, and you don't have to apologize for not knowing what to write about. We enjoy hearing everything you tell us about, and I would be overjoyed if Ida would once also include a few words for me. Also, you haven't told us where your mother-in-law is living and if there are still brothers and sisters. Is there a church or house of God close to where you live, and how are things in regard to the salvation of your soul, and have you consecrated your children to God, who sends us blessings? And then we may not forget to thank God accordingly ... are doing well ... .

We haven't received any news from Gustav for close to an entire year. He wrote that he wasn't doing well with his ... business, and that he was going to move. That is why be is not writing to us, he doesn't know how many worries and sorrow he is causing us because of this. We now would like to write to him, haven't you heard anything from him yet.

You appear to have heard from Josephine, and ... also has told you everything. You have to put up with my scribbling, I can no longer write well. I have pain in my arms, and cannot write well, old age is accompanied by quite a few hardships. Aunt Petersen and Julius are sending best wishes and heartfelt regards to you. Father and Therese want to write, so I'm ending for today with my most heartfelt regards to you and to your dear wife and children. I regret nothing more than not being able to see you and the children at least once. Goodbye and keep in mind your old Mother who loves you.

Josepha Klier

---

[1] *... torn and missing paper; marked throughout this entire page by "........"*

The following was a letter from Sister Antonie (Toni) in Germany to Wilhelm Klier, Fredericksburg, referring to Ida's loss –the death of Ida's father, Johan Striegler. After 11 years, Wilhelm Klier was associating with the Ranslebens again. Father Klier (who has not retired) sold the house on *Herrenstrasse (a street in Muenster)* and moved to an apartment next to Royal Bank *(Koenig Bank in Muenster)*. Therese Klier Schlickum lives on *Mauritz* Street, Germany, and 19-year-old Catharine Schlickum lives with her Uncle Otto Schlickum in Gelsenkirchen, Germany.

Letter #36

Muenster

January 6th[1] ,1873

Dear Wilhelm,

The first letter I'm writing in the New Year is directed to you, to ensure that you're finally going to receive another message from us. To begin with I'm wishing a very blessed and happy New Year to you, your Ida, and to your children. May this year hold all the good things you are wishing for. We were sorry to hear of Ida's recent and difficult loss. Relate to her our heartfelt sympathy and let her know that we are feeling this bitter pain together with her. This loss must have been very difficult for your mother-in-law as well. May the good Lord bestow strength and fortitude on her, so she can bear, and submit herself to, this test with patience.

You cannot imagine how happy we are that you are associating with Ranslebens again. After all, you did spend so many years with them, and the children must certainly have like you so much. It is such a great relief for us to know that you are supporting each other again. You must have suffered a lot, since you were the only ones who are close to each other.

Chances are that our last letter to Josephine has arrived, and that you have heard from her how we are living now after having sold the house at the *Herrenstrasse* and moved to the place next to the Royal Bank. We have a very comfortable apartment and like it quite well here. Father and Mother are rather happy with it. We are living secluded here as we are not directly facing the street, but we can go for the nicest walks on the *Domplatz,* right in front of our door. Father was quite sick for several weeks this winter, he had a bad cough and difficulties breathing as never before, and Mother and I did our best to care for him. Hopefully, he'll retire soon now, so he can rest and look out for his health. He has toiled much during his entire life, and it will certainly do him good to finally be able to retire. Therese lives on Mauritz, right behind Lindenbrink *[streets in Muenster]*, which you surely still remember, she has a nice little house there, with a small garden. Kathchen is currently in Gelsenkirchen with Otto Schlickum. His wife isn't completely healthy either, and Kathchen can help out there quite a bit. Aunt Petersen turned 84 a few months ago. Lately she was feeling very week and is often quite frail. Although she is still going for walks, this is often a challenge for her, to the extent that is only able to accomplish the bare necessities every day and getting dressed and undressed is a major task for her. Her mind is still rather clear, she is asking about everyone and wants to know everything. We are still receiving letters from Fellingers regularly. Yesterday Richard joined a paint and dye factory as a partner, where he had been a manager for several years. He has one child, a strong boy by the name of Richard, according to his letters. Little Therese is staying with him. Hermann is in Hagen. Lina, the wife of Dr. Küster, is in Dusseldorf, however she has no children, the first one died when it was 3 weeks old, causing her quite a heartbreak. Much has changed over the years at Wolters in Dahlen since you had been there. Aunt and Uncle Peter are getting older and are rather worried about their income, as they now only have a small inn. Karl and Peter are in America as well. Peter is married there to the daughter of his boss. According to his last letter, Karl is planning a major venture, and he is hoping to become a rich man if he succeeds. He is in the process of digging for an oil well, and finding the right place depends much on luck. Lilly is still spending most of her time with her parents. Jettchen, who was a widow with 9 children, was remarried a few weeks ago. Josephine, who is Wolters' youngest, is here in Munster with the countess of ...² rode as a governess of ... ³ their youngest daughter ... and Heinrich, whose wife died last year, as well. His only child is currently in England and is working as a waiter. Fritz is in Cologne working in an inn. And now I would like to report about your acquaintances. Eduard Cortain [Certain], who is still in Wolbeck where he owns a pharmacy, has 2 children just like you, and is a happy person. At Cortains [Certains] we often talk about you, and you and Eduard should both come to visit together with your families. August and Heinrich Bevermann returned again from America about 2 years ago. The old Mr. Bevermann has died, and Bernhard, who had taken over the place of the father, died two years ago as well. At this time, the Bevermanns are no longer involved with the Schlossgarten (a restaurant). Herrmann has bought into the Weinburg [vineyard], close to Kinderhaus [a district in Muenster, Germany]. He was married this year, and August is living with him. Heinrich bought a place just before *Felgte* [street in Muenster], where he lives with his 5 children. He has hired a housekeeper, who takes care of his household. Mrs. Bevermann and Marie are now living with Settchen at the *Sandstrasse* [street in Muenster], who has a profitable business. Several weeks ago, the president of Dresberg [North Rhine-Westphalia, Germany] died as well, he had been retired for one and a quarter year. Vicar and preacher Kaal at the Cathedral, whom you and Josephine knew well, died also. He had been a preacher at the Cathedral for 40 years and my confessor for 23 years; he is in heaven now, and chances are that he will come fetch all of us as well. Enough for today, Mother and Father, and Therese want to join in and write to you also. Mother has difficulties with writing, as she still suffers from gout in her right arm and hand. Give my regards to your wife and children, and please write again very soon. If you visit Josephine, you can let her read this letter. Now ... [4] your loving sister ... [5].

Antonie

---

[1]*day is unclear/unsure due to tape that appears to have been applied over a tear in the page.*

[2]*Page torn, words missing.*

[3]*Page torn, words missing.*

[4]*Page torn, words are missing.*

[5]*Page torn, words are missing.*

The following was a letter from Sister Toni, Muenster, Germany, to her brother Wilhelm Klier, in Fredericksburg, referring to Ida Striegler Klier's loss—the death of Ida's father, Johan Striegler. Wilhelm Klier had reconciled with Julius and Josephine Klier Ransleben. This seems to be a duplication of the letter dated January 6, 1873. Wilhelm Klier was associating with the Ranslebens again.

Above: Today's Stiftsherrenstrasse #5 (formerly Herrenstrasse), Muenster Germany

Father Klier (who will retire soon) sold the house at *Herrenstrasse* and moved to an apartment next to the Royal Bank. Therese Klier Schlickum lives on Mauritz, and 19-year-old Catharine Schlickum lives with her Uncle Otto Schlickum in Gelsenkirchen, Germany.

Letter #37

Muenster

January 26th[1] , 1873

Dear Wilhelm,

The first letter I'm writing in the New Year is directed to you, to ensure that you're finally going to receive another message from us. To begin with I'm wishing a very blessed and happy New Year to you, your Ida, and to your children. May this year hold all the good things you are wishing for. We were sorry to hear of Ida's recent and difficult loss. Relate to her our heartfelt sympathy and let her know that we are feeling this bitter pain together with her. This loss must have been very difficult for your mother-in-law as well. May the good Lord bestow strength and fortitude on her, so she can bear, and submit herself to, this test with patience.

You cannot imagine how happy we are that you are associating with Ranslebens again. After all, you did spend so many years with them, and the children must certainly have like you so much. It is such a great relief for us to know that you are supporting each other again. You must have suffered a lot, since you were the only ones who are close to each other.

Chances are that our last letter to Josephine has arrived, and that you have heard from her how we are living now after having sold the house at the *Herrenstrasse* and moved to the place next to the Royal Bank. We have a very comfortable apartment, and like it quite well here. Father and Mother are rather happy with it. We are living secluded here as we are not directly facing the street, but we can go for the nicest walks on the Domplatz, right in front of our door.

Father was quite sick for several weeks this winter, he had a bad cough and difficulties breathing as never before, and Mother and I did our best to care for him. Hopefully, he'll retire soon now, so he can rest and look out for his health. He has toiled much during his entire life, and it will certainly do him good to finally be able to retire. Therese lives on *Mauritz* [street in Muenster], right behind *Lindenbrink* [street in Muenster], which you surely still remember, she has a nice little house there, with a small garden.

Kathchen is currently in Gelsenkirchen with Otto Schlickum. His wife isn't completely healthy either, and Kathchen can help out there quite a bit. Aunt Petersen turned 84 a few months ago. Lately she was feeling very week and is often quite frail. Although she is still going for walks, this is often a challenge for her, to the extent that is only able to accomplish the bare necessities every day and getting dressed and undressed ins a major task for her. Her mind is still rather clear, she is asking about everyone and wants to know everything.

We are still receiving letters from Fellingers regularly. Yesterday Richard joined a paint and dye factory as a partner, where he had been a manager for several years. He has one child, a strong boy by the name of Richard, according to his letters. Little Therese is staying with him. Hermann is in Hagen. Lina, the wife of Dr. Küster, is in Duesseldorf, however she has no children, the first one died when it was 3 weeks old, causing her quite a heartbreak.

Much has changed over the years at Wolters in Dahlen since you had been there. Aunt and Uncle Peter are getting older and are rather worried about their income, as they now only have a small inn. Karl and Peter are in America as well Peter is married there to the daughter of his boss.

According to his last letter, Karl is planning a major venture, and he is hoping to become a rich man if he succeeds. He is in the process of digging for an oil well, and finding the right place depends much on luck. Lilly is still spending most of her time with her parents. Jettchen, who was a widow with 9 children, was remarried a few weeks ago. Josephine, who is Wolters' youngest, is here in Muenster with the countess of ... [2] rode as a governess of ... [3] . Their youngest daughter ... and Heinrich, who wife died last year, as well. His only child is currently in

England and is working as a waiter. Fritz is in Cologne working in an inn.

And now I would like to report about your acquaintances, Eduard Cortain [Certain], who is still in Wolbeck where he owns a pharmacy, has 2 children just like you, and is a happy person. At Cortains [Certains] we often talk about you, and you and Eduard should both come to visit together with your families. August and Heinrich Bevermann returned again from America about 2 years ago. The old Mr. Bevermann has died, and Bernhard, who had taken over the place of the father, died two years ago as well. At this time, the Bevermanns are no longer involved with the Schlossgarten. Herrmann has bought into the Weinburg, close to Kinderhaus. He was married this year, and August is living with him. Heinrich bought a place just before *Felgte* [street in Muenster], where he lives with his 5 children. He has hired a housekeeper, who takes care of his household. Mrs. Bevermann and Marie are now living with Settchen at the *Sandstrasse* [street in Muenster], who has a profitable business.

Several weeks ago, the president of Dresberg died as well, he had been retired for one and a quarter year. Vicar and preacher Kaal at the Cathedral, whom you and Josephine knew well, died also. He had been a preacher at the Cathedral for 40 years and my confessor for 23 years; he is in heaven now, and chances are that he will come fetch all of us as well.

Enough for today, Mother and Father, and Therese want to join in and write to you also. Mother has difficulties with writing, as she still has suffers from gout in her right arm and hand. Give my regards to your wife and children, and please write again very soon. If you visit Josephine, you can let her read this letter. Now......... [4] your loving sister ... [5].

Antonie

---

[1]*Day is unclear/unsure due to tape that appears to have been applied over a tear in the page.*

[2]*page torn, words missing.*

[3]*page torn, words missing.*

[4]*page torn, words missing.*

[5] *page torn, words missing.*

The Klier family sold the house on *Herrenstrasse* and moved to an apartment next to the Royal Bank. At that time, they lived in *Rudolfstrasse* 38 (*today's house number 2*).

Left: Rudolfstrasse 38 Apartment

The following was a letter to Wilhelm Klier in Fredericksburg from his sister, Therese Klier Schlickum, in Germany (dated in either March or May of 1873).

Letter #38

March or May 1873[1]

My dear Wilhelm,

Mother and Toni have already written to you, and now it's my turn. To begin with I also am wishing a very joyous and happy New Year to you and to your dear ones. All of us, without any exception, have started the New Year healthy and jovially, and we are hoping the same of you. And to your dear wife I'm sending special wishes, hoping that time, the great healer, will soon mend the wound caused by the death of her dear Father.

Today, on January 3rd, the schools have reopened following 2 weeks of vacation. I'm happy that the boys are occupied and back in their routine again, as Julius and Hugo are both at the age that is rightfully called the "awkward age." Especially the youngest one, Hugo, is keeping me on my toes, it is horrendous. He is a very quick-witted boy who has much talent, is of a kind disposition, but unbelievably wild and fickle beyond all description. He is quite developed for his age (on M.[1]11th he turned 11) and is in seventh grade[2], but one has to push him into doing anything he doesn't consider fun. Although it is true that nowadays an awful lot is being demanded of the children. They are being pestered all day and have barely one hour left for recreation, but what can you do, these days no one can get anywhere without a good education. Julius on the other hand enjoys studying all the more, and with more ease, and he is actually quite passionate about learning. Thank goodness the boys have grown much stronger since we have moved to *Mauritz*. Currently, for the new year, a clergyman who is also a professor has moved in with us. He is a kind man who is assisting the boys somewhat with their studies.

As you were writing, your three children are quite a burden at this time, however over there these feelings only last mostly for the first few years. Then they grow up without you really noticing. May the good Lord keep them in good health for you, and you as well, and then everything will turn out well. We are always happy to receive letters from you. Please send kind regards to Josephine and Ransleben. Last time I did not include a letter to them, as the letter had already been sent when I came to visit the parents. However now we have agreed to write each other more often, since that's all we have.

Minna and Kath.[3]Schl. are sending many regards to you and to your dear wife, both are still doing well. Otto Schlickum is doing well again. Kath. has been there already for nearly 2 months; she has grown to be a tall, strong girl. As soon as she returns again, I'm planning to have a photograph taken of the children and will send a picture to all of you. I will end for today and am sending thousands of heartfelt regards to you and to your dear wife.

In old and faithful love,

Your sister Therese

---

[1]*Abbreviated "M" — it March or May is unclear.*
[2]*Or third grade of higher education at the "Gymnasium."*
[3]*Hath, or Kath.*

John Walter was elected sheriff of Gillespie County in 1874. Richard Coke became Governor of Texas on January 15, 1874. The following was a letter from Father Klier, Mother Klier, and Toni, who are living in Coblenz,

Germany, to Wilhelm Klier in Fredericksburg. Wilhelm's brother, Gustav Klier, had become engaged. Father Klier stated that he was 75 years old, and congratulations were extended on the birth of Wilhelm and Ida's third son, Hugo, who was born on March 17, 1874. Wilhelm Klier's birthday was December 9, 1874 (not May 28 as stated in letter).

Letter #39

Coblenz, May 27, 1874

Dear Wilhelm!

Your letter of April 17, according to the postmark was mailed on April 23, was received here on May 14. So, it took only 3 weeks to get here. We waited to hear from you day after day; so, I don't want to wait any longer to write and congratulate you on your newborn son, Hugo. That he is a crybaby and that you had to get a cradle for him, you can blame yourself for. For the same reason we had to get a cradle after your birth.

We have not heard from Gustav either since his announcement of his engagement. On the other hand, Minna Schlickum recently received a paper clipping out of one of your papers there with an ad of Gustav's wedding.

Here in Coblenz, it is very nice. You could not find a more pleasant place to live if it wasn't for the sharp air and the disagreeable wind that blows all the time. My left eye has been afflicted and I have had it operated on here, but it has not fully healed. Because of the wind, I also suffer from rheumatism from the sharp wind. Hopefully, it will all get better soon as I take good care of myself and follow my diet. At my high age of over 75 years, I may have to move to some other place of my health doesn't improve.

It is probable that we would move to Dahlen to Ohm Peter or that we together would search for another homesite. So that you and Josephine will have an idea of how I look now, I am enclosing a recent photograph taken here and I will also enclose one in my next letter to Josephine. Mother also wants to have a photograph made, which really isn't necessary as she still looks as good as she did in the photograph you have, on which you, Toni and our late Maria were also present.

We receive weekly letters from Muenster. Therese has been here for a few days visit us again as soon as she recovers from a long illness and has taken a salt-water bath cure in Erwitte where Minna lives; maybe next month. Her Katchen is now 18 years old and is a very capable young lady. Her Hugo is in his thirteenth year. He went to first communion recently and was confirmed yesterday. Although he is smart and skillful, he is not a very good student, being restless and wild. He is a good athlete.

Our good old Aunt Petersen died on March 21 (your mother's birthday) in her 86th year.

We're very happy over your letter and are surprised that you haven't forgotten how to write in German and that you could express yourself as being very content in your life there. Stay on this track so that your dear children will grow up to be capable, caring people, even if they have to live in limited circumstances. Greetings to your wife and all your children. May God bless you and keep you. So that you can see with your own eyes that your Mother and Toni are well they will add a few words to this. Greetings also to Josephine, her husband, and children. For your birthday, (Wilhelm, May 28), which is tomorrow we send congratulations and hope this letter will travel as fast to you as your last letter to us. If you want to send us a short message, you could write a postcard like Gustav did when he announced his engagement. You can only write what is meant for everyone to read.

With unending love,

Your true old *Papa Klier*

Another thing!

Josephine complained in her last letter that I didn't have her address correct or that the letter was delayed. Whichever one of you writes next, please send correct address. I believe I omitted the ... .

May 27, 1874 (continued)

Dear Wilhelm!

Since Father has already written all the news, I want to send my best wishes on the birth of your third son, Hugo. May the little cry baby grow up to your joy as a brave man. I can well believe that your dear Ida has plenty to do with 4 children. It takes a lot of work and care but if they are healthy, that is the important thing.

Greet Ida and the children. We are now here on the beautiful Rhine. It is really pretty here. We have become accustomed to living here but Father cannot stand the strong wind who blows here so he wants to see about moving to another place as he wrote you.

Our good old Aunt Petersen was finally released from all her ailments which come with age. She has prayed for this. Lina Fellinger had her first son, Max, on April 28th. . She is very happy about this.

For your birthday tomorrow I wish you blessings and good luck. Write again soon.

Greetings to all of you, Your sister, *Toni*

Dear Wilhelm, for your third son, Hugo, I send you our hearty best wishes. *(The rest of Mother Klier's message is not legible.)*

On August 10, 1874, Louis Doebbler was awarded a contract to build a new Gillespie County Jail. The amount of the contract was $1,645.00. The jail was erected south of the County Courthouse and had since been reworked several times and a second story was added. It was subsequently razed. John Walter was elected sheriff of Gillespie County in 1876. Richard B. Hubbard becomes Governor of Texas on December 1, 1876.

The following was a letter from Toni in Germany to her brother, Wilhelm Klier, in Fredericksburg. She mentioned the birth of Wilhelm and Ida's fifth child, Waldemar, (born December 30, 1875). Toni mentioned their move to Coblenz, then to Dahlen, and their move back to Muenster, Germany.

Letter #40

Muenster, January 27, 1876, mailed April 8, 1876.

Dear Wilhelm!

Yesterday we received your letter of the 2nd of this month, wherein you told us of the increase in your family. We wish you and dear Ida the best of luck. May God grant that you will have much joy from this little one as well as the other four outlaws (as you call them).

You finished the old year well with this event. Best wishes for the New Year. Heaven's riches blessings to you for your house, field and pasture in peace and happiness.

You complained in your letter that you hadn't heard from us in a long time, and I have to admit that. However, if you had been in my place, you would probably not done any different. With our moving around from place to place, packing and unpacking and getting organized, there was no desire to write. And writing is one thing you can put off till later. But I hope that now that we are in our old home again, we will settle down as Father does not think about moving away again, and we can catch up on what we missed as we have a lot to tell you.

What did you think about our moving; first to Coblenz then to Dahlen barely a year and then back to Muenster? Coblenz was very nice and after we had gotten settled and acquainted there, we liked it so well that we would like to have stayed there if Father could have accepted it. It was beautiful there on the Rhine with its mountains, a beautiful panorama. Also, church wise, we had everything we wished for, and we could have forgotten our old home, but Father could not stand the air there and it was lonesome because he did not have any friends there and he did not make new ones.

Then we went to Dahlen where he hoped to find a home with Ohm and Tante. But it was not to be; father couldn't accept it. It was sad what we found there; not at all like the old days. We did not know what to believe; from all sides, we heard the circumstances. It seemed that financially they had gone backwards. Ohm had provided well for his two sons, Heinrich, and Karl, and spent his entire fortune in this manner. But this was not the worst of it. Their friends and acquaintances had virtually abandoned them as Lily, unfortunately, had an affair with a tanner who, at the same time, had gotten another young lady into trouble, so both of them had been betrayed. Lily saw that she could not expect anything from this man so she attached herself to another tanner who promised her that he would marry her and adopt her child. However, he was a widower and had his whole family against him. Nevertheless, he kept Lily hanging on from one year to the next until last year when we wanted to move from Coblenz to Dahlen when Father wrote to the Ohm that for us to move there, Lily would have to be married; we only knew of this last relationship and had no inkling of what had gone before.

When we were in Dahlen about four years ago and witnessed this acquaintance with the widower, named Siemes, I asked Lily "But why do you not get married?" That is why father had insisted that, if we were to move there, Lily must be married; they promised this would take place, not immediately, but at the beginning of October.

We arrived there on September 9 and then heard the whole story. We could do nothing but feel sorry for them as there was no way we could help. Then came the beginning of October and the end of October but no wedding; so, also November and December. As we had been promised that Lily would be married or out-of-the house, Lily had written to Karl who, as you know, lives in Pittsburgh in America, about a position with him and he had written her to come and even sent her a ticket. This came the beginning of December and as Lily now believed that Siemes would never marry her, she made up her mind and departed on December 31st, the day that Father and

Mother celebrated their Golden Wedding Anniversary. The trip went as well as you could expect in wintertime.

But now Siemes reacted by crying and complaining that Lily must come back; he would marry her. No one believed him but he wrote to Lily and sent her the money so she could come back. Soon the word went around that Lily had come back and was living in Köln [Cologne]. That turned out to be true. She was living with a friend. Siemes now had to make all arrangements for them to be married and after all the difficulties, it came about on August 14th. We had left Dahlen on August 12th, so we did not see Lily again.

We were glad to be back in Muenster. As you can imagine, it was not very pleasant to be there any longer. I could tell you much more, but this is enough for now. This much is evident, the Wolter children are all not in the best of circumstances. Jettchen married her second husband but she herself is very weak and has 11 children. Pauline was married to a man name Schumann who had to go to war in 1870-and came back with a lung sickness. He suffered all these years and died week before last. She now had the fabric business.

You can see that through all of this there was no pleasure in writing. However, I think it will get better. Now, stay well, greet Ida and the children, also your mother-in-law and sister-in-law and especially you are heartily greeted from your sister.

Toni

After an adventurous life, Ferdinand Schlickum passed away on November 12, 1876, in Austin, Texas.

Richard B. Hubbard was elected as Governor of Texas on December 1, 1876. Wilhelm Klier turned 42 years old on December 9, 1876. Rutherford B. Hayes became the President of the United States in 1877. The first newspaper in Gillespie County was the German-language *Fredericksburg Wochenblatt,* established in 1877. Antonie Klier, second daughter of Wilhelm and Ida Striegler Klier, was born on April 14, 1877, in the Meusebach Creek Community, Gillespie County, Texas. On October 28, 1877, Julius, and Josephine Klier Ransleben celebrated their 25th wedding anniversary.

The first four children of Wilhelm and Ida Klier attended the Meusebach Creek log cabin school on the Fritz Lochte place—Frederick, Gustav, Signe, and Hugo. Ida Striegler Klier's brother, Ove W. Striegler, was the teacher; he taught at Meusebach Creek from 1877 to 1881. Erected on land owned by local resident Fritz Lochte, the 1869 original structure was a 96 square foot shingle-roofed log cabin near the creek. The walls consisted of logs filled with mortar. The only openings in the building were a door and a window. The bare interior revealed only a stove, long benches, and the teacher's desk. The floor was made of rough planks. The log building was razed when a larger stone structure was built in 1881.

The following was a letter from Josephine Klier Ransleben to her sister, Therese Klier Schlickum, in Germany. Wilhelm Klier had six children (Antonie born on April 14, 1877); and the Ranslebens celebrated their 25th anniversary *(they were married October 28, 1852)* with the Wilhelm Kliers and other family and friends.

Letter #41
Pedernales, Texas
Dec. 9, 1877
My dear Therese,

You have surely wondered why I have allowed your very dear letter and your heartfelt, well-intentioned wishes to go unanswered. Quite rightly so, for I received your dear lines on Oct. 15, just exactly on your name's day. On that morning I told Julius and the children at the breakfast table, today is Aunt Schlickums name's day, three days ago her birthday, so after breakfast I'm going to write her and congratulate her. That afternoon my son, Julius, who had gone to town, came riding back, shouting loudly, "Father, Mother, a letter from Germany!" Casting all my work aside, I grabbed it and opened it, exclaiming "Holla, it's from Aunt Schlickum."

And that's the remarkable thing: I spoke of you this morning; said I wanted to write you and then got a letter from you. You cannot imagine the joy as I read it. I wept heartily with joy, you good true soul! You haven't forgotten us. Your dear dear good-natured lines bear witness of your deep feelings. How hard, how infinitely hard it must be for you ... to send wishes for such a rare celebration that my dear sister didn't take part in. (*Passage is unclear because of missing words.*)

You poor woman, you have had to suffer so much and deprive yourself of so much in your young life. Yet, dear heart, even if it will be difficult for you to make your way, you still have good children, thank God. Let them be your comfort and your happiness. You know the Lord cares mostly for widows and orphans. But I don't want to make your heart heavy. From your letter I learned to my great joy that our parents are also writing to us. We received [one] last on Nov. 15. On Oct. 28, we celebrated our silver anniversary with Wilhelm (*Klier, her brother*), along with his wife and six children, some neighbors and Mrs. Schertz, also Louis, little Marie, and Louise. We couldn't hold it on a grand scale because of space and it would also cost too much. We enjoyed a good dinner and supper and a good glass of beer along with cake. Our oldest sons along with Josephine offered up everything to surprise and to please us.

I had hoped that Carl would have gotten engaged the same day, but he doesn't want to yet, since times are still bad. His business is going well, only the money doesn't come in right away for the transports(?) all had bad harvests this year. So, all the young girls are still waiting for him. He is a particularly charming and handsome boy who understands his business very well to this point is the best wheelwright in Fredericksburg. He understands everything and he makes each order good and attractive. He also helped his uncle build a house. My Max would like very much to get married, but farmers are losing their courage. The harvests are getting too bad.

(?) enjoyed our silver wedding anniversary very much. Mrs. Schertz (?) gave me a silver bridal wreath and Julius a silver bouquet. We all drank a toast to you several times and decorated all your portraits. You all could have made an appearance in our midst, and we would have been so boundlessly happy. But oh Lord, would we have recognized one another after 25 years?

Yes, Therese, we would have seemed old enough. We see each other reflected in our children. You can imagine how stirred up the wish has become, to see you and above all our old parents whom you depicted so vividly for us, but since this probably won't happen in our lifetime, we must write one another the more often. That is the one single thing that the great distance leaves for us yet. I would certainly like to write, but I always am afraid that you would always have to hear the same thing, our bad outlook, and bad harvests.

I was surprised that you moved (?) again but your reasons justify your decision, and you are right. `You wrote so much news about relatives and acquaintances which gave me unending joy. I thought so much about my earlier years I had to tell my oldest about it all and even the young people amused themselves well. God, Therese, who would have thought that you laugh and wonders how you could make such jokes and how you could make life so easy. And how our friends are so scattered in the world, each one hearing so little from one another. How I should like to see Linna Sch ... (*Schlickum*) again with her children. Most our mends are married and have many children. I wonder if we would know each other again. I still remember your little daughter so clearly, such a lively hearty little girl. How I should like to have her here once, particularly with my Josephine, two dear cousins after all, for I believe that Josephine's disposition would correspond to that of Katie.

If only I could send you a picture. I am so angry that still no photographer is coming by and even if one does come, he takes bad pictures. And we never go to Austin or to San Antonio. That is the single fault that we have put of writing because we were told that the end of November a very good photographer was coming, that he could come by any day, but I couldn't wait any longer for father's (birthday?) wishes would arrive too late. So don't be angry with us, I'll try to make it up to you. How happy I was that your two dear sons, Hugo, and Julius, are making such good progress and also that they love their little sister so much. All my boys also love their dear little sister, she is everyone's darling. She looks up from under her brothers like a sweet sleeping beauty, guarded and watched by her cavalier-like brothers. She has become 16, slender, a hand's width taller than I and Carl is afraid that she will grow taller than he. She is diligently learning to sew and embroider from Miss Schertz (?) in Fredericksburg and it has become her main pleasure.

You would like to hear the news from here? For the last three weeks, we've had a nice amateur theater in which the principal ladies' roles are the ladies of the town. Mrs. Brockmann; Miss Fanny Schild, Postmaster Schild, Adolph Lenkwitz (Lungkwitz?), Robert Fersenius [Fresenius], our Carl as the director, Wilhelm Bahse [Basse] and many more. They are playing magnificent theater in Mr. Niemecz (*Nimitz?*) big hall, every month a comedy or drama and afterwards a dance until 2 o'clock. Only members are permitted; it is a closed society, and we belong to it, my three sons and Josephine also go along to see it. Since Carl and Os live next to Niemecz [Nimitz], it is convenient for us.

Just think, the old pharmacist (?) Miller is a widow and quite ... (?) She is a ward of the city, and her irresponsible son, a saddler in Austin, neglects her altogether. He is thoughtless and a toper (?). The Lungkwitz (?) family lives in Austin; they are doing well. Martha is married to a teacher in an elementary school, a good-looking young man, Jakob Bichler. They have two young children. Lug (?) is said to have aged a lot; the two twins are very handsome, have lots of admirers but no ... (?) since they put on airs. Max is a gunsmith and earns very well, a very good-looking young man who would like to get together with a rich merchant's daughter. Then Mrs. L. still has a little son eleven years old and a young daughter of 14 or 15 named Eva whom I haven't seen for years. Mrs. Kuechler has her own big house in Austin; they have two sons, the oldest and the youngest. Rolf was shot with a pistol by his school friend through carelessness ... (?) You can't imagine what immeasurable sorrow and misfortune that ... (?). How recklessly children here go around with weapons.

We were invited to Comfort by the Flags [Flachs] last July 4 and we had a good time there, the four of us. They send their best regards. I would be please to tell you even more, but everything has changed so that I scarcely know who your acquaintances were. Mrs. Schertz sends her regards along with little Marie and little Luise if you still remember them. They are two very pretty girls and are considered hard-working, good, and skilled milliners with a lot to do here.

It does me good that you are writing me of the many deaths; it seems that the Ohms and the Schlickums have been hard beset. I am so sorry for poor dear Minna, also for Chatinka. Please give them my regards. I would be so unendingly happy to hear from them since they can write letters better. I am really out of practice for I speak better than I write. You can believe me when I say that I think of them often and am thankful for and interested in everything that you all write.

You have more material to write about than I. My main entertainment is my narrow circle of family and our farm. Since we seldom go out otherwise, only occasionally to Wilhelm. He is at the moment expanding his house since his family ... too quickly. You should see this little tribe sometime, just like the pipes of an organ, all however pretty attractive strong children. Wilhelm also is looking better, and Ida is as round as a [butter] ball and very industrious. Yet it would be good if this exceedingly great blessing of children would soon cease. W. has had a good wheat crop, also very good corn and cotton and he has very good fruitful land, if only rain and no grasshoppers would come. Our horse has ruined all of our wheat and the grasshoppers our corn and the drought our cotton. There were only four bales. But now dear Therese, in closing Julius' and my heartfelt thanks for your good wishes and your letter. Our regards to your son and to all who still remember me.

Heartfelt kisses from your faithfully loving sister,
Josephine Ransleben

Chapter XII - After Reconstruction (1878-1899)

In 1878, the Friedrich Wilhelm Klier family moved to *Clemenstrasse* 22, Muenster, Germany. (*The present day address is an der Clemenskirche 14.*)

An der Clemenskirche 14

Egon Klier, fifth son of Wilhelm and Ida Striegler Klier, was born on September 5, 1878, in the Meusebach Creek Community, Gillespie County, Texas. Wilhelm Klier turned 44 years old on December 9, 1878. Oran Milo Roberts took the oath of office as the Governor of Texas on January 21, 1879.

The following is a letter from Toni Klier in Germany to her brother, Wilhelm Klier, regarding the death of

Friedrich Wilhelm Klier (Father Klier) on May 1, 1879; and that he became a child of the Catholic Church before his death. Mother Klier's angst over Wilhelm not raising his children Catholic, was revealed when she wrote a letter to Father Tarrillion, St. Mary's Catholic Church, in Fredericksburg, Texas, inquiring if the Klier children had been baptized. Father Tarrillion replied that they had not been baptized; that is, not in the Catholic faith.

German-born Father Tarrillion fell in love with the Hill Country when he first visited Fredericksburg in 1856, nine years after the city was first settled. When he became the pastor of St. Mary's Catholic Church in 1867, he remained for 32 years. He was born in Edlingen, Lothringen in 1821, as an only child. He came to America in 1852 and continued his studies in a Missouri seminary. He was ordained into the priesthood in Galveston, Texas, on March 25, 1855, and celebrated his silver jubilee as priest at Fredericksburg on March 31, 1880.

Letter #42

Muenster, August 25, 1879

Dear Wilhelm!

Gladly would I have answered your letter sooner, but your letter brought us much grief and pain as you, upon receiving the news of our dear Father, did not say one word of gladness that he, before his death, became a child of the Catholic church. You so coldly stated that he is resting in the cool earth; that all is well with him now, that his suffering is over. These words hurt me very much and we fear that you have no belief at all anymore. The message from Pastor Father Tarrillion of Fredericksburg, to whom we wrote to learn what the status of your religious life is, stated that you, as well as Josephine, are known to him only by name and that not one of your children has been baptized. This is shocking, that you, who were so well taught, can live like that. I feel it is my duty to remind you, in sisterly love, of your duty. Mother is overcome with grief and pain since your eternal welfare weighs heavily on her heart. Daily she prays for you. When we received the letter from Father Tarrillion, she said that she would rather had had the news that all of you had died a blissful death. In her eyes, you are now dead; she will withdraw her hand from yours since you have ignored her teachings and warnings that life is short and eternity is long; and, as you live, so shall you die. Think of the sorrow and pain that Mother had, when you were here in 1860, that you had strayed from belief and truth. She says to tell you that you might pray daily to Jesus and Maria that God would show you and your family the right way and would lead you there. Visit the good Pastor Father Tarrillion, greet him for us, thank him in our name and ask him to help you again be a good child, a good son of the Catholic church. We want to unite in praying to God; pray also for our dear Father.

I am enclosing a few death notices. Pray for the poor souls in purgatory. Write soon to our dear Mother so she will have hope that you are again as of old. Otherwise, I fear that her sorrow and pain will be too heavy for her. Pray, pray, pray, and think of the end.

Your sister, *Toni.* A.W.G. (All with God).

*Left: Sister
Antonie Klier
(1845-1893)*

Gillespie County's population was 5,228 in 1880. The 1880 Gillespie County Census listed the following household members: Wilhelm Klier, farmer, age 45; Ida, age 35; Friedrich, age 11; Gustav, age nine; Signe, age seven; Hugo, age six; Waldemar, age four; Antonie, age three; Egon, age one; and Baby, age one month. A daughter was born to Wilhelm and Ida Striegler Klier in April 1880 but died in infancy a month later at Meusebach Creek community, Gillespie County, Texas. The daughter was included in the census.

Catharine Schlickum, age 26, married Johann Heinrich Rieb on August 29, 1880, in Germany. Catherine was the daughter of Therese Klier Schlickum and the late Julius Schlickum.

The following was a letter by Julius Ransleben, living in Fredericksburg, to his sister-in-law, Therese Klier Schlickum, in Germany.

<u>Letter #43</u>

(Letter by Julius Ransleben[1] only one page is left -)

Fredericksburg,

December 12th, 1880

Dear Sister-in-Law,

We received your valued letter on October 10th, and I'm making haste to answer it myself as Josephine has been very sick for 8 weeks already. She is getting better again now, God be thanked. I'm hoping that we can get Josephine back to the farm again next week. We had to bring her to Carl who lives in town, in order to have a doctor handy. She contracted typhus[2] and things got so bad, we were worried that she might not survive. — In regard to the young man, neither Wilhelm nor we can arrange a permanent job for him here, but if he likes to work, he certainly should be able to find employment at a farm at any time, however he has to be here in person.

Many young people have come here without any means at all, have found good work, and in time started out on their own. But we cannot take the responsibility to coax the young man into coming here, as everyone has to find their own way here. Nobody has to starve who likes to work and has perseverance. But we, and also Wilhelm, and Ida, can take him in and support him until he can find employment, as long as he doesn't reproach us, saying that we suggested for him to come over here. He'll have to change his lifestyle and learn completely new ways, as the relationship between workers and employers are different from Germany, and here he'd be treated more like a friend of the family. If he, however, isn't afraid of work, it wouldn't be difficult for him to find good income. This is how I see the matter, and the young man has to decide by himself if he is strong enough to tackle our conditions here.

You, my dear Sister-in-Law, know well enough from your own experience how things look like here, and that there are lots of things one has to do without. Nevertheless, I'd never want to exchange it again with life in the old homeland; at least we can ensure our children's financial future here. If the young Falk[3] still has the courage to come here after considering all of that, we'll gladly help him. In that case, please make sure to notify us if he is coming, or not. Perhaps he can bring along a few little items for us, such as the flute that belonged to our dear, late Father, and that he had gifted to Carl, but which hasn't come into our possession yet until this day.

This year we suffered quite numerous illnesses. First Julius was laid up for 4 months with a fever, thereafter Hilmar, age 17, Guido, age 11, and finally our Mother. Work in the fields is suffering because of this, to the extent that we are still in the process of picking cotton. It rained so much this year as never before in Texas, so all harvests were delayed, and we got stuck with the ploughs. We were especially late with sowing wheat, and now everything is happening helter-skelter.

Our children Carl and Louise in Fredericksburg are doing well, considering the circumstances. They have blessed us with a little girl who is about 5 months old and is everyone's joy. Max, age 26 is building his house now and would like to enter holy matrimony soon as well. Oskar is working in San Marcos in a large smith's shop and makes 1 1/2 $ a day.

---

[1] *Transcriber spelled the name alternately Ransleden and Ransleben.*

[2] *Translator's note: "Gallenfieber" can also describe jaundice or cholangitis.*

[3] *Transcriber was unsure of the name.*

John Walter was elected sheriff of Gillespie County in 1878 and 1880. The following was a letter from Toni Klier and Therese Klier Schlickum, living in Germany, to Wilhelm Klier, in Fredericksburg. Trunks (often called boxes) were sent to Texas with items for Josephine Ransleben and Wilhelm Klier containing some of the following items: pictures of Father Klier's parents; a picture of Father Klier as a little boy with the little dog; *coopererschen* books from Father's library; red bedspread for Josephine; items from Mother Klier for Josephine; pants and overcoat for Josephine's sons; *durch nahter* Rock coat for Josephine; articles from Father Klier for Wilhelm; lightweight bedspread; a feather-filled cover; watch and chain for Wilhelm; gilded cups and plates for both Josephine and Wilhelm; memoirs of our loving parents; Father Klier's pipes; books; and sacred books. Both Josephine and Wilhelm married spouses who were

Lutheran, and Toni was trying to persuade them to return to the Catholic faith. Mother Klier passed away April 7, 1881, at age 77 years.

Letter #44

(Letter from sisters Toni & Therese to Wilhelm)

Muenster,

July 17, 1881

Dear Wilhelm:

Last week Monday I received the letter from you that I had looked forward to for such a long time. I have packaged many items in a heavy box, which I will now forward to you. I am carrying out the wishes and will of our parents, and you as the oldest son in the family, it was the wish of Father, that you should have the pictures of his parents and the picture of him as a young boy with the little dog. I had Father's permission to keep them for a while but since I, too, want you to have them because of your birthright as the oldest son, and because I may not have a chance to send them later.

I am placing them safely among other articles. During the many years that you have been separated from us, I feel that I have been exceptionally lucky to have lived so long close to our dear parents and I believed it would be a delight for you to have them as a remembrance. When Father and I discussed this matter, I told him that I would have these portraits photographed so that all the other family members could have copies of the pictures.

I have enclosed a photocopy for Josephine (*Wilhelm's sister who married Julius Ransleben*). They are placed among the cooperschen books from Father's library, which have gone out of print and are no longer available. The box is addressed to you in care of the forwarding agent that Ransleben named in his letter. The shipment left yesterday. I have made a list of everything that is in the box and as I have been advised here, I am sending it with shipping charges to be paid at the port of entry, to assure its safe arrival. I suggest that you open the box before paying duty on it and check the contents against my list.

When you and Ransleben come to claim the shipment, please bring another box with you so that you can take the articles tagged for you and place them immediately in this box. That would be the simplest way to do it since I carefully packed all of Josephine's in the bottom of the box. You should easily recognize the items that are yours from the ones that are hers.

In the bottom is a red bedspread (*Stechdecke?*) [*bettdecke*] for Josephine. On top of the spread are other items from Mother for Josephine. Since Josephine has sons that are almost grown, the pants and the overcoat will be practical. Also, for Josephine there is a (*durch nahter Rock*) coat from Lina Fellinger who surprised us with gifts often when our aunt was still living and frequently gave toys to Therese's children. (*Therese was the sister of Wilhelm and Toni, and the great-great grandmother of Hans Dahlmanns*[1]).

In the top I have placed the articles from Father for you. There are only a few such things because Mother gave many to Therese's children and found joy in giving presents to the needy. And of course, you remember how in her weakness, she found pleasure in cheering the underprivileged. Even though I often pleaded with her to save these family possessions in order that we could send them to America, she avoided the task by saying it was too costly and nixed the idea. Father also thought it was too troublesome. Although I was not able to persuade Father or Mother, I always yearned to send small gifts of appreciation to both of you. In the end Father's will always prevailed and he sent money instead --- but back to the subject. On top in the trunk, you'll find a lightweight bedspread and near the center is a feather-filled cover *(Daumen ober Bett),* which Mother had ordered made a few years before Father's death. It is practically brand new. Most of the items on top of this cover are for you and those underneath are for Josephine, except for the watch and chain wrapped in silk in the small box with your name on it. The gilded cups and plates are to be divided equally between you and Josephine, plus other items, which I can do without here, are enclosed as memoirs of our loving parents. Father had the habit of giving away many of his personal things to his friends, but a few of his favorite pipes are enclosed. You may keep all of the books and loan them to Ransleben to read or you divide them as you please. I am enclosing some of our sacred books which I hope you will read in order that your soul may be nourished.

Dear Wilhelm, you did not answer my question in my last letter in reference to this matter, but I can take a hint, no answer is an answer. I am aware of the pressure that surrounds you, living under circumstances which you cannot always control, but God through His grace, will lead you in the proper direction and that is the way our dear parents would have wanted it to be. Remain true to your vow, and as the duty of the oldest brother, encourage

Ransleben and Gustav by your example. Be particularly kind to Julius Ransleben, he may have certain peculiarities, I agree, but if you and Josephine had remained steadfast in your belief, the situation might have resolved itself in your behalf. (*Both Josephine and Wilhelm married spouses who were Lutheran, and Toni is trying to persuade them to return to the Catholic faith.*)

Dear Wilhelm, I wish you could have observed how our father struggled and suffered as he fought his way through the maze of the material world and the teachings of the church. How liberated he felt when the Holy Spirit moved him to find himself as a child of God. He proclaimed many times, "Why didn't I experience this inner peace in the past 50 years?" In retrospect, he spoke of you and Josephine and how he would have enjoyed sharing this faith with you. Even in his latter days he prayed that he might be forgiven had he failed in guiding you in our religious upbringing.

0, dear Wilhelm, what a precious father we had, who in his old age gave his will entirely to God as he journeyed safely to his eternal home. I could go on and on telling you about the happiness that prevailed in our home until he died, but I must get back to the purpose of this letter. The trunk has been delivered to the freight depot and it is eight days later, now July 25th, since I began this letter, and it is time to get it mailed. I am enclosing a listing of every article in the trunk as was required by the forwarding agent. The value of each item as declared is my own estimation. This is considerably higher than market value. Even though they could be lost in transit; I believe you would rather have the family treasure than the money.

I wrote Josephine and Julius that I want to send 100 (*type of money*) but until I receive the receipt or certificate (*Beglaubigungsheine*) I cannot collect or raise any money. Please send it as soon as possible. Please give my greeting to your dear wife (*Ida Striegler Klier*) and children. With love from your sister,

> Toni

Mein Lieber Wilhelm:

Space and time limit me to say only a few words. Greetings to your dear Ida and lovely children. I hope all is well and please keep us informed of your activities. Let's not forget our family ties, though time and space prevent us from being together. With love, your sister,

> Therese

¹Actually great grandmother, as per Hans Dahlmanns' statement in his letter; along with an Akhenaten family genealogy file provided in the "Schlickum" letters and original papers submitted by Hans in 1997. (Note: It is not certain if the reference to Gustav was the brother who moved to St. Louis, MO, or the 2nd oldest son of Wilhelm, who was also named.)

Left: Trunk #1 from Germany (July 17, 1881)

Above: Trunk #2 from Germany (July 17, 1881)

Trunk #1 had been kept in the Klier home at Stonewall and Trunk #2 had been stored in a barn at the Stonewall homeplace. The trunks from Germany have been handed down through six generations of the Klier family.

In 1881, the Meusebach Creek log cabin school was replaced by a larger stone structure in the Fritz Lochte pasture. The other Klier children attended the stone structure until the family moved to Stonewall in 1896. The second Meusebach Creek School was completed in 1881. The stone structure was more spacious, being 15' X 20.' It had four windows and one door, which was also an improvement over the original building. The interior was neatly plastered in white and green, and the furniture included such innovations as bookshelves and coat hangers. Flowers and pot plans often filled the wide windowsills, and long benches were placed in the center of the floor.

Remnants of the Second Stone Meusebach Creek School

The first Gillespie County Fair, oldest continuously operated county fair in Texas, was first held at Braeutigam's Garten, the site old Fort Martin Scott in 1881. James Abram Garfield was elected as the 20th President of the United States in 1881. On July 2, 1881, Charles J. Guiteau, a disappointed and delusional office seeker, shot Garfield at the Baltimore and Potomac Railroad Station in Washington D.C. The wound was not immediately fatal, but he died on September 19, 1881, from infections caused by his doctors. Chester A. Arthur succeeded to the presidency upon the assassination and the subsequent death of President Garfield. Arthur, a Republican, had been the Vice President of the United States.

Arthur Klier, sixth son of Wilhelm and Ida Striegler Klier was born on November 19, 1881, in the Meusebach Creek Community, Gillespie County, Texas. Wilhelm Klier turned 47 years old on December 9, 1881. The second Gillespie County Courthouse, 115 West Main Street, was completed in 1882 for the cost of $23,000; it was a two-story rusticated limestone structure. It was designed by

Former Second Gillespie County Courthouse

Alfred Giles, English Architect turned Texas Sheep Rancher. John Walter was elected sheriff of Gillespie County in 1882 and 1884. John Ireland became the Governor of Texas on January 16, 1883.

Hannah Klier, daughter of Wilhelm and Ida Striegler Klier, was born on January 19,1883, in the Meusebach Creek Community, Gillespie County, Texas. Fernanda Klier, daughter of Wilhelm and Ida Striegler Klier, was born May 14, 1884, in the Meusebach Creek Community, Gillespie County, Texas. Wilhelm Klier turned 50 years old on December 9, 1884.

Grover Cleveland became the President of the United States in 1885. The Gillespie County jail (The Old Jail), 117 West San Antonio Street, was built in 1885; it was the fourth jail in Gillespie County. Of the first three jails, one burned down and two were razed when better ones were needed. The jail was completed in December 1885 at a cost of $9,962.

Left: Old Jail, 117 W. San Antonio Street, Fredericksburg

Wilhelm Klier purchased 971.84 acres of land on the north side of the Pedernales River near Stonewall, on December 9, 1885, for $2,672.57. He was 51 years old on December 9, 1885. Friedrich Klier, son of Wilhelm and Ida Striegler Klier, passed away in 1886, in Gillespie County, Texas. He was 17 years old and is buried in Der Stadt Friedhof. John Walter was elected sheriff of Gillespie County in 1886.

The Evangelical Protestant Church of the Holy Ghost (*Heilige Geist*), later to be known as Holy Ghost Lutheran Church (*present day 113 E. San Antonio Street, Fredericksburg*), split from the *Vereins Kirche* congregation in 1886. Wilhelm and Ida Striegler Klier worshipped at Holy Ghost Lutheran, Fredericksburg until the turn of the century.

"Holy Ghost (Heilige Geist) Evangelical Protestant Church Marker Inscription. This congregation traces its origins to the first Protestant services held in Fredericksburg by the Rev. Henry Basse in 1846. Members worshiped at the old Vereins Kirche until 1888 when Carl Priess gave this lot for a new building. The first portion of the structure was dedicated in 1893. The tower houses an original bell from the Vereins Kirche. In 1948-49 the building was remodeled and enlarged, and the congregation became Holy Ghost Lutheran Church."
Recorded Texas Historic Landmark – 1981

Josephine Klier, daughter of Wilhelm and Ida Striegler Klier, was born on July 6, 1886, in the Meusebach Creek Community, Gillespie County, Texas. Lawrence Sullivan "Sul" Ross became the Governor of Texas on January 18, 1887.William Klier, seventh son of Wilhelm and Ida Klier, was born on November 8, 1887, in the Meusebach Creek Community, Gillespie County, Texas. Telephones came into existence in Gillespie County in 1887. Lawrence S. Ross becomes Governor of Texas on January 18, 1887.

J. J. Hagen was elected sheriff of Gillespie County in 1888.The White Elephant Saloon was built at 242 E. Main Street in 1888. The *Gillespie County News* newspaper was established in 1888 in Willow City; it was the first English language newspaper in the county. The corner stone for the new Holy Ghost Lutheran Church was laid on June 6, 1888, under the ministry of Pastor Pfaeffle. The building, designed by Mr. James Wahrenberger of San Antonio, is of Romanic-Gothic type of architecture and cost $10,450.

Holy Ghost Lutheran Church

The following was a letter from Julius Ransleben, living on the Pedernales, to his brother-in-law, Wilhelm Klier, living in Fredericksburg. Josephine Klier Ransleben died June 29, 1888. The ill-feeling which existed between Wilhelm Klier and Julius Ransleben (brother-in-law) was due to the circumstance when Wilhelm arrived at the Ransleben residence to hide out after escaping the Nueces Battle (1862) and then, unfortunately, being "captured" when Julius went to town seeking advice, had innocently let it get out that Wilhelm was at the ranch, resulting in word getting to the Confederates ....Wilhelm's capture....and ultimate sentence of forced conscription service in the Confederate forces.

<u>Letter #45</u>

(Letter from Julius Ransleben, brother-in-law, to Wilhelm Klier. Most of letter is missing. Dote of letter is calculated by date of death of Josephine; 6/29/1888, at age 62.)

June 29, 1888

Mr. W. Klier

Snerbenkorg[1]

Petemales, ... [2] June

Dear brother-in-law,

Since it is too late now, I shall send some of my wrath to you, as things turned out like ...[3].

We had awaited Mother all week, but last night when the sun went down, our last hope sank with it as well. We blame You for all of this.

Father had to ... alone to ... examination ... [4]

(Note: This highly damaged letter 'appears' to have been sent to Wilhelm ("brother-in-law") by Julius Ransleben, husband to Wilhelm's sister Josephine. The heading of 'Perdernales' matches another letter in the collection, from Josephine to Theresa, wherein Josephine also shows the location at the beginning of that letter. This reference is to the location of the Ransleben ranch which is just outside city limits of Fredericksburg. Referring to the date of June, and to the reference of "Mother," along with the phrase "last nite," it appears to match the death of Josephine in 1888 on June 29th. The reference to "wrath" appears to match the apparent wrath that existed between the brothers-in-law due to the circumstances when Wilhelm arrived at the Ransleben residence (to hide out) after escaping the Nueces Massacre, and then unfortunately being `captured' when Julius went to town seeking advice ... had (innocently) let it get out that Wilhelm was at the ranch resulting in word getting to the Confederates ... Wilhelm's capture ... and ultimate sentence of forced conscription service in the Confederate forces. Carrol KLIER Timmerman ... Great granddaughter of Wilhelm Klier.)

---

[1] *The place name appears to be Snorbenkorg. Snarbenkarg, or Snorbenkorg?*

[2] *Page torn, date missing.*

[3] *Page torn. Word is illegible/unsure.*

[4] *Page torn, words are missing, and the rest of the following page is missing as well.*

The following was a letter by Julius Ransleben, living in Fredericksburg, to Therese Klier Schlickum in

Germany. Ransleben was married to Josephine Klier, Therese's sister. This letter was obviously the answer to Therese's letter of condolence after the death of Josephine Klier Ransleben on June 29, 1888. Julius mentioned that he is now living in town with his son, Carl Ransleben. Julius stated that Wilhelm was quite old (he is 54 years old) and working hard to pay off land he purchased 12 miles below Fredericksburg on the Pedernales.

<u>*Letter #46*</u>

(This letter is obviously the answer to
Therese's letter of condolence after the death of Josephine
on June 29, 1888)

Fredericksburg,
October 4th, 1888
My dear Sister-in-Law,

I have received your dear letter dated August 22nd and am thanking you for the sympathy you extended therein to me and to my children. From this letter you can see that I don't return tit for tat, as I'm fulfilling your wish and am telling you now as much as possible about all of us. Regrettably, I'm not at all in the right frame of mind to keep my thoughts completely together and since the death of my dear Josephine I'm suffering from chest- and stomach problems, sometimes so much so that I have to stay in bed for days, and at the same time I also suffer from breathing problems.

I moved to Carl who lives in town, where I'm taken care of, and I have a doctor close by. And all of the children don't wish for me to work anymore. Uncle Klier[1] has to toil quite a bit with his 11 children that are still living (3 of them died already). He is getting quite old now but is still in good health and working tirelessly. He also bought our land at the lower Pedernales, 12 miles below Fredericksburg, and is picking cotton right now together with his children. Hopefully, his harvest will be good, so he can pay off his land.

My oldest son Carl is living quite nicely in Fredericksburg, he built a large, beautiful house for himself, where he lives together with his wife and 4 children — 3 girls and 1 boy. His shop has an added machine and wagon[2] Agency, and he makes quite a bit of money with it. Oskar, my third, works with him and lives next door in his own house, with his wife and three children — 2 boys and one girl. Max, my 2nd, lives alone on the farm together with his wife and 2 children — 1 boy and 1 girl. I gave him 150 acres of land, with which he has to manage. Last year he had lots of bad luck with his wife. She has been constantly sick for one year, and that always costs a lot of money. But I'm hoping, and it also looks now as if she is improving.

Julius, the fourth, is also living on my farm, I gave him 100 acres as well, where he and his wife, and his little son are keeping house. Julius has an excellent wife, who looked out for me and also for Guido since Mother's death. As you know, Josephine is married to Theodor Boos and has 2 girls and 1 boy and is living in our neighborhood. Hilmar is married in Boerne and has a nice business there, and no children yet, but they are on their way.

And now to my youngest (Guido)[3], since my poor Hermann has died. He works that part of the farm that belongs to me, and he'll inherit it when I die. He is a hard worker and has to toil heavily; while Mother was still alive there were three of us, but now he has to do the work by himself. However, Anna, Julius's wife, takes very good care of him (... ?) washes his laundry and cooks, and looks out for his comfort in general.

Now you know about everything, dear sister-in-law, and can picture somewhat how we are living. From our dear Tony's letter, we learned that she had bad luck with her finances, and it appears that she isn't doing very well; please tell me in more detail about it, so that we won't have to keep guessing. — After Grandmother died, Toni wrote that she would like to come here, and she would have had a much better life here with Josephine and the children, as she wouldn't have had to worry about anything, and here she could have invested the little money she has securely at 8%.

Now the situation has changed since I'm alone and am living with the children, and so I can no longer renew any of the invitations. If Toni however would like to come here, she would be kindly taken in at the farm, or with any of the children. But these are just thoughts that would be difficult to implement. Now I have told you everything you might be interested in, dear Sister-in-Law, but I have to ask for your forgiveness if the letter isn't quite...? I can't think clearly anymore, and writing is very difficult for me, but please be satisfied with what I'm writing, and still keep for love for me in times to come.

Your sincere Brother-in-Law

Julius Ransleben

I wrote to Toni yesterday and sent it to the Muenster address.

[1]*Wilhelm Klier, Therese's brother, who emigrated in 1849 together with Julius (see following letter).*

[2]*Translator's note literally: Maschinen Wagen, Machine vehicle or wagon/cart.*

[3]*Transcriber added the name and question mark.*

Benjamin Harrison became the President of the United States in 1889. Gillespie County's population in 1890 was 7,056. James Stephen Hogg became the Governor of Texas on January 20, 1891.

The following was a letter by Wilhelm Klier, living in Fredericksburg, to his sister, Therese Klier Schlickum in Germany. Therese's son, Dr. Julius Schlickum, had announced his engagement to Paula Doedter. Dr. Julius Schlickum was the son of Therese Klier Schlickum and nephew of Wilhelm Klier. Wilhelm and his family were living on the 150-acre farm (Meusebach Creek) he purchased after the Civil War from Fritz Lochte. Four years ago, Wilhelm purchased approximately 1,000 acres of land at $4 an acre in Stonewall.

Letter #47(From Wilhelm Klier[1] to his sister, Therese)
December 21, 1891
Dear Therese,

You'll be saying: after years of silence, a letter from Texas! Likely a long time has passed since I wrote to you last time; regrettably, my last letters remained unanswered, until about 5 months ago when your son Dr. Julius Schlickum announced his engagement to Miss Paula Doedter. It was sent to me by Mrs. Doedter, widow of Town Mayor Doedter from Hagen in Westphalia. Since you know my tremendous passion for writing letters, I ask you to please give my apologies to the young couple for only thinking of them this late. Please, dear Therese, be so kind and relate to them regards from me, my wife, and children, as well as best wishes to their engagement.

Since I'm just talking about the topic of engagement or respectively marriage, I'm herewith announcing the marriage of my oldest daughter Jensine[2] with Mr. Wilh. Wehmeier [*Wehmeyer*], which took place in spring. The latter owns a farm where the Dry Creek flows into the Pedernales, about 10 miles from our farm; you might remember that I bought a piece of land of about 150 acres here after the War from Fritz Lochte that backs up to the creek, and then settled on it.

We still live in this place, but since our family became bigger, I had to buy more land. About 4 years ago I bought about 1000 acres of land 3-4 miles below from where the Dry Creek and the Pedernales meet. We cleared the land right away, as we had to pay for the land with the profits from the harvest; last year we had so much cotton that I can pay off the rest. It cost me about 4 Dollar per acre. Land prices are rising here tremendously, to the point where my land couldn't be bought for less than 6 to 7 Dollars now! Since slavery was abolished everyone, here is planting cotton, and as a result people have more money as ever before, and the farmers are all doing well now. We grew 23 bales (a bale at 500 pounds). The price is lower this year compared to past years, about 7 cents per pound. Other than that, we have harvested 250 bushels of wheat and about 400 bushels of corn, and enough fodder for the horses and cattle. On December 9th, my 57th birthday, we had a small party, and the old Ransleben and some of his sons attended as well. Ida's brother, Owe[3] Striegler, is the schoolteacher in our district, and at the same time also the conductor at our local Choral Society, and he came to serenade us in the evening. All of us had a very good time! — Before ending my letter, I should probably write something about our family. Three children, a boy and 2 girls, were torn from us by death — the following are still with us:

the oldest, Gustav 20 years

Antonie 15

Hugo   Johanna

Waldemar   Fernando

Egon   Josephine

Arthur

the youngest, Wilhelm   4 years

I probably won't have to tell you that raising such a big family is accompanied by so much fear, worry, and work, especially for a mother; one is contented if only everyone remains healthy! Judging from newspaper articles from Europe it appears as if there might soon be a war with Russia that would be horrible! Chances are that once it would be going on, all major powers would be pulled into it, and then there would be no end in sight.

I haven't heard from Toni since our parents died; none of my last letters were answered. I also don't know anything about you! Have the two of you, that is you and your Julius, taken up your residence in Hagen, or are you living there only temporarily? And where does Toni live?

Please write to me soon and tell everything that is of interest! I'm giving my best to the young couple and to the widow, Mrs. Doedter, and am ending for today, and am sending many regards to all of you, also from my wife and children.

Your brother *Wilhelm Klier,*

Heartfelt Holiday Wishes to all, especially also to Toni!

---

[1] *Wilhelm had managed to find his way home after the Battle at Nueces Springs.*

[2] *Translator's Note: this appears to be a deciphering error by the transcriber unless it is a "pet name."*

[3] *Translator's note possibly "Ove."*

The addition to the rear of Holy Ghost Lutheran Church and the porch on the parsonage were built in 1892 through the cooperative efforts of the congregation and the pastor. In 1892, the Gillespie County Fair moved to a new site. Present day South Adams, East Ufer, South Lincoln, and East Park Streets bounded the new fair grounds. The first Gillespie County fair held at the new site was on September 24-28, 1892. F.J. Morgan was elected sheriff of Gillespie County on July 20, 1892. George B. Riley was elected sheriff of Gillespie County in December 1892. Grover Cleveland became the President of the United States in 1893.

The following was a letter written by Wilhelm Klier, living in Fredericksburg, to his sister, Therese Klier Schlickum in Germany. Wilhelm mentioned that his nephew, Guido Ransleben, passed away October 15, 1892 (at the age of 23) from Typhoid fever. He left behind his wife, Mina Bonn Ransleben, and a little daughter named Cora. Typhoid fever was transmitted by eating food or drinking beverages improperly handled by an infected person with *salmonella typhi* or if contaminated water containing the bacteria was used for washing food or drinking. Wilhelm Klier was 59 years old. Enclosed with this letter to Therese was a picture of the Personnel of the Wm. Klier Family in 1892. Wilhelm mentioned the Gillespie County Fair which was held at Fort Martin Scott from 1881 through 1889; thereafter, it was moved to Fredericksburg.

Letter #48

Gillespie County, Texas,

February 4th, 1893

Dear Therese,

Time keeps going by without stopping, and in the meantime, one is getting old! According to your wishes I'll be sending a sign of life from us to you every now and then! About two or three months ago I had sent a picture of my entire family to you, hoping that you would enjoy it a little. According to my calculations it should have arrived there shortly before Christmas. Hopefully, it arrived there on time! Our area used to be considered quite good for one's health in the past, but about 3 — 4 months ago we were afflicted by typhoid fever, infecting mostly younger people.

The Ransleben family was hit very hard. Guido Ransleben, the youngest, died from the fever after a short time, leaving behind his wife and a little daughter of not quite 2 years; thereafter Max Ransleben's wife became sick, and died from it a short time later. She leaves behind her husband and three little children. Josephine Ransleben, who is married to Theodor Boos, was actually the first one to get this treacherous disease and was hovering between life and death for a long time. She survived the disease and now is doing very well again. May God grant respite from diseases again!

As far as my family, I can report that we are all doing well and are in good spirits and hope it will remain thus as well. We are leading a quiet life on the countryside, and our only distraction are family visits every now and then, or when a singer comes to the settlement every so often, or there is a Fair featuring shooting matches. On those occasions acquaintances and relatives meet and have a chance to chat to their fill. Other than that, we all have to work if we want to keep everything in order, and if I didn't have such a hard-working wife as my Ida, I would have no idea how things could be kept in such good order!

I have to end my letter for today with the expectation that you'll write immediately upon receipt of this one. Many regards from my entire family, and from me, your Brother, and am remaining yours sincerely,

Wilhelm Klier

Wilhelm and Ida Striegler Klier

Above – The Klier family in 1892

The following pictures depict what Main Street looked like in 1892 during the life of Wilhelm and Ida Striegler Klier.

East Main Street, Fredericksburg, 1892

A view looking west from the 400 block of East Main Street shows the famous old Nimitz Hotel started in 1855 and built by Charles H. Nimitz, grandfather of Fleet Admiral Chester W. Nimitz. Note the steamboat observation tower. This historic old hotel, in which Admiral Nimitz played as a child, was torn down and remodeled in 1926. Today it is known as the "Admiral Nimitz Museum," a museum and a state commission, honoring Admiral Nimitz, and all men in the U. S. Armed forces.

The two-story structure at left foreground is the first such native limestone building erected in Fredericksburg built by the pioneer citizens Friedrich Kiehne and Mary Kreinsen in 1848.

Other structures in the next block are the Keidel Hospital building, on right, the White Elephant Saloon, and on the opposite (left side) the Peter Kleck building where the Cotillion club held club dances upstairs. A little further to the left is the two-story rock building, formerly Probst Hardware and Kolmeier and Klier. The first part of the structure was built by John Schandua in the 1890's and the remainder by his brother Henry Schandua, in 1902, the building housing the Schandua Hardware store. Mrs. Felix Pehl, Ella Schandua, surviving daughter of John Schandua (died in 1900) recalls that the Masonic Lodge held their meetings in a large hall upstairs, where dances were also held.

West Main Street, Fredericksburg, 1892

Looking East from the 200 Block of West Main Street we can see the historic Herman Ochs Saloon, later Otto Meurer's Buckhorn Saloon, then the Plaza Hotel, operated by John Stehling. The building was bought by Arthur Stehling from his father and then sold to Security State

Bank and Trust, which incorporated the original rock walls into the bank building. To the right of the Saloon is the first Gillespie County Courthouse behind which was the first jail. *(Herman Ochs, incidentally, was at one time Gillespie County Sheriff)*. The large two-story rock building, standing off to the right in the middle of the block is the second Courthouse, completely restored and renovated in 1967 by Mr. and Mrs. Eugene McDermott of Dallas.

Immediately to the left foreground is the old Schwarz General Merchandise Store *(before Schwarz built the larger two-story rock structure now occupied by Fredericksburg Firestone.)* The same place was used for a time by the late R. L. Kott as a pool hall and in the early 1920's by Felix, Emil and Leo Blanchard Sr. where they had an auto and bicycle repair and accessories shop. The historic *Vereins Kirche*, known as the "Die Kaffee Muehle" (Coffee Mill), was built by the pioneers (*Adelsverein*) in 1847 to serve as a house of worship for all creeds, as a school, public meeting place, and as a haven for protection against Indians. It was torn down – demolished – in 1897. In 1934-35 a replica was built by the citizens of the City and WPA; the late Lee Kiehne, son of Mr. and Mrs. Otto Kiehne, serving as architect. The *Vereins Kirche*, the imposing octagonal replica, stands in the middle of Market Square, 300 feet removed to the left from the original site where it stood for half a century in the center of Fredericksburg's historic wide Main Street.

Wilhelm and Ida Klier's first granddaughter, Olga Lene Wehmeyer, was born on July 14, 1892, to William and Signe Klier Wehmeyer. Wilhelm Klier turned 58 years old on December 9, 1892. Antonie (Toni) Klier, sister of

Wilhelm Klier, passed away in the year of 1893 in Germany, at the age of 48. Holy Ghost Lutheran Church building was dedicated in March 1893. Wilhelm and Ida Klier's first grandson, Louis Wehmeyer was born to Wm. And Signe Klier Wehmeyer, on September 10, 1893. Wilhelm Klier turned 59 years old on December 9, 1893. Gustav Klier, second son of Wilhelm and Ida Striegler Klier, died on September 25, 1894, at age 23 years.

October 12, 1894
Cemetery – Vol. 4, Pages 290-291

On October 12, 1894, eleven community members which included Wilhelm Klier purchased the land for the Meusebach Creek Cemetery in the amount of $12, i.e., Borchers, Klier, Gerhardt, Lochte, Kirchhoff, Kuhlmann, Kuhlmann, Feller, Striegler, and Stroeher.

Charles A. Culberson becomes the Governor of Texas on January 15, 1895. Wilhelm Klier and his wife, Ida, sold their 150-acres of land in the Meusebach Creek Community to Louis Lochte (son of Friedrich "Fritz" Lochte), on October 4, 1895. They had lived on this property for 25 years.

On November 14, 1895, Wilhelm Klier purchased 362 acres in the amount of $1,810.00 for land on the north side of the Pedernales River adjoining the east side of the 971.84 acres of land he purchased in 1885. Wilhelm Klier turned 61 years old on December 9, 1895.

The Wilhelm Klier family moved to the Stonewall Community in 1896, where Wilhelm had purchased a farm and ranch, some years previously (1885). The Klier children attended the Stonewall School. Wilhelm Klier owned around 1,500 acres of land, from the Pedernales River all the way up to the Double Horn Road. The home place was on the northwest corner of the Pedernales River; they had about a mile of riverfront property. The Pedernales River furnished the large family with fishing and swimming holes.

About 200 yards south, southwest of the house, through the Vogel's easement gate and past the old clay pit, yellow clay was burned for a mortar mixture used to cement the limestone rocks together for their house. They got the rock at the quarry located at Double Horn Road and Gellerman Lane. The homeplace was built by a Mr. Duecker who resided in the Cave Creek area.

The large home in the country had four bedrooms; two upstairs and two downstairs. The original, two-story limestone structure was L-shaped. The home had a shingle roof. The upstairs bedrooms were on opposite ends of the "L" and the downstairs bedrooms were adjoining. The boys' bedroom was the larger of the upstairs, and the other was the girls' bedroom. Downstairs, the one on the top of the "L" was Wilhelm and Ida's bedroom and the one adjoining was another bedroom. The younger children shared the bedroom downstairs.

This was the days before electricity (in the country), indoor plumbing, and refrigerators. Kerosene lamps and candles were used for lighting. A cistern and windmill with a tank house were used as the primary source of water for the household. An outhouse was used as a toilet. An icebox was a kitchen appliance that kept their food cold. Back in those days wood was the primary source of heat for warmth and cooking. The wood used for this purpose usually consisted of oak trees that were chopped down. They were stacked throughout the pasture until the wood was needed for cooking or the wood stoves. The larger pieces were usually split with an axe, four ways, to conveniently fit into the cooking stove. The pot-bellied heating stoves could use the larger pieces, whole.

On the farm, Wilhelm planted corn, wheat, oats, and cotton. The farm had apple trees, and pear trees. Common farm equipment during this period was a 2-bottom gang plow, disk and peg-tooth harrow, binder, thresher, two-row planters, wagons, and horses. Wilhelm and his large family spent time trying to squeeze a living out of the stone and rock fields.

Klier Homeplace, Stonewall, Texas

The Hollmig Property (private property), 3085 Gellermann Lane, Stonewall, Texas (2021) (Previously Klier Homeplace)

The town of Fredericksburg got its first electric light company in 1896. Kerosene lamps and candles were used for lighting; otherwise, houses were dark at sundown. Henry Ford built his first experimental car in a workshop behind his home in Detroit in 1896. By creating the first automobile that middle-class Americans could afford, he converted the automobile from an expensive curiosity into an accessible conveyance that profoundly impacted the landscape of the 20th century.

Gustav Hugo Wehmeyer, third child of Wm. And Signe Klier Wehmeyer, and third grandchild of Wilhelm and Ida Klier was born on March 29, 1896.

The *Vereins Kirche* stood in the middle of Main Street in Fredericksburg, Texas until 1896. The building was partially dismantled for Fredericksburg's Golden Jubilee celebration when the walls were removed, and it was transformed into an open pavilion for the celebration. The 50-year anniversary of the Foundation of the Colony of Fredericksburg was held on May 8, 9, 10, 1896 on the Market Square in Fredericksburg. The original *Vereins Kirche*, which stood on San Saba Street (now Main Street), was demolished in 1897. William McKinley became the President of the United States in 1897. Joseph D. Sayers take office as Governor of Texas on January 17, 1899. Hugo Klier, son of Wilhelm and Ida Striegler Klier, was married to Emma Kolmeier on June 6, 1899.

Chapter XIII - Background of the Gustav Klier Family

Gustav Rudolph Emil Ferdinand Klier, son of Friedrich Wilhelm and Josephine Klier, brother of Wilhelm Klier, was born April 27, 1843, in Germany. He was baptized at *Liebfrauen-Uberwasser Katholische*, Muenster, Westfalen, Germany. The letters from Gustav Klier are among the Klier papers.

Left: Liebfrauen-Uberwasser Katholische, Muenster, Germany

Father Klier took Gustav out of grammar school two weeks before his university-entrance exam for which he had all the qualification per the professors. Gustav had been very successful at school. All professors (teachers at grammar school in Germany at that time had the title of "Professor") were angry with Father Klier because the date of the examination was only four weeks after Gustav had to leave school. Because of his early exit, Gustav Klier could not pass his *"Abitur,"* a school leaving exam and university entrance exam at the same time but equal to the associate degree at college. Before emigrating to America, Gustav worked for the Councilor of Commerce in Versmold, Germany.

According to a letter dated July 30, 1866, Gustav Klier was to immigrate to New York on either August 4, 1866, on the ship *Bremen* or on August 11, 1866, on the ship *America*, at the age of 23 years old. In a letter dated January 21, 1867, Carl Wolters stated that Gustav had previously arrived in New York. Letters from Gustav Klier in St. Louis, Missouri began on March 9, 1867.

At the age of 31 years, Gustav Klier married Mrs. Ernestine Miller on February 21, 1874, in St. Louis, Missouri. Ernestine Wilhelmine Prange was born April 19, 1848, and baptized on April 30,1848 in Westfalen, Germany. On November 7, 1849, Ernestine Prange (at the age of six months) immigrated with her family from Le Havre, France on the ship *Harmonia*. Her mother was Christine Prange, and her father was Ferdinand Prange. Fredrich William Klier was born October 31, 1876, in St. Louis, Missouri.

The 1880 St. Louis, Missouri Census shows Gustav, age 36, living with his wife, Ernestine, age 32; three sons: Willie Klier, age four; John Miller, age 13; Gustav Miller, age 10; and three cousins: Selma, age 10; Hana, age 10; and Ernestine Miller, age 64 years. Gustav Klier was a letter carrier.

Ernestine Prange Klier died July 25, 1897, age 49, in St. Louis, Missouri. The 1900 St. Louis, Missouri Census indicated that Gustav Klier, age 55, a letter carrier and widowed, had a stepson, Gustav Miller, age 25, living in his household. Gustav Klier died July 13, 1908, age 65, in St. Louis, Missouri.

Chapter XIV - Turn of the Century (1900-1907)

The population in Gillespie County was 8,229 in 1900. The 1900 Gillespie County Census consisted of the following household members in Stonewall, Texas: Wilhelm Klier, farmer, age 64; Ida, age 55; Waldemar, age 24; Antonie, age 23; Egon, age 21; Arthur, age 18; Hannah, age 17; Fernanda, age 16; Josephine, age 14; and William, age 12. John Klaerner was elected sheriff of Gillespie County in December 1900. Wagons or buggies had been the only means of transportation, but automobiles came into use early in 1900. This affected everyday life in the 20th century and in Gillespie County. Ida Wehmeyer, fourth child of William and Signe Klier Wehmeyer, and fourth grandchild of Wilhelm and Ida Striegler Klier, was born on December 10, 1900. On June 15, 1901, Waldemar Klier, son of Wilhelm and Ida Striegler Klier, and Auguste Grobe were united in marriage, in Fredericksburg, Texas. Theodore Roosevelt was elected President of the United States from 1901 to 1909.

In 1902, the first church of the Evangelical Trinity Lutheran Church of Albert was built in Stonewall which was converted into a parsonage when the second church was built. The Lutheran Church had been a mission church at the Williams Creek School in Albert, Texas. At the turn of the century, Wilhelm and Ida Klier transferred their membership to the Lutheran Church at Stonewall, Texas. This church was much nearer to their home.

"This congregation traces its history to 1902, when it was organized in the Albert Schoolhouse. A sanctuary built

here in 1902 was replaced in 1904, and this structure was erected in 1928. Worship services were conducted in the German language until 1950. A fine example of the Gothic Revival style of architecture, the church features fine details in its arched window and door openings, Gothic steeple, and original pressed metal siding." -- Recorded Texas Historic Landmark

On January 14, 1902, Antonie Klier and Emil Ad. Eckert were united in marriage in the Holy Ghost Lutheran Church. Wilhelm W. Klier, oldest child of Waldemar and Auguste Grobe Klier, and grandchild of Wilhelm and Ida Striegler Klier, was born October 9, 1902, at Stonewall, Texas. Samuel W.T. Lanham takes office as Governor of Texas on January 20, 1903.

On November 5, 1903, Wilhelm Klier purchased 236-acres, for $3,750 from Phillip Ellebracht. Waldemar Klier received the 236-acre tract which Wm. Klier (F. W. Klier) bought in 1903, and is recorded in Vol. 9, Pages 495-496. The location of the 236-acre tract is near the intersection of Highway 290 and Ranch Road 1623 and went all the way to the Pedernales River. Ida and all the children signed the Partition Deed, which conveyed the 236-acres to Waldemar Klier; that is how he got title to the land.

The mission church became Trinity Lutheran Church in 1904 *(present day 4270 Ranch Road 1, Stonewall, Texas)*. The cornerstone and surrounding stones formed the foundation for the second church which was dedicated in 1904 in Stonewall. Wilhelm and Ida Klier were members of this congregation. Its original cornerstone rests beside the current church, though the original 1904 church was

Trinity Lutheran Church, Stonewall, Texas

situated in the current location of the stone-veneered parsonage. The historical marker is near Stonewall, Texas, in Gillespie County. The marker can be reached from Ranch Road 1. The marker is located near the church to the right of the front entrance.

In 1905, the first telephone system of any size came to Fredericksburg. On February 2, 1905, Arthur Klier, son of Wilhelm and Ida Klier, and Clara Ottmers were united in marriage. Paula Doedter, wife of Dr. Julius Schlickum, passed away on April 1, 1905, in Germany. Dr. Schlickum was the nephew of Wilhelm Klier. In 1905, Therese Klier Schlickum passed away in Germany at the age of 77 years. Elgin Klier, eldest child of Arthur and Clara Ottmers Klier, and grandson of Wilhelm and Ida Klier, was born on November 10, 1905, at Cave Creek, Gillespie County, Texas. Catharine Schlickum Rieb, daughter of the late

Julius Schlickum and Therese Klier Schlickum died December 26, 1906, in Germany, at the age of 52 years. Wilhelm Klier turned 72 years old on December 9, 1906. Wilhelm would not live to celebrate his birthday his next birthday in 1907. In 1907, the *Gillespie County News* becomes the *Fredericksburg Standard.* Thomas M. Campbell takes the oath of office as the Governor of the State of Texas on January 15, 1907.

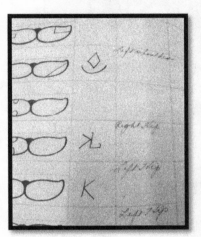

Above: Klier Cattle Brand

The town of Fredericksburg got its first ice factory in 1907. Wilhelm and Ida Klier have, too, had their share of heartaches. They had 14 children and four have passed away *(Friedrich, the oldest son, died in his 17th year; Gustav, their second son died in his 24th year; one daughter died in infancy in 1880; and another daughter died in infancy, date unknown).*

Wilhelm Klier died on June 22, 1907, at Fredericksburg, Gillespie County, Texas in his 73rd year. He is buried at the *Der Stadt Friedhof* in Fredericksburg, Texas. Ida died at her home at Stonewall, Texas, November 8, 1911, in her 67th year. The Rev. Max Heinrich of Trinity Lutheran Church conducted the funeral services at the home of her son, Hugo, and at *Der Stadt Friedhof* in Fredericksburg, Texas. She was a wonderful wife and mother. Her genial disposition and ready humor endeared her to all who knew her.

Above: William Friedrich Klier and Ida Agathe Striegler Klier, Der Stadt Friedhof, corner of East Schubert Street and Lee Street, Fredericksburg, Texas (Section D, Row 08, Plots 32 and 33)

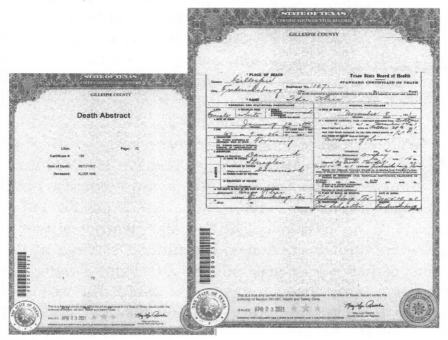

After the death of Wilhelm Friedrich Klier, a copy of the Partition Deed of Wilhelm Klier's Farm (F.W. Klier should be W.F. Klier) spells out how much each son had to pay to a specific sister and to their mother Ida in order to receive their land ($567 to a specific sister and $600 to Ida Striegler Klier). Waldemar paid Antonie and Ida; Egon paid Hannah and Ida; Wilhelm (Wm.) paid Josephine and Ida (plus Ida and daughters reserve the use of the dwelling house for Ida's natural life); Hugo paid Signe and Ida; and Arthur paid Fernanda and Ida.

The County Clerk's Online Probate Records was checked for Wilhelm and Ida Striegler Klier's wills. There is no probate record of either of their wills, but a "Proof of Heirship" was recorded in Volume 24, Page 141. That is how the sons received title to their parcels. The Partition Deed was signed and recorded August 17, 1907, only about two months after Wilhelm Klier passed away.

"Proof of Heirship" dated December 3, 1953, recorded in Volume 71, pages 345-346, Deed Records, stating that Wilhelm Friedrich Klier was also known as F.W. Klier. Wilhelm Friedrich Klier died June 22, 1907, leaving as his heirs his wife, Ida Striegler Klier and his children, Signe Wehmeyer, Hugo Klier, Waldemar Klier, Antonie Eckert, Egon Klier, Arthur Klier, Hannah Klier, Fernanda Eckert, Josephine Klier, and William Klier.

Partition Deed dated August 17, 1907, executed by Mrs. Ida Klier, Signe Wehmeyer, Hugo Klier, Waldemar Klier, Antonie Klier, Egon Klier, Arthur Klier, Hannah Klier, Fernanda Eckert, Josephine Klier and Wilhelm (Wm.) Klier, conveying to Wilhelm (Wm.) Klier 315 acres of land, recorded in Volume 13, pages 270-275, Deed Records.

Throughout their home were many examples of Wilhelm's handicraft. He made most of the furniture for their home. Once, at Christmas time, they were unable to get trimmings for their tree, so he carved the chains to decorate the tree, out of wood, making perfect links within one another, as neatly, as if they had been machine made. These chains were used year after year. He also made all his axe handles, plow handles, plow stocks and beams.

Wilhelm Klier had survived the Nueces massacre! He carried on after almost being hung during the Civil War. Wilhelm and other Germans did not want to be instrumental in tearing up one of the most beautiful forms of government the world had ever seen, in order to build a new government founded solely on the principle of expansion of human slavery. Wilhelm had participated in preserving this wonderful form of democracy and standing up for his beliefs.

Wilhelm went on to be married after the Civil War to an amazing woman and had 14 children. Wilhelm and Ida Striegler Klier raised their family in a Christian faith. Wilhelm had accomplished the American dream of being free and owning land. Upon Wilhelm's death, he owned 1,569.84 acres of land in Gillespie County, Texas. He outlasted numerous trepidations while prospering and flourishing in the Texas Hill Country. The huge Klier family owes its existence to the founder of the Klier family in Texas, Wilhelm Friedrich Klier. Wilhelm was known to be held in high esteem, known for his honesty, had a pleasing personality, and was well-liked by all his friends.

These traits and characteristics have been passed down to Wilhelm Friedrich Klier's descendants. We exist today in Texas and beyond because of this brave, inspiring and humble soul. Wilhelm, *Mein Lieber Wilhelm, Gross Opa,* your blood will flow through our veins forevermore!

On June 19, 2021, Wilhelm Friedrich Klier was remembered by the Former Texas Rangers Association and the Klier family with a Texas Ranger Memorial Cross Dedication, for his service. Texas Rangers were known as Minute Men and during the Civil War era, frontier ranging companies were generally referred to by several different designations, including Texas State Troops (TST). These Texas Ranger units were specially assigned to frontier defense and did not serve under or engage against Union or Confederate Forces. These men are considered Texas Rangers because the service they performed was that of the Texas Frontier Defense against Indians and outlaws, not fighting with the Confederacy against Union soldiers.

On February 25,1861, Wilhelm Klier became a member of the Minute Company, Gillespie County, Texas State Troops (TST) as Private Wilhelm Klier; Commanding Officer, Captain Phillip Braubach, Wilhelm's age was listed as 26 years.

Right: Texas Ranger Memorial Cross Dedication Program, June 19, 2021

Left and below: Texas Ranger Memorial Cross Dedication, June 19, 2021

Genealogy

The Wilhelm and Ida Striegler Klier Children
(Married November 6, 1867)

1. Friedrich Klier, born in1868, at Meusebach Creek, Gillespie County, Texas; died in 1886, in Fredericksburg, Texas, at the age of 17 years.

2. Gustav Klier, born March 15, 1871, at Meusebach Creek, Gillespie County, Texas; died September 25, 1894, in Fredericksburg, Texas, at the age of 23 years.

3. Signe Klier Wehmeyer, born June 17, 1872, at Meusebach Creek, Gillespie County, Texas; died September 27, 1929, in Kerr County, at the age of 57 years.

4. Hugo Klier, born March 17, 1874, at Meusebach Creek, Gillespie County, Texas; died December 2, 1920, in Fredericksburg, Texas, at the age of 46 years.

5. Waldemar Klier, born December 30, 1875, at Meusebach Creek, Gillespie County, Texas; died June 17, 1948, in Fredericksburg, Texas, at the age of 73 years.

6. Antonie Klier Eckert, born April 14, 1877, at Meusebach Creek, Gillespie County, Texas; died March 25, 1966, Fredericksburg, Texas, at the age of 89 years.

7. Egon Klier, born September 5, 1878, at Meusebach Creek, Gillespie County, Texas; died July 4, 1951, in Fredericksburg, Texas, at the age of 73 years.

8. Baby Klier was born April 1880, Meusebach Creek, Gillespie County, Texas (one month old on 1880 Census); died in infancy, Fredericksburg, Texas.

9. Arthur Klier, born November 19, 1881, at Meusebach Creek, Gillespie County, Texas; died June 7, 1967, in Fredericksburg, Texas, at the age of 86 years.

10. Hannah Klier Sohm, born January 19, 1883, at Meusebach Creek, Gillespie County, Texas; died March 9, 1979, in San Bernardino, California, at the age of 96 years.

11. Fernanda Klier Eckert, born May 14, 1884, at Meusebach Creek, Gillespie County, Texas; died June 19, 1970, in Fredericksburg, Texas, at the age of 86 years.

12. Josephine Klier Vogel, born July 6, 1886, at Meusebach Creek, Gillespie County, Texas; died September 19, 1968, in Fredericksburg, Texas, at the age of 82 years.

13. William Klier, born November 8, 1887, at Meusebach Creek, Gillespie County, Texas; died January 20, 1972, in Fredericksburg, Texas, at the age of 85 years.

14. Daughter died in infancy.

The Julius and Therese Klier Schlickum Children
(Married September 27, 1849)

1. Catharine Schlickum Rieb was born in 1854, in Gillespie County, Texas; married Johann Heinrich Rieb on August 29, 1880; and died September 26, 1906, in Germany, at the age of 52 years.

2. Dr. Julius Schlickum was born November 22, 1859, in Bexar County, Texas; married Paula Doedter (1867-1918); had six children; and died October 30, 1936, in Muenster, Germany, at the age of 77 years.

3. Hugo Otto Schlickum, born January 14, 1862, in Boerne, Kendall County, Texas; married Helene Zimmermann; died September 2, 1934, in Dorsten, Nordrhein-Westfalen, Germany, at the age of 72 years.

The Julius Johann and Josephine Klier Ransleben Children
(Married October 28, 1852)

1. Carl Ludwig Ransleben, born June 13, 1853, in Comfort, Kendall County, Texas; died October 31, 1918, in Gillespie County, Texas, at the age of 65 years.

2. Gustav Rudolph Ransleben (Max), born December 15, 1854, in Gillespie County, Texas; died February 27, 1941, in Gillespie County, Texas, at the age of 86 years.

3. Oskar (Oscar) Wilhelm Ransleben, born February 15, 1856, Gillespie County, Texas; died October 25, 1927, in Kendall County, Texas, at the age of 71 years.

4. Julius William Ransleben, born May 11, 1858, in Gillespie County, Texas; died December 8, 1941, in Fredericksburg, Texas, at the age of 83 years.

5. Fritz Ransleben, born in 1860, in Gillespie County; died in 1863, in Gillespie County, Texas, at the age of 3 years.

6. Josephine Marie Ransleben Boos, born October 1, 1861, in Gillespie County, Texas; died February 23, 1934, in Fredericksburg, Texas, at the age of 73 years.

7. Friedrich Hilmar Ransleben, born December 23, 1863, in Gillespie County, Texas; died March 2, 1938, in Fredericksburg, Texas, at the age of 75 years.

8. Guido Eduard Ransleben, born July 15, 1869, in Gillespie County, Texas; died October 15, 1892, in Fredericksburg, Texas, at the age of 23 years.

9. Hermann Wilhelm Ransleben, born February 12, 1870, in Gillespie County, Texas; died November 12, 1887, in Fredericksburg, Texas, at the age of 17 years.

The Johan Frederick Gottlieb and Jensine Amalie Adamine Fredericke Lange Striegler Children
(Married January 15, 1837)

1. Antoinette Striegler Otte, born June 9, 1837, in Svendborg, Denmark; died May 24, 1883, in Fredericksburg, Texas, at the age of 47 years.

2. A daughter born in 1838 died in infancy.

3. Olfert Striegler, born March 7, 1839, in Svendborg, Denmark; died September 26, 1923, in Menard County, Texas, at the age of 85 years.

4. Arthur Striegler, born August 10, 1840, in Nakskov, Denmark; died May 10, 1915, in Fredericksburg, Texas, at the age of 75 years.

5. Ove William Striegler, born May 18, 1842, in Nakskov, Denmark; died December 30, 1919, in Fredericksburg, Texas, at the age of 78 years.

6. Attila Nicolai Striegler, born July 2, 1843, in Nakskov, Denmark; died February 5, 1912, in Comfort, Texas, at the age of 69 years.

7. Ida Striegler Klier, born January 13, 1845, in Nakskov, Denmark; died November 8, 1911, in Fredericksburg, Texas, at the age of 67 years.

8. Olga Emilie Striegler, born August 7, 1847, in Svendborg; died November 16, 1847, in Svendborg, Denmark, at the age of 3 months.

9. Frederick C. Striegler, born October 5, 1848, on the Island of Funen, Denmark; died January 25, 1935, in Fredericksburg, Texas, at the age of 87 years.

10. Amailie Striegler Nelson, born December 31, 1851, in Svendborg, Denmark; died February 22, 1934, in Boerne, Texas, at the age of 82 years.

11. Inetz Striegler Pickett, born March 25, 1855, in Svendborg, Denmark; died January 31, 1931, in Sand Springs, Oklahoma, at the age of 76 years.

12. Fernanda Striegler Falder, born May 14, 1857, in Fredericksburg, Texas; died June 2, 1911, in Sedalia, Missouri, at the age of 54 years.

13. Alice Striegler, born in 1859, in Fredericksburg, Texas; died in 1861, in Fredericksburg, Texas, at the age of 2½ years.

The Gustav Rudolph Emil Ferdinand and Ernestine Prange Miller Klier Family

(Married February 21, 1874)

1. Fredrich William Klier, born October 31, 1876, in St. Louis, Missouri; died January 23, 1932, in St. Louis, Missouri, at the age of 55 years.

The Friedrich Wilhelm and Anna Josepha Baar Klier Children

(Married December 31, 1824)

1. 1.Josephine Wilhelmine Klier Ransleben, born August 1, 1826, in Muenster, Germany; died June 29, 1888, in Gillespie County Texas, at the age of 62 years.

2. Caroline Therese Klier Schlickum, born October 12, 1828, in Muenster, Germany; died May 16, 1905, in Germany, at the age of 77 years.

3. Hugo Klier, born in 1832, (unknown).

4. Wilhelm Friedrich Eduard Klier, born December 9, 1834, in Muenster, Germany; died June 22, 1907, in Fredericksburg, Texas, at the age of 73 years.

5. Toni Klier, born about 1845, in Muenster, Germany; died about 1893, in Germany, at the age of 48 years.

6. Carl Georg Franz Klier, born October 14, 1839, in Muenster, Germany; died in 1861, Gillespie County, Texas, at the age of 22 years.

7. Maria Friederica Klier Neuhaus, born November 20, 1841, in Muenster, Germany; died July 1, 1867, in Germany, at the age of twenty-six years.

8. Gustav Rudolph Klier, born April 27, 1843, in Muenster, Germany; died July 13, 1908, in St. Louis, Missouri, at the age of 65 years.

<u>The (Johann) Jakob Schlickum and Katharine Pokorny Schlickum Children</u>

(Married in 1823)

1. Wilhelmine Minna Schlickum, born in 1824, in Prussia; date of death is unknown.

2. Jakob Julius Schlickum, born October 27, 1825, in Muenster, Prussia; died October 27, 1863, in Matamoros, Mexico, at the age of 38 years.

3. Catharine (Kathinka) Schlickum, born August 5, 1827, in Muenster, Prussia; date of death is unknown.

4. Carl Ferdinand Schlickum, born October 12, 1829, in Coblenz, Prussia; died November 12, 1876, in Austin, Texas, at the age of 47 years.

5. Albert Schlickum, born March 9, 1833, in Coblenz, Prussia; date of death unknown.

6. Otto Schlickum, born March 1, 1835, in Westfalen, Prussia; date of death unknown.

<u>The Johann Abraham and Christina Boeck Klier Children</u>

(Married August 15, 1797)

1. Maria Christina Klier 1798
2. Friedrich Wilhelm Klier 1799
3. Johann Jacob Klier 1801
4. Abraham Klier 1802
5. Isaac Klier 1802
6. Christine Therese Klier 1812

Source Notes

Chapter I

Ancestry.com. Germany, Select Births and Baptisms, 1558-1898 [database on-line]. Provo, UT, USA: Ancestry.com Operations, Inc., 2014.

Ancestry.com. Germany, Select Marriages, 1558-1929 [database on-line]. Provo, UT, USA: Ancestry.com Operations, Inc., 2014.

Ancestry.com. Germany, Select Deaths and Burials, 1582-1958 [database on-line]. Provo, UT, USA: Ancestry.com Operations, Inc., 2014.

Ancestry.com. U.S., Find a Grave Index, 1600s-Current [database on-line]. Provo, UT, USA: Ancestry.com Operations, Inc., 2012.

Dahlmanns, Hans, Christoph Dahlmanns, Chuck and Carrol (Klier) Timmerman, "Book of Schlickum-Klier Letters and Pictures," June 2012.

Striegler, Selma Weyrich, *The Johan Frederick Gottlieb Striegler Family History, A Detailed Genealogy of the Descendants of Pioneer Citizens of Gillespie County, Texas, 1940 to January 1952.* Compiled, Edited and Published Under the Direction of Selma Weyrich Striegler, Family Historian; Fred Mathisen; Attila N. Striegler, Business Managers; and Mabel Zimmermann, Revising Editor.

Chapter II

Ancestry.com. Germany, Select Marriages, 1558-1929 [database on-line]. Provo, UT, USA: Ancestry.com Operations, Inc., 2014.

Ancestry.com. Germany, Select Births and Baptisms, 1558-1898 [database on-line]. Provo, UT, USA: Ancestry.com Operations, Inc., 2014.

Dahlmanns, Hans, Christoph Dahlmanns, Chuck and Carrol (Klier) Timmerman, "Book of Schlickum-Klier Letters and Pictures," June 2012.

Penniger, Robert, *The First Fifty Years*, Translated from the German text by C. L. Wisseman, Fredericksburger Wochenblatt, Fredericksburg, Texas, May 1896.

Chapter III

Ancestry.com. Germany, Select Marriages, 1558-1929 [database on-line]. Provo, UT, USA: Ancestry.com Operations, Inc., 2014.

Ancestry.com. Germany, Select Births and Baptisms, 1558-1898 [database on-line]. Provo, UT, USA: Ancestry.com Operations, Inc., 2014.

Ancestry.com. Germany, Select Deaths and Burials, 1582-1958 [database on-line]. Provo, UT, USA: Ancestry.com Operations, Inc., 2014.

Ancestry.com. Missouri, U.S., Death Records, 1850-1931 [database on-line]. Provo, UT, USA: Ancestry.com Operations, Inc., 2008.

Ancestry.com. Texas, U.S., Death Certificates, 1903-1982 [database on-line]. Provo, UT, USA: Ancestry.com Operations, Inc., 2013.

Ancestry.com/Kruse Heuthen Family Tree.

Dahlmanns, Hans, Christoph Dahlmanns, Chuck and Carrol (Klier) Timmerman, "Book of Schlickum-Klier Letters and Pictures," June 2012.

Penniger, Robert, *The First Fifty Years*, Translated from the German text by C. L. Wisseman, Fredericksburger Wochenblatt, Fredericksburg, Texas, May 1896.

Striegler, Selma Weyrich, *The Johan Frederick Gottlieb Striegler Family History, A Detailed Genealogy of the Descendants of Pioneer Citizens of Gillespie County, Texas, 1940 to January 1952"* Compiled, Edited and Published Under the Direction of Selma Weyrich Striegler, Family Historian; Fred Mathisen; Attila N. Striegler, Business Managers; and Mabel Zimmermann, Revising Editor.

Worm, Peter, Lord Mayor, Town of Muenster, Germany, e-mail 10/13/2021 and 10/15/2021.

Chapter IV
Ancestry.com. U.S. and Canada, Passenger and Immigration Lists Index, 1500s-1900s [database on-line]. Provo, UT, USA: Ancestry.com Operations, Inc, 2010.

Dahlmanns, Hans, Christoph Dahlmanns, Chuck and Carrol (Klier) Timmerman, "Book of Schlickum-Klier Letters and Pictures," June 2012.

Deutsche Auswanderer-Datenbank.de.

https://www.indianolatx.com/history.html.

https://www.thetrainline.com/en/train-times/bremen-hbf-to-munster-westf-hbf.

Juenke, Carlos, *The Orphan – The Caspar Fritz Story*, Xlibris Corporation, 2011.

Striegler, Selma Weyrich, *The Johan Frederick Gottlieb Striegler Family History, A Detailed Genealogy of the Descendants of Pioneer Citizens of Gillespie County, Texas, 1940 to January 1952.* Compiled, Edited and Published Under the Direction of Selma Weyrich Striegler, Family Historian; Fred Mathisen; Attila N. Striegler, Business Managers; and Mabel Zimmermann, Revising Editor.

Chapter V
Dahlmanns, Hans, Christoph Dahlmanns, Chuck and Carrol (Klier) Timmerman, "Book of Schlickum-Klier Letters and Pictures," June 2012.

Goff, Myra Lee Adams, "Many trails converge in New Braunfels," Around the Sophienburg, Sophienblog, February 5, 2017.

https://www.hmdb.org/The Historical Marker Database.

https://www.tshaonline.org/handbook/entries/.

https://www.tshaonline.org/handbook/entries/fisher-miller-land-grant.

https://www.tshaonline.org/handbook/entries/indianola-tx.

https://www.tshaonline.org/handbook/entries/pinta-trail.

Juenke, Carlos, *The Orphan – The Caspar Fritz Story*, Xlibris Corporation, 2011.

Manken, Bernard, "Hardships of a German Family," *J. Marvin Hunter's Frontier Times Magazine*, July 18, 2018.

Morgenthaler, Jefferson, *The German Settlement of the Texas Hill Country*, Mockingbird Books, 2007.

Striegler, Selma Weyrich, *The Johan Frederick Gottlieb Striegler Family History, A Detailed Genealogy of the Descendants of Pioneer Citizens of Gillespie County, Texas, 1940 to January 1952.* Compiled, Edited and Published Under the Direction of Selma Weyrich Striegler, Family Historian; Fred Mathisen; Attila N. Striegler, Business Managers; and Mabel Zimmermann, Revising Editor.

Ward, Amanda Eyre, "A Relative of German Settlers Retraces Her Ancestors' Arduous Path to the Texas Hill Country," *Texas Highways*, May 31, 2019.

Chapter VI

Ancestry.com. 1850 United States Federal Census [database on-line]. Provo, UT, USA: Ancestry.com Operations, Inc., 2009. Images reproduced by FamilySearch.

Ancestry.com. Germany, Select Births and Baptisms, 1558-1898 [database on-line]. Provo, UT, USA: Ancestry.com Operations, Inc., 2014.

Ancestry.com/Germany, Births and Baptisms, 1558-1898. Salt Lake City, Utah: FamilySearch, 2013.

Dahlmanns, Hans, Christoph Dahlmanns "Book of Schlickum-Klier Letters and Pictures," June 2012.

Gillespie County Courthouse Records.

https://www.en.wikipedia.org/wiki/List_of_governors_of_ Texas.

https://www.fbgtxgensoc.org/timeline.

https://www.sites.rootsweb.com/~txgilles/gillespiesheriff s.html.

https://www.tshaonline.org/handbook/entries/meusebac h-john-o.

https://www.tshaonline.org/handbook/entries/twohig-john.

https://www.whitehouse.gov/about-the-white-house/presidents/.

Juenke, Carlos, *The Orphan – The Caspar Fritz Story*, Xlibris Corporation, 2011.

Kowert, Elise, *Old Homes And Buildings Of Fredericksburg*, Fredericksburg Publishing Company, Fredericksburg, Texas, 1977.

Penniger, Robert, Fredericksburg, *The First Fifty Years*, Fredericksburg Publishing, 1971.

Striegler, Selma Weyrich, *The Johan Frederick Gottlieb Striegler Family History, A Detailed Genealogy of the Descendants of Pioneer Citizens of Gillespie County, Texas, 1940 to January 1952.* Compiled, Edited and Published Under the Direction of Selma Weyrich Striegler, Family Historian; Fred Mathisen; Attila N. Striegler, Business Managers; and Mabel Zimmermann, Revising Editor.

Chapter VII

Ancestry.com. Germany, Lutheran Baptisms, Marriages, and Burials, 1500-1971 [database on-line]. Lehi, UT, USA: Ancestry.com Operations, Inc., 2016.

Ancestry.com. U.S. and Canada, Passenger and Immigration Lists Index, 1500s-1900s [database on-line]. Provo, UT, USA: Ancestry.com Operations, Inc, 2010.

Ancestry.com. 1870 United States Federal Census [database on-line]. Provo, UT, USA: Ancestry.com Operations, Inc., 2009. Images reproduced by FamilySearch.

Ancestry.com. Texas, U.S., Select County Marriage Index, 1837-1965 [database on-line]. Provo, UT, USA: Ancestry.com Operations, Inc., 2014.

Ancestry.com. U.S., Find a Grave Index, 1600s-Current [database on-line]. Provo, UT, USA: Ancestry.com Operations, Inc., 2012.

Ancestry.com/1860 census/Gillespie County.

Dahlmanns, Hans, Christoph Dahlmanns, Chuck and Carrol (Klier) Timmerman, "Book of Schlickum-Klier Letters and Pictures," June 2012.

Gillespie County Historical Society, *Pioneers in God's Hills*, Von Boeckmann-Jones, Austin, Texas, 1960.

https://www.immigrantships.net.

Kowert, Elise, *Old Homes and Buildings of Fredericksburg*, Fredericksburg Publishing Company, Fredericksburg, Texas, 1977.

Ransleben, Guido E., *A Hundred Years of Comfort in Texas*, The Naylor Company, 1954.

Striegler, Selma Weyrich, *The Johan Frederick Gottlieb Striegler Family History, A Detailed Genealogy of the Descendants of Pioneer Citizens of Gillespie County, Texas, 1940 to January 1952*. Compiled, Edited and Published Under the Direction of Selma Weyrich Striegler, Family Historian; Fred

Mathisen; Attila N. Striegler, Business Managers; and Mabel
Zimmermann, Revising Editor.
www.Fbgtxgensoc.org/lists/immigration.

Chapter VIII
Ancestry.com. Germany, Select Births and Baptisms,
1558-1898 [database on-line]. Provo, UT, USA: Ancestry.com
Operations, Inc., 2014.
Ancestry.com. U.S. and Canada, Passenger and
Immigration Lists Index, 1500s-1900s [database on-line].
Provo, UT, USA: Ancestry.com Operations, Inc, 2010.
Ancestry.com/1860 census/Gillespie County.
Ancestry.com/Year: 1860; Census Place: San Antonio
Ward 2, Bexar, Texas; Page: 370; Family History Library Film:
805288.
Bexar County Courthouse records.
Boerne Convention and Visitors Bureau, Boerne, Texas.
Burrier, Wm. Paul, *Confederate Military Commission Held
in San Antonio, Texas, July 2 – October 10, 1862*. Watercress
Press, San Antonio, 2014.
Dahlmanns, Hans, Christoph Dahlmanns, Chuck and
Carrol (Klier) Timmerman, "Book of Schlickum-Klier Letters and
Pictures," June 2012.
Gillespie County Courthouse records, Fredericksburg,
Texas.
https://www.bing.com/wagoner.
https://www.en.wikipedia.org/wiki/List_of_governors_of_
Texas.
https://www.fbgtxgensoc.org/timeline.
https://www.fortconcho.com.
https://www.hmdb.org/.
https://www.hmdb.org/campsansaba.
https://www.kendall.org.

https://www.sites.rootsweb.com/~txgilles/gillespiesheriff s.html.

https://www.texasfortstrail.com/fortmason.

https://www.thc.texas.gov/historic-sites/fort-mckavett-state-historic-site.

https://www.tshaonline.org/handbook/entries/fort-mason.

https://www.whitehouse.gov/about-the-white-house/presidents/.

Kowert, Elise, *Old Homes and Buildings of Fredericksburg*, Fredericksburg Publishing Company, Fredericksburg, Texas, 1977.

Striegler, Selma Weyrich, *The Johan Frederick Gottlieb Striegler Family History, A Detailed Genealogy of the Descendants of Pioneer Citizens of Gillespie County, Texas, 1940 to January 1952*. Compiled, Edited and Published Under the Direction of Selma Weyrich Striegler, Family Historian; Fred Mathisen; Attila N. Striegler, Business Managers; and Mabel Zimmermann, Revising Editor.

Chapter IX

Ancestry.com Operations, Inc., 2008. Staatsarchiv Hamburg. Hamburg Passenger Lists, 1850-1934 [database on-line]. Provo, UT, USA:

Ancestry.com. 1860 United States Federal Census [database on-line]. Provo, UT, USA: Ancestry.com Operations, Inc., 2009. Images reproduced by FamilySearch.

Ancestry.com. Texas, U.S., Select County Marriage Index, 1837-1965 [database on-line]. Provo, UT, USA: Ancestry.com Operations, Inc., 2014.

Ancestry.com/Year: 1860; Census Place: Precinct 4, Gillespie, Texas.

Gillespie County Historical Society, *Pioneers in God's Hills*, Von Boeckmann-Jones, Austin, Texas, 1960.

Striegler, Selma Weyrich, *The Johan Frederick Gottlieb Striegler Family History, A Detailed Genealogy of the Descendants of Pioneer Citizens of Gillespie County, Texas, 1940 to January 1952.* Compiled, Edited and Published Under the Direction of Selma Weyrich Striegler, Family Historian; Fred Mathisen; Attila N. Striegler, Business Managers; and Mabel Zimmermann, Revising Editor.

Chapter X

Ancestry.com. Year: 1860; Census Place: Bexar, Texas.

Ancestry.com. Texas, U.S., Muster Roll Index Cards, 1838-1900 [database on-line]. Provo, UT, USA: Ancestry.com Operations, Inc., 2011.

Ancestry.com/1860 census/Gillespie County.

Ancestry.com/National Park Service. U.S., Civil War Soldiers, 1861-1865 [database on-line]. Provo, UT, USA: Ancestry.com Operations Inc, 2007.

Anderson, Val, "The Lands and Legacy of Dr. Ferdinand Ludwig Herff Magical History Tour," October 17, 2017.

Barr, Alwyn, "Records of the Confederate Military Commission in San Antonio, July 2 – October 1861," edited by Alwyn Barr in '*Southwestern Historical Quarterly,*' Volume LXXI, No. 2, October 1967.

Barr, Michael," The Dreaded Haengerbande," *Fredericksburg Standard Radio Post*, October 17, 2018.

Benedict, John "Caleb Thomas' Log Cabin", Boerne Visitors' Center.

Boerne Convention and Visitors Bureau, 282 N. Main Street, Boerne, TX 78006.

Burrier Sr., W. Paul, *Confederate Military Commission Held in San Antonio, Texas, July 2 – October 10, 1862*, Watercress Press, 2014.

Burrier, Sr., Wm. Paul, *Nueces Battle and Massacre, Facts....Myths*, Watercress Press, San Antonio, 2015.

Cardenas, Hector, San Antonio Fire Department Retirees, e-mail, July 12, 2021.

Dahlmanns, Hans, Christoph Dahlmanns, Chuck and Carrol (Klier) Timmerman, "Book of Schlickum-Klier Letters and Pictures," June 2012.

https://www.americancivilwar101.com/pow/confederate.html.

https://www.bing.com/Ft+Sumter+is+fired+upon.

https://www.bing.com/search?q=camp+davis+gillespie+county+texas+1862.

https://www.bing.com/search?q=headwaters+of+the+South+Fork+of+the+Guadalupe+River+hunt+texas.

https://www.bing.com/search?q=jefferson+davis+provisional+governor+of+texas+1861.

https://www.bing.com/search?q=West+Prong+of+the+Nueces+River+Texas.

https://www.bing.com/search?q=what+is+a+morgen+of+land&form=.

https://www.bing.com/search?q=what+is+the+definition+of+headwaters.

https://www.cibolo.org/.

https://www.colt.com/.

https://www.en.wikipedia.org/wiki/Cascade_Caverns.Cave.

https://www.en.wikipedia.org/wiki/Colt_M1861_Navy.

https://www.en.wikipedia.org/wiki/John_Wilkes_Booth.

https://www.en.wikipedia.org/wiki/List_of_governors_of_Texas.

https://www.en.wikipedia.org/wiki/Nueces_River.

https://www.en.wikipedia.org/wiki/Partisan_Ranger_Act.

https://www.en.wikipedia.org/wiki/Typhoid_fever.

https://www.fbgtxgen.soc/specialprojects/timeline of Gillespie County Historical Events.

https://www.Fbgtxgensoc.org/Browse Veterans of Gillespie County List.

https://www.fbgtxgensoc.org/lists.

https://www.fbgtxgensoc.org/lists/10 Aug 1862 - Unionists Participating in Battle at Nueces River.

https://www.fbgtxgensoc.org/Lists/Military Lists/1860-80s-Texas Rangers.

https://www.fbgtxgensoc.org/Military Lists/Gillespie County Minute Company, Feb 1861 to Feb 1862.

https://www.fbgtxgensoc.org/timelines.

https://www.fbgtxgensoc.org/Veterans/Veterans of Gillespie County.

https://www.google.com/maps/search/Boerne+family+practice+on+corner+of+Blanco+and+Main@29.7941638.-98.7360508.16z.

https://www.historic.one/tx/kendall-county/historical-marker/.

https://www.hmdb.org/KendallCoTexas.

https://www.hmdb.org/KerrCoTexas.

https://www.kendallcountysheriff.com/john-sansom.

https://www.loc.gov/item/today-in-history/april-14.

https://www.mapcarta.com/.

https://www.merriam-webster.com/dictionary/yellow fever. https://www.mycivilwar.com/pow/confederate.html.

https://www.ncpedia.org/substitutes-civil-war.

https://www.researchonline.net/txcw/unit65.htm Taylor's 8th Cavalry.

https://www.sites.rootsweb.com/~txgilles/gillespiesheriffs.html.

https://www.texashistoricalmarkers.weebly.com/dr-ferdinand-ludwig-von-herff.html.

https://www.texashistoricalmarkers.weebly.com/old-military-headquarters.html.

https://www.texashistory.unt.edu.

https://www.tshaonline.org/handbook/entries/bullhead-creek-real-county.

https://www.tshaonline.org/handbook/entries/cascade-caverns.

https://www.tshaonline.org/handbook/entries/degener-edward.

https://www.tshaonline.org/handbook/entries/frontier-regiment.

https://www.tshaonline.org/handbook/entries/kampmann-john-herman.

https://www.tshaonline.org/handbook/entries/kuechler-jacob.

https://www.tshaonline.org/handbook/entries/north-prong-of-the-medina-river.

https://www.tshaonline.org/handbook/entries/thirty-third-texas-cavalry.

https://www.tshaonline.org/handbook/entries/west-frio-river.

https://www.tsl.texas.gov/ref/abouttx/secession/1march1861.html.

https://www.tsl.texas.gov/treasures/earlystate/secess-01.html.

https://www.tsl.texas.gov/treasures/giants/houston-01.html/Houston/Clark.

https://www.whitehouse.gov/about-the-white-house/presidents/.

Juenke, Carlos, *The Orphan, The Caspar Fritz Story*, Xlibris Corporation, 2011.

Kammlah, Joe, "Area Germans Remembered at Massacre site in Comfort," *Fredericksburg Standard Radio-Post*, August 22, 2012.

Kendall County Courthouse records.

Moon, Bryden, So early in the Civil War, 1862....very crude and very short-lived, called "Prison Town." E-mail dated August 7, 2020.

Morgenthaler, Jefferson, *The German Settlement of the Texas Hill Country*, Mockingbird Books, 2007.

National Register of Historic Places, United States Department of the Interior, Section 8, 3rd paragraph Page 13, Herff-Rozelle Farm, Boerne, Kendall County, Texas (Rev. 01/2009).

Penniger, Robert, Fredericksburg, *The First Fifty Years*, Fredericksburg Publishing, 1971.

Ransleben, Guido E., *A Hundred Years of Comfort in Texas*, The Naylor Company, 1954.

Sansom, John W., and R. H. Williams, *The Massacre on the Nueces River*.

Schwartz, Stephan, *Twenty-Two Months Prisoner of War*, A. F. Nelson Publishing Co., St. Louis, MO., 1892.

Spellman, Paul N., *This Fateful Revolution, Letters of a German-Texan Unionist, 1862-1863*, edited by Paul N. Spellman, Vol. CXXI, Southwestern Historical Quarterly, January 2018.

Striegler, Selma Weyrich, *The Johan Frederick Gottlieb Striegler Family History, A Detailed Genealogy of the Descendants of Pioneer Citizens of Gillespie County, Texas, 1940 to January 1952*. Compiled, Edited and Published Under the Direction of Selma Weyrich Striegler, Family Historian; Fred

Mathisen; Attila N. Striegler, Business Managers; and Mabel Zimmermann, Revising Editor.

Texas State Historical Association, Letters July 1862 Military Commission Source: "Records of the Confederate Military Commission in San Antonio, July 2 – October 10, 1862." *The Southwestern History Quarterly*, October 1967,Vol. 71, No. 2 (October 1967) pp. 247-278. Published by: Texas State Historical Association.

texashistory.unt.edu/ark:/67531/metapth2409/m1/29 headwaters of Turtle Creek.

Underwood, Rodman L., *Death on the Nueces*, Eakin Press, Austin, Texas, 2000.

Van Winkle, Irene, "Henderson has long history in West Kerr County," *West Kerr Current*, Ingram, Texas, February 16, 2006.

Chapter XI

Ancestry.com. Maria Friederica Klier/Stammbaum.

Ancestry.com. Germany, Select Marriages, 1558-1929 [database on-line]. Provo, UT, USA: Ancestry.com Operations, Inc., 2014.

Ancestry.com. Texas, U.S., Death Certificates, 1903-1982 [database on-line]. Provo, UT, USA: Ancestry.com Operations, Inc., 2013.

Ancestry.com. Texas, U.S., Select County Marriage Index, 1837-1965 [database on-line]. Provo, UT, USA: Ancestry.com Operations, Inc., 2014.

Ancestry.com. U.S., Find a Grave Index, 1600s-Current [database on-line]. Provo, UT, USA: Ancestry.com Operations, Inc., 2012.

Ancestry.com. Year: 1870; Census Place: Fredericksburg, Gillespie, Texas; Roll: M593_1587; Page: 305A.

Barr, Michael, *"The dreaded Haengerbande,"* *Fredericksburg Standard-Radio Post*, Fredericksburg, Texas, October 17, 2018.

Dahlmanns, Hans, Christoph Dahlmanns, Chuck and Carrol (Klier) Timmerman, *"Book of Schlickum-Klier Letters and Pictures,"* June 2012.

Engelke, Louis B., "He Got the Drop on Waldrip," *San Antonio Light*, San Antonio, Texas, January 3, 1954.

Fbgtxgensoc.org/timeline.

Gillespie County Courthouse Records.

historicschools.org/Meusebach creek school.

https://www.en.wikipedia.org/wiki/List_of_governors_of_ Texas.

https://www.fbglodging.com/fredericksburg-rentals/properties/meusebach-creek/Bonn.

https://www.fbgtx.org/208/History/Wochenblatt.

https://www.fbgtxgensoc.org.

https://www.genealogytrails.com/tex/hillcountry/gillespi e/1870census_gil_fbg.html.

https://www.sites.rootsweb.com/~txgilles/gillespiesheriff s.html.

https://www.texaspolitics.utexas.edu/.../us-constitution-and-civil-war-amendments.

https://www.txhillcountrytrail.com/plan-your-adventure/historic-sites-and-cities/sites/treue-der-union-monument.

https://www.washingtonian.com/2015/07/03/lincoln-co-conspirators-hung-1865-lewis-powell-mary-surratt-david-herold-george-atzerodt-old-arsenal-penitentiary-dc-fort-mcnair/.

https://www.whitehouse.gov/about-the-white-house/presidents/.

Juenke, Carlos, *The Orphan – The Caspar Fritz Story*, Xlibris Corporation, 2011.

Kammlah, Joe, "Area Germans Remembered at Massacre Site in Comfort," *Fredericksburg Standard-Radio Post*, August 22, 2012.

Morgenthaler, Jefferson, *The German Settlement of the Texas Hill Country*, Mockingbird Books, 2007.

Ninety Years of Education at Meusebach Creek (leaflet).

Ransleben, Guido E., *A Hundred Years of Comfort in Texas*, The Naylor Company, 1954.

Striegler, Selma Weyrich, *The Johan Frederick Gottlieb Striegler Family History, A Detailed Genealogy of the Descendants of Pioneer Citizens of Gillespie County, Texas, 1940 to January 1952.* Compiled, Edited and Published Under the Direction of Selma Weyrich Striegler, Family Historian; Fred Mathisen; Attila N. Striegler, Business Managers; and Mabel Zimmermann, Revising Editor.

Worm, Peter, Lord Mayor, Muenster, Germany, e-mail 10/13/2021.

www.hmdb.org.

Chapter XII

Ancestry.com. AnneMarieJosephaElisabethaJuditha Baar/Eckhardt-Familienstammbaum/Death of Mother Klier April 7, 1881.

Ancestry.com. Germany, Select Births and Baptisms, 1558-1898 [database on-line]. Provo, UT, USA: Ancestry.com Operations, Inc., 2014.

Ancestry.com. Germany, Select Marriages, 1558-1929 [database on-line]. Provo, UT, USA: Ancestry.com Operations, Inc., 2014.

Ancestry.com. Hesse, Germany, Deaths, 1851-1958 [database on-line]. Provo, UT, USA: Ancestry.com Operations, Inc., 2016.

Ancestry.com. Texas, U.S., Select County Marriage Index, 1837-1965 [database on-line]. Provo, UT, USA: Ancestry.com Operations, Inc., 2014.

Ancestry.com.Year: 1880; Census Place: Fredericksburg, Gillespie, Texas; Roll: 1305; Page: 260B; Enumeration District: 061.

Dahlmanns, Hans, Christoph Dahlmanns, Chuck and Carrol (Klier) Timmerman, *"Book of Schlickum-Klier Letters and Pictures"*, June 2012.

genealogytrails.com/tex/hillcountry/gillespie/history_county.html.

Gillespie County Courthouse Records.

historicschools.org.

https://sites.rootsweb.com/~txgilles/gillespiesheriffs.html.

https://www.175th.org/2021/04/restoring-fredericksburgs-forgotten-history/Tarrillion.

https://www.bing.com/search?q=1890+labor+and+farming&form/Farm Equipment.

https://www.bing.com/search?q=when+did+fredericksburg+texas+get+its+first+electricity.

https://www.en.wikipedia.org/wiki/Henry_Ford/1896.

https://www.en.wikipedia.org/wiki/List_of_governors_of_Texas.

https://www.fbgtxgensoc.org/timelines.

https://www.history.com/this-day-in-history/president-garfield-shot/.

https://www.hmdb.org/The Historical Marker Database.

https://www.medical-dictionary.thefreedictionary.com/typhoid.

https://www.tshaonline.org/handbook/entries/gillespie-county.

https://www.whitehouse.gov/about-the-white-house/presidents/.

Klier, Harold Victor, *Down on the Farm, 1933 to 1951*, 2012.

Kowert, Elise, *Old Homes and Buildings of Fredericksburg*, Fredericksburg Publishing Company, Fredericksburg, Texas, 1977.

Ninety Years of Education at Meusebach Creek (leaflet).

Penniger, Robert, *Fredericksburg, The First Fifty Years*, Fredericksburg Publishing, 1971.

Striegler, Selma Weyrich, *The Johan Frederick Gottlieb Striegler Family History, A Detailed Genealogy of the Descendants of Pioneer Citizens of Gillespie County, Texas, 1940 to January 1952.* Compiled, Edited and Published Under the Direction of Selma Weyrich Striegler, Family Historian; Fred Mathisen; Attila N. Striegler, Business Managers; and Mabel Zimmermann, Revising Editor.

The Radio Post, Fiftieth Anniversary Commemorative Edition, Fredericksburg, Texas, October 1972.

Worm, Peter, Lord Mayor, Muenster, Germany, e-mail 10/13/2021.

Chapter XIII

Ancestry.com. Year: 1880; Census Place: Saint Louis, St Louis (Independent City), Missouri; Roll: 727; Page: 476C; Enumeration District: 060.

Ancestry.com. Germany, Select Births and Baptisms, 1558-1898 [database on-line]. Provo, UT, USA: Ancestry.com Operations, Inc., 2014.

Ancestry.com. Missouri, U.S., Death Records, 1850-1931 [database on-line]. Provo, UT, USA: Ancestry.com Operations, Inc., 2008.

Ancestry.com. New Orleans, Passenger Lists, 1813-1963 [database on-line]. Provo, UT, USA: Ancestry.com Operations, Inc., 2006.

Ancestry.com. Texas, U.S., Select County Marriage Index, 1837-1965 [database on-line]. Provo, UT, USA: Ancestry.com Operations, Inc., 2014.

Ancestry.com. U.S., Find a Grave Index, 1600s-Current [database on-line]. Provo, UT, USA: Ancestry.com Operations, Inc., 2012.

Ancestry.com.Germany, Births and Baptisms, 1558-1898. Salt Lake City, Utah: FamilySearch, 2013.

Dahlmanns, Hans, Christoph Dahlmanns, Chuck and Carrol (Klier) Timmerman, "Book of Schlickum-Klier Letters and Pictures," June 2012.

Chapter XIV

Ancestry.com. U.S., Find A Grave Index, 1600s-Current [database on-line]. Provo, UT, USA: Ancestry.com Operations, Inc., 2012.

Ancestry.com. Year: 1900; Census Place: Justice Precinct 1, Gillespie, Texas; Page: 17; Enumeration District: 0031; FHL microfilm: 1241638.

Ancestry.com. Hesse, Germany, Deaths, 1851-1958 [database on-line]. Provo, UT, USA: Ancestry.com Operations, Inc., 2016.

fbgtxgensoc.org/timelines.

Gillespie County courthouse, Fredericksburg, Texas.

https://www.bing.com/search?q=population+of+gillespie+county+texas+1900.

https://www.en.wikipedia.org/wiki/List_of_governors_of_Texas.

https://www.fbgtx.org/208/History/1905 first Telephone in Fredericksburg.

https://www.fbgtx.org/208/History/Ice factory.

https://www.findagrave.com/cemetery/422870/der-stadt-friedhof-cemetery.

https://www.hmdb.org/The Historical Marker Database.

https://www.sites.rootsweb.com/~txgilles/gillespiesheriff s.html.

https://www.trinitylutheranstonewall.com/about.html.

https://www.whitehouse.gov/about-the-white-house/presidents/.

Striegler, Selma Weyrich, *The Johan Frederick Gottlieb Striegler Family History, A Detailed Genealogy of the Descendants of Pioneer Citizens of Gillespie County, Texas, 1940 to January 1952*. Compiled, Edited and Published Under the Direction of Selma Weyrich Striegler, Family Historian; Fred Mathisen; Attila N. Striegler, Business Managers; and Mabel Zimmermann, Revising Editor.

www.thehenryford.org/collections-and-research/.

End Notes & Picture Credits

Friedrich Wilhelm Klier (1799-1879), photo courtesy of the Alton Klier Family Collection, page 1.

Johann Abraham Klier (1771-1843), photo courtesy of the Alton Klier Family Collection, page 2.

Anna Christina Charlotte Boeck Klier (1776 - ?), photo courtesy of the Alton Klier Family Collection, page 2.

Julius Schlickum (1825-1863), photo courtesy of Hans Dahlmanns, Christoph Dahlmanns, and Chuck and Carrol (Klier) Timmerman, page 8.

Sankt Ludgeri Katholische, Muenster, Germany, photo courtesy of the Parish of *Sankt Lamberti Katholische*, Muenster, Germany, page 17.

Schloss, Muenster, Germany (Former Episcopal Castle) and *Schlossplatz (Neuplatz)*, photo by Rüdiger Wölk, www.woelkimages.com, page 19.

Muenster, Germany, photo courtesy of Worldatlas.com, page 21.

Bremen, Germany, photo courtesy of Worldatlas.com, page 23.

Map of Fisher-Miller Land Grant, courtesy of Gillespie County Historical Society, page 33.

Trail from Indianola to Gillespie County, courtesy of Gillespie County Historical Society, page 37.

Meusebach Treaty with Penateka Comanche Indians –
Marketplatz, photo courtesy of Gillespie County Historical
Society, page 49.

Vereins Kirche, photo courtesy of Gillespie County Historical
Society, page 51.

The Kammlah House (Pioneer Museum), photo courtesy of
Gillespie County Historical Society, page 51.

Nimitz Hotel, photo courtesy of Gillespie County Historical
Society, page 58.

Karl Ferdinand Schlickum (10/12/1829-11/12/1876), Austin,
Texas, photo courtesy of Hans Dahlmanns, Christoph
Dahlmanns, and Chuck and Carrol (Klier) Timmerman, page
62.

Julius and Josephine Klier Ransleben, photo courtesy of Hans
Dahlmanns, Christoph Dahlmanns, and Chuck and Carrol
(Klier) Timmerman, page 66.

First Gillespie County Courthouse, photo courtesy of Gillespie
County Historical Society, page 69.

Sankt Martini Katholische, Muenster, Germany, courtesy of
Sankt Martini Katholische, page 74

Historical Marker, Fort Martin Scott, Fredericksburg, Texas,
hmdb.org, photo by Cosmos Marine, page 76.

Fort Mason, Mason, Texas, photo courtesy of Mason County
Chamber of Commerce, page 76.

Fort McKavett, Menard, Texas, photo courtesy of the Fort McKavett State Historic Site, page 77.

Denmark map courtesy of Worldatlas.com, page 86.

Private Wilhelm Klier's Enlistment Card, fbgtxgensoc.org, page 93.

Two-Story St. James Hotel on the left; location of "Schlickum and Holzapfel" Store, photo courtesy of Dietert Historical Archives, Patrick Heath Public Library, Boerne, Texas, page 96.

Private Wilhelm Klier's Enlistment Card, fbgtxgensoc.org, page 97.

Wilhelm Klier's Colt .44 Navy Revolver and Holster, photos by Alan Saenger, page 99.

211 N. Main (left two-story building) + 402 Blanco Road, Boerne (home & windmill on hill, upper left in the background), photo courtesy of Dietert Historical Archives, Patrick Heath Public Library, Boerne, Texas, page 107.

U. S. Army Headquarters, 205 East Houston Street, San Antonio, Texas, hmdb.org, Old Military Headquarters Historical Marker, photo by Brian Anderson, page 109.

Confluence of Menger and Cibolo Creek, Cibolo Nature Center, Boerne, Texas (location where Wilhelm Klier was almost hung), photo by Alan Saenger, page 141.

Treue der Union Monument, Comfort, Texas, photo courtesy Julia Hayden, page 233.

Wilhelm Klier (1834-1907), photo courtesy of Alton Klier Family Collection, page 265.

Marriage License, Gillespie County Courthouse, page 267. Caroline Therese Klier (10/12/1828-5/16/1905), photo courtesy of Hans Dahlmanns, Christoph Dahlmanns, and Chuck and Carrol (Klier) Timmerman, page 274.

East End of Old Klier House (Meusebach Creek), Inside of Old Klier House with Water Well in the Left Corner, Northeast Corner of Old Klier House, photos by Alan Saenger, pages 282-283.

Today's *Stiftsherrenstrasse* (formerly *Herrenstrasse*), Muenster, Germany, MediaWiki, page 292.

Rudolfstrasse 38 Apartment, MediaWiki, page 296.

An der Clemenskirche 14, MediaWiki, page 313.

Sister Antonie Klier (1845-1893), photo courtesy of Hans Dahlmanns, Christoph Dahlmanns, and Chuck and Carrol (Klier) Timmerman, page 316

Trunk #1 from Germany (July 17, 1881), photo by Alan Saenger, page 324.

Trunk #2 from Germany (July 17, 1881), photo by Lesa Brown-Valades, page 325.

Remnants of the Second Stone Meusebach Creek School, photo by LaVerne Heiner, page 326.

Former Second Gillespie County Courthouse, photo courtesy of Gillespie County Historical Society, page 327.

Old Jail, 117 W. San Antonio Street, Fredericksburg, photo courtesy of Gillespie County Historical Society, page 328.

Holy Ghost Lutheran Church, photo courtesy of Gillespie County Historical Society, page 330.

Wilhelm and Ida Striegler Klier, photo courtesy of Kim Otte Gibbs, page 341.

The Klier Family in 1892, Striegler book, page 342.

East Main Street, Fredericksburg 1892, Radio Post, Commemorative Edition, October 1972, page 343.

West Main Street, Fredericksburg 1892, Radio Post, Commemorative Edition, October 1972 Edition, page 344.

Klier Homeplace, Stonewall, Texas, photo courtesy of LaVerne Heiner, page 348.

The Hollmig Property (private property), 3085 Gellermann Lane, Stonewall, Texas 2021 (previously Klier Homeplace), photo by Alan Saenger, page 349.

Liebfrauen-Uberwasser Katholische, Muenster, Germany, photo courtesy of *Liebfrauen-Uberwasser Katholische*, page 351.

Trinity Lutheran Church, Stonewall, Texas, hmdb.org, photo by Duane Hall, page 353.

Klier Cattle Brand, photo by Patrick Klier, page 357.

Wilhelm Friedrich Klier and Ida Agathe Striegler Klier, Der Stadt Friedhof, (corner of East Schubert and Lee Street, Fredericksburg, Texas, Section D, Row 08, Plots 32 & 33), photo by Mark Alberthal, page 358.

Death Abstract and Death Certificate of Wm. Klier and Ida Klier, Gillespie County Courthouse, page 358.

Texas Ranger Memorial Cross Dedication Program, June 19, 2021, Former Texas Rangers Association, page 361.

Texas Ranger Memorial Cross Dedication, June 19, 2021, photo by Martelle Luedecke/Luedecke Photography, page 362.

Texas Ranger Memorial Cross Dedication, June 19, 2021, photo by Martelle Luedecke/Luedecke Photography, page 362.

CPSIA information can be obtained
at www.ICGtesting.com
Printed in the USA
BVHW042045240722
642921BV00001B/3